Dancing Away

Dancing Away

Dancing Away
A Covent Garden Diary

Deborah Bull

Methuen

For Patricia Linton, who showed me what I might do with the gifts I was fortunate enough to inherit.

Published by Methuen in 1998

1 3 5 7 9 10 8 6 4 2

First published in the United Kingdom in 1998 by
Methuen Publishing Limited
20 Vauxhall Bridge Road, London SW1V 2SA

Random House Australia (Pty) Limited
20 Alfred Street, Milsons Point, Sydney, New South Wales 2061, Australia
Random House New Zealand Limited
18 Poland Road, Glenfield, Auckland 10, New Zealand
Random House South Africa (Pty) Limited
Endulini, 5A Jubilee Road, Parktown 2193, South Africa

Photographs © Marcel Imsand, Ross MacGibbon, Lawrie Lewis, Leslie Spatt,
Dee Conway, Robbie Jack, University of Derby, Country Life 1998

Methuen Publishing Limited Reg. No. 3543167

A CIP catalogue for this book is available from the British Library

ISBN 0 413 72600 2

Typeset by SX Composing DTP, Rayleigh, Essex
Printed and bound in Great Britain by The Bath Press, Bath

Acknowledgements

My first thanks must go to those people at the Royal Ballet who help me to juggle the hours in each day, especially Anthony Dowell, Jeanetta Laurence, Christopher Newton, Georgie Perrott, Anthony Russell-Roberts and Louise Shand-Brown. I am also indebted to Monica Mason for support both in and out of the studio over several years. Amanda Jones, Head of Press at the Royal Opera House, has given me invaluable advice, and Janine Limberg and Simon Magill of The Royal Ballet press office have both been extremely helpful.

Thanks also to Scott Royal of the Arts Council press department; Jane Blackburn of the Royal Opera House development office; David Buckland, David West and my mother for taking and supplying photographs; Johanna Adams for providing information on various theatrical technicalities and Mary Ann Kurtz for reading and advising on the final draft. Very special thanks to all my family; to my agent, Pat Kavanagh; to Michael Earley, for his extraordinary generosity and countless hours of fun during the editorial process; and to Torje Eike, for researching facts and offering constant support.

Prologue

7.20 p.m. Five minute call. The shoes are on my feet and sewn on to my tights, my head-dress is pinned firmly in place and Sue has finished negotiating the array of poppers and hooks which fasten the tutu. I pick up my water bottle and head for the stage. I feel fairly calm; after all, there is a sense, more than anything, of inevitability about a performance. Short of divine intervention, it *will* happen, and however nervous I feel, I'm too much of a professional to head back to my room, take off the costume and go home. On-stage, behind a closed curtain, I put the bottle down and sample a variety of steps from my solo while dancers mill around me, practising, chatting, repeating a joke about something that happened earlier in the day. For the rest of the company, this is just another performance in a run of twelve, and I can't expect them to share the same cocktail of fear and nervous excitement which is coursing through my veins. With five minutes to go before curtain up, I realise I've been short-changed on the excitement, and the mixture is stronger on fear. I felt fine on the brief walk from my dressing-room. Now I feel as if I'm wearing someone else's legs. I can't find my balance, and the last diagonal of the solo, a series of sustained turns, repeated three times, is going from bad to worse. I know that rehearsing in these last few moments is tantamount to useless, and the way it goes now, curtain down, will most likely bear no relation whatsoever to the way it goes later, curtain up. I give in, hand my fate over to the gods, and say good luck to a soloist who looks as tense as I feel.

7.30 p.m. The overture begins. The full dramatic swell of the plot – the dark portents and the triumph of good over evil – prescient in two or three minutes of sublime music. At stage management's command, the curtain rises on our cloistered and esoteric world and the ballet begins. I have a while before my first entrance and I pace up and down the wings, quickening to a jog and then stopping to stretch out my left calf muscle. On-stage, the action continues, and I catch occasional glimpses of it; a friend is having trouble with a difficult step in her solo, and I position myself to see how it goes, fingers crossed and willing her to succeed. It's passable. She won't be pleased, but the audience won't have noticed anything amiss. More jogging, then a sip of water. About five minutes to go now. The *corps de ballet* rush past me, off stage, and down to their dressing-room for a quick change; they'll be back again before I finally go on, lining up for their next entrance, different costumes for a different role. From nowhere, the stagehands appear, and in a short pause between acts, they change the set from palace gates to moonlit lakeside. I'm starting to focus inwards now, less concerned about what's going on around me and more interested in calming my pounding heart. I try to think about the character, about who I will be on the stage, where I've come from and what's made me the way I am, but all the time rogue elements shoot through my mind. Did I switch on the answerphone before I left home? It doesn't matter. Don't think about it. My calf feels tight already. It's just nerves. Don't think about it. But I can't do it. I'm a fraud. It shouldn't be me. There are plenty of dancers who could do this better than I will. I know that last diagonal won't work. Don't think about it.

The Prince runs on – it's exactly the piece of music which begins every rehearsal, when Monica or Sasha calls across to the pianist, 'Let's go from the Prince's entrance, shall we?', as if we had any option. Something clicks inside me and the sense of inevitability gains pace. It *will* happen. It's about to happen. Inside, I say a tiny, unfocused prayer, a general cry for help to anyone who might be listening, and my body starts to shift into gear. Two or three quick *relevés* to remind my feet to point and imperceptible stirrings in my back as I picture my arms moving up and down in time to the music. Another rogue thought is banished. Just focus. Don't let it get to you. You've wanted this for so long. You mustn't blow it now. Three sustained, tremolando chords, ascending the scale, and I run on. I land from my *jeté* to a ripple of applause, and then stillness. I'm alone on an empty stage. It's quiet out there. I feel as lonely as I've ever felt in my life, despite the silent presence of two thousand people watching me from the auditorium. Someone coughs. I'm settled centre stage and the conductor has paused, his baton in the air. It's up to me to make the next move, but I'm not sure that I can. The music won't start without me, so what would happen if I just didn't move? It's tempting. After all, I could pretend I'd suddenly been taken ill, or that I'd hurt my ankle as I landed from the jump. I'm sure I'd get away with it. The next step, a simple *posé* on my right leg, takes all the nerve of diving off a cliff, but my ingrained sense of duty wins out, and I do it. Not bad. Could have held it a bit longer, but not bad. Once more, the same step. Better. Third time, and I'm gaining courage. The courage to dare.

I'm back in the wings now, hot and sweaty after the long *pas de deux* and pulling on leg warmers to try and retain the heat until my next entrance. I retrieve my bottle from the prop table nearby and take thirsty sips. On-stage, four girls are linked together in one of ballet's most familiar and most parodied moments, the stuff of television commercials and endless mickey-taking. I stretch out cramped muscles, tease the blood back into the left foot which will take the brunt of this evening's exertions, and fuss over my shoes. I knew they wouldn't feel right. I think about rushing back to my dressing-room to change them for the pair I've laid out, ready for the next act, but there just isn't time. They'll have to do. The staccato music is replaced by a generous and lilting waltz and two girls soar through the next, brief, number. As they start out on their last step I peel off the leg warmers, scuff in the resin box and check that the knots in the ribbons on my shoes are tucked out of sight. The girls take their call and leave the stage. It's my turn. I let the mood settle, waiting for a few seconds before I set out on the longest walk of a dancer's career, the silent procession to the centre of the stage where the solo begins. I take my position and draw both arms up over my head. The music starts and I fold one wing after the other to a pose of neatly crossed wrists just above the net skirt of my tutu. The variation opens with three controlled *ronds de jambe relevés*, each one melting from the height of the extension back to the ground in a hopeless sigh. They've been working well in rehearsals and tonight they go smoothly. Pleased with myself, I manage to crash land the next step before I return to the centre to repeat the whole sequence on the other foot. I try to put the mistake behind me and concentrate on the present, but it's unnerved me and the first *rond de jambe* is clumsy. I can't afford to do it wrong again, and I focus my attention on the leg which is holding me up rather than the one describing circles in the air – left leg, right leg. It brings me back on track, but I can feel the dull ache start up in my left calf. The rigours of the next act flash through my mind. Don't think about it now. Step at a time.

I pause in fifth position on *pointe* and take a deep breath before the next phrase, a mixed series of jumps and balances which alternates bursts of explosive energy with still and suspended poise. I strike it lucky, hitting an *arabesque* on *pointe* which momentarily freezes time and then grows outwards, reverberating with the clarinet in the orchestra. On the left side, the balance is more difficult to find, and besides, I'm acutely aware now of the pain in my calf. The constant ache is threatening to take over, to destroy all the work that I've put in for my one performance of this ballet, but I won't allow it. Focus. Go back to the route map; tight fifth position, soft arms, drop the head down over the front leg and then pull up the top of the thigh as I *relevé*. Left shoulder back. Good.

A linking step, and I'm almost on to the traumatic diagonal. 'Work out the pitfalls,' a teacher used to tell me, but now I wish I didn't know about them. I wish I didn't know that I've failed in this step as many times as I've succeeded. I'm tired, too. It's the end of the solo; I'm breathing heavily and my left calf is throbbing. I steal a demi-semiquaver of music from the step beforehand and try to arrive in the upstage corner with an extra second to catch my breath. Just concentrate. Think of what Monica would say – top of the left leg. Don't try and make the calf do all the work on its own. And my secret trick, putting the heel down before the double – no one will notice and it helps to keep my weight back. First one – good. Exactly. Same thing again. Just do it the same way. No – don't try too hard. Relax. *Let* it work, don't stop it working. Third one. Yes. Perfect. Now, controlled *chaînées*, feet close together – ignore the people sitting in the wings. They don't matter. Just control it – deep *plié* to put the brakes on and step on the right foot into the final pose. Soft arms. Mouth closed. Breathe through your nose. Hold it.

Applause. I must have done it. Ten minutes on-stage, and I'm dancing away.

May 1997

Up with the lark after a very late night. I'm never good in the mornings, and particularly not after too little sleep. Last night was the first performance of Glen Tetley's *Amores*, his first work for The Royal Ballet in about eighteen years, and we celebrated the occasion with a post-performance dinner at Bank, the latest mega-sized and pricey restaurant to open in the Covent Garden area. Unfortunately we have a matinée today at midday – unusually early and much too close to the time I got to bed. I have to be at the Opera House by 9.30 this morning.

More importantly than all that, today was the general election – the first election, I'm ashamed to admit, at which I've been politically awake. I've voted occasionally in the past, but more often than not, elections have coincided with touring, and I've been out of the country. A likely excuse, I know, but I'm sticking to it. I remember one year when an election was announced, fought and concluded all during the course of a tour. Until recently, it never seemed to matter. Politics were the last thing which concerned me. I didn't smoke (still don't), drink (do, a bit), or drive (do, a lot) and as I was earning a dancer's wage and barely eligible to pay tax, budgets and fiscal affairs went straight over my head. Mostly, though, I was focused so intently on 'being a dancer' that the rest of the world just didn't intrude. Now that I'm growing up a bit, politics concern me enormously. I've shed my blinkers and I don't always like what I see. The arts are being sidelined as 'élitist', irrelevant and the role they have to play in human development is often totally ignored. It infuriates me that people in power don't seem to do anything to set things straight.

But perhaps there is hope ahead, as it seems that there will be, without a doubt, a change of government. It can't be a coincidence that the election was scheduled for Labour Day. The Tories have held the fort for eighteen years – since Tetley's last piece for the company, in fact. My entire working life has been carried out under Tory rule, and I still wondered, even as I cast my vote, if the 'better the devil you know' route might be the way to jump. I certainly thought long and hard about where to put my cross. Change is fine, as long as it's for the better. But will it be better? The cynic in me is inclined to wonder.

By 10 p.m. I was struggling to keep my eyes open after two strenuous shows in fifteen hours and precious little sleep between them. Sensing that something momentous was going on and eager to be there as it happened, I did my best to keep pace with the *Newsnight* Swing-o-meter. But election coverage is difficult to follow at the best of times, and the political analysts weren't helping a bit. Nor did it help that my eyelids were getting heavier by the minute, and for about half an hour I fought to stay awake in the vain belief that with just a bit more concentration I would surely figure out what was going on. When the first result came in the pundits predicted a record landslide victory for Tony Blair and his Labour Party. I knew as much as I needed to know. You can't fight the inevitable. I guess the Tories realised that too. I certainly did. Fatigue won out. By midnight I was out for the count, and Blair, so it seemed, was in.

2nd May 1997, London
I wake up to a different world. I very rarely watch TV over breakfast, but this morning I feel obliged to turn it on to catch the pictures of last night's events – the ones I slept through. I am amazed, stunned by the cheering crowds who lined the streets in the middle of the night. It doesn't resemble an election victory so much as a liberation, and Tony and Cherie Blair greet the crowd like conquering heroes. Whichever way you lean politically, there is no ignoring the strength of feeling which lies behind this. The people have spoken, and they've opted for change.

I spend longer than usual getting up and making my tea, and then it dawns on me that I'm inventing delays because I don't want to go out. I feel as if the landscape will have shifted in some way, and when a friend calls, I ask if it's safe to leave the house. It seems that where there is so much passion and strength of feeling in the air, there must surely be some physical manifestation to demonstrate it. Perhaps the speed limits will have altered, or Tony Blair's head will be on the currency. Something radical must have changed. I brave it, and go out to buy the papers, intrigued to read the detailed dissection of the election results and, tucked away in the arts pages, the odd hundred words on *Amores*. The reviews are mixed, not very excited, and my name doesn't feature. And nothing out there has changed, except the weather. It's glorious, and will undoubtedly be taken by those who believe in such things as a good omen. People are smiling a bit more than usual, I find. But when the newsagent asks one of his regulars what she thinks about the new government, she simply replies, 'I don't like politicians.'

I spend the rest of the morning at the BBC recording a voice-over for one of a series of short programmes celebrating the centenary of the Tate Gallery. The idea is that experts in a given field will talk about well-known works of art in the Tate which reflect aspects of our knowledge. I have been asked to talk about Degas' *Little Dancer*, the tiny, pained creature who decorates the lids of endless chocolate boxes. My voice will be played while the camera roves over and around the statue, probing and poking into places Degas never meant us to see. Being a conscientious sort of person, I've been down to see her beforehand, and taking notes on her wrinkled tights (she pre-dates lycra), her *retroussé* nose and her unlikely posture, and the whole thing takes less than fifteen minutes.

The remainder of the day is mine, and I stay indoors, still unsure about the new world outside.

5th May 1997, London
Saturday, and we had a matinée, the third performance of *Amores*. As usual, I drove down to Covent Garden expecting to be able to enjoy free parking from 1.30 p.m. onwards. The single yellow lines were surprisingly empty, so I pulled over, suspicious, to check the regulations on a nearby meter. And there it was; the physical manifestation of the new government that I've been waiting for. No more free parking in Covent Garden on Saturday afternoons. Seriously disgruntled, I fed a quarter of my week's salary into the slot and went to work. Although I was still tired from the week's excitement, the show went well. Unfortunately, Glen Tetley wasn't here to see it. He left hurriedly after the first night to get back to his beloved grapes in Tuscany. I was rather sad to see him go. For me, Tetley is a living part of dance history, and working with him was a huge privilege. When I was a dance student in the seventies, he was very much a 'happening' thing, creating several important and innovative works – *Pierrot Lunaire* and *Field Figures* among them – for The Royal Ballet and Ballet Rambert. He fused what we used to call contemporary dance (I think it's 'alternative' now) with classical technique, introducing flexed feet, deep contractions and lycra to a generation of ballet dancers. Twenty years later, I'm not sure we got the very best out of him. It could be argued that at the grand age of

seventy-two, it's inevitable that his best has already been given. But I do think that if we had had longer to get used to each other (an impossible luxury in our packed rehearsal schedule), it would have been a more successful collaboration.

I spent the rest of this bank-holiday weekend at the computer. I'm hard at work on my first book, an antidote to all the nonsense that gets written about dieting, and I've set myself a tough deadline, promising my publishers, Dorling Kindersley, that they'll have the as yet untitled manuscript by the end of this month. Back home from the matinée, I crack on and write about 6,000 words. By this evening, my springs have gone. But writing is such a different discipline from dancing that I don't mind putting in several hours of work at the end of the day. For a start, it's wonderful to be able to see the results instantly – there they are, words on the screen, and you can play with them, manipulate them, make changes and sleep on them before you take the decision to go public. No such luxury in dancing. You create and deliver at the same time; the ultimate deadline. And very rarely do you have something to hold on to after the event. Unless a performance is filmed, it evaporates as soon as it appears. Sooner, in fact; step erases step, with all the longevity of footprints in wet sand. The idea of a lasting creation, such as a book, is entirely novel to me, and I am relishing the challenge.

6th May 1997, London
Back to work after the long weekend. Following rehearsals I went to see Michael Earley at Methuen. I received a letter from him last week, suggesting that we should meet. He has read several of my articles over the last year and wonders if I would be interested in writing something about dance, perhaps a personal account of the coming year.

At the Opera House we're all embarking on a fascinating year. Not only are we living under a new Labour government, one that is traditionally much kinder and more sympathetic to the arts, but for the first time in The Royal Ballet's history, we will be homeless. While the Opera House undergoes its extensive and controversial redevelopment, we will be dancing away from it, following a peripatetic existence which has attracted criticism even before it starts. There will be plenty of people examining the year ahead from every conceivable political angle, but I am interested in recording the effects of all this upheaval on one individual within the system. Me. As I write this, it occurs to me that we're not in for an easy ride.

It's been a long time since I've kept a diary, but over the last year, I've been writing a lot, and I've started once again to keep a journal of daily events. Between the ages of seven and twenty-one, I was extremely diligent and kept a daily record of everything that went on. The early ones are nothing more than scribbled reminders of what I did every day: 'got up, went to ballet class, had beans on toast for tea'. Really riveting stuff. As I got older and my life became more interesting, the entries expanded until I was writing several thousand words a day. It was at that point that I gave up. I simply couldn't afford the time any longer. Today I found myself offering to do it again.

Now I record the day's events in a slightly different fashion, one much more in tune with the electronic age. My Norwegian, Torje (I hate any of the usual words – partner, boyfriend, other half. Lover tends to embarrass people) spends most of his life at the moment away from home. He's a physiotherapist who 'looks after' certain athletes and performers, keeping them fit and, where possible, preventing injuries. I have known him for about five years and for three of them he has been on the road with the Rolling Stones. In the early days we spent a lot of time on the telephone, but when a four-figure bill arrived from British Telecom, I decided it was time to find another way of communicating. From faxing we progressed to e-mail, a wonderful invention which seems to me to combine the spontaneity of a phone call with the permanence of a letter, until, that is, it gets lost in cyber space. At the end of our first long separation – at least a year – our exchanges remained as a complete diary of the period we were apart.

7th May 1997, London
More cast changes at The Royal Ballet. Darcey Bussell's ankle is dodgy, and it looks as if she won't be able to cope with the very heavy work-load at the weekend. We have two performances of the triple bill (*Amores*, *Symphony in C* and *Judas Tree*) on Saturday, followed hot on the heels by shows on Wednesday and Thursday. It would probably be too much to manage at the best of times. On top of this, we are opening with *Sleeping Beauty* in California next week, and Darcey is scheduled to dance the first night. So Zenaida Yanowsky and Inaki Urlezaga have to take over the matinée performance of *Amores*, and they have three days to prepare. I can only wish them luck. I'm glad it's not me, but nevertheless, a tiny part of me longs, wistfully, for that adrenalin rush which comes with stepping in and saving the day. Three days might

sound like a long time, but *Amores* involves a tricky and exhausting *pas de deux* which comes right at the end of the piece, when you've been dancing for twenty minutes already. I'm sure they'll get their limbs around the technicalities, but it's physiologically impossible to improve stamina in three days. In anything else so physically demanding, athletics, for instance, the three days prior to performance would involve tapering off the training and eating well in order to rest the muscles and restock the energy stores. Not so in the dance world. Too often the day before a première is the day of the dress rehearsal. In the worst cases, the dress rehearsal happens on the afternoon of the first night. For some companies this is normal practice, which leads people to think it's right. I often hear dancers, on the day before performance, saying 'I need to do my solo to build stamina'. For a dancer to give themselves a pre-performance rest day would involve going completely against the grain, trashing everything they believe in. Psychologically, it might prove difficult. Physically, they'd be doing themselves an enormous favour.

I had a performance of *Anastasia* this evening, a full month after the last one. I play the Russian ballerina Mathilde Kschessinska, who was, allegedly, the mistress of Tsar Nicholas II and Inaki and I dance a *pas de deux* in the second act, at a 'coming out' ball for the eponymous heroine. The *pas de deux* is really just a *divertissement*, an excuse for some quality dancing. Except tonight, when it was an excuse for some mediocre dancing. It's a strange number, as it comes out of nowhere; no preamble, no chance to build up a character. You walk on, the music starts, and off you go. Tonight, right from the beginning, it fell apart. The lights were dazzling and I couldn't seem to make firm contact with the floor. It was like one of those anxiety dreams made flesh, where everything you touch turns to dust and slips through your fingers. And we had done so well last time. Tonight everyone on stage knew I'd blown it. It was all pretty depressing and afterwards I slunk towards the stage door in dark glasses clutching my ill deserved flowers.

Afterwards, I had the most bizarre experience. Torje had arranged to come and collect me, and I waited, collar up and eyes down, at the stage door in Floral Street. And I waited. And waited. After about half an hour, I called him to see if he had forgotten, and got no reply. It was about this time that panic set in, and I can see now why panic is often described as 'blind'. This one overtook me so completely that I couldn't see straight. I headed home, absolutely convinced that I had lost him, and sure enough, when I arrived at the flat, he wasn't there. No sign of him. Vanished. I tried to run through all the logical explanations, yet none of them seemed to add up. The only answer that struck me as rational was the least rational of them all, that he had somehow disappeared off the face of the earth. I started to call around; the hospitals, the police, and then my poor, long-suffering friend, David. I was even put through to 'custody', in case he had been arrested for being drunk and disorderly. (Even in my distressed state, I could see the comedy here. Torje has never been drunk and disorderly in his life, unless you count the time he and David, then both Crystal Palace physios, shared in the celebrations following their league cup victory over Everton.) At about midnight, when I had started to rewrite my life story without him in it, my car pulled up outside the flat, and out stepped Torje, who looked up at me from the street in total bemusement. As always, he had been waiting by the ballerina statue, outside Bow Street Magistrate's Court just across from the Opera House. He has waited there at least once a week since I first met him, but for some reason this evening, I chose to forget our routine. Bad performances can really throw you.

9th May 1997, London
Still feeling a bit depressed and generally exhausted, though I'm not quite sure why. I need to pull myself together, as the company leaves on tour in a week's time and there's an awful lot to do between now and then. We will be away for six weeks, two in California and four in Japan. As I'm not involved in *Romeo and Juliet* and I'm not cast, this time, as Kitri in *Don Quixote*, I'm only needed for the Californian fortnight and the last week of the Japan trip. I'm a bit upset that I won't be dancing *Don Q.* I thought it was one of my better roles and I loved doing it. But the mysteries of casting are way beyond my comprehension, and I shall look on the bright side; at least I'll be able to pop home after California, giving me a chance to do my laundry and finish writing the DK book before I head off to Japan. Even so, there's a lot of preparation involved, packing 'normal' luggage as well as two 'blue boxes', the foot square containers which transport pointe shoes, tights, make-up and all the rest of a dancer's paraphernalia. The company traditionally has a day off before we leave on tour to deal with all this housekeeping, but I'm booked up for my first photographic shoot for the illustrations in the DK book. Just when am I supposed to shop and pack? Stress is building up. This morning my throat was sore and I didn't like the taste in my mouth,

so I made one of my rare visits to the doctor. Sure enough, I have a throat infection. Great timing. I have two shows to get through tomorrow. No wonder I've been feeling down. As the doctor says, I'm not very ill, but I'm not very well either.

Yesterday I had another meeting with the editorial team at DK, a round table of women who will transpose my text on to the printed page. Halfway through it, I realised that I was in a completely unfamiliar position. For the first time in my life, people were listening to me. Within reason, what I say goes. You can't imagine how unusual this is for a dancer. It's not quite a case of 'don't think, just do', but dancers are generally there to mutely express someone else's ideas, not to spout their own. Although I have a reputation for being outspoken, I can see this shift in roles is going to take a bit of getting used to.

After the meeting I was thrown abruptly back into my Royal Ballet persona when I dropped into the Opera House to come clean to Amanda Jones, the company's press officer, about all this book writing. I have avoided saying anything before now in the belief that the minute I mentioned it, the whole thing would fall through. Now I have to back track a bit and make sure there are no objections before I go ahead and sign the contract with DK. I haven't mentioned this diary yet. I wonder how that will go down in a year's time?

Today was Labour's – sorry, New Labour's – first cabinet meeting, and it was all carefully choreographed to set a different tone from cabinet meetings of the past. The formalities and titles were gone, jackets were off, and the room was bustling with women. Tony and the Tonettes have arrived.

They have come up with a list of twenty-two new laws to be passed, several of which are related to education. Amongst them is the scrapping of the assisted places scheme. I guess it's all to do with an attempt to even out society. I think it's a myth that all children need the same education. This might be true if they were all starting from the same point. Inevitably, however, some children arrive at school with a head start on the others because of the five years that have gone before. Even if we were all born with the same equipment, there is a hell of a lot to influence it before the education system gets hold of us. All children should have good education, but this doesn't necessarily mean they should have the *same* education. What is good for one will not automatically be good for another. And I have to speak up for assisted places; without them I wouldn't be where I am now.

God, I sound like a Tonette. It must be contagious. Someone pass me a soapbox.

13th May 1997, London

As I tucked into my morning muesli with natural yoghurt, Radio 4 announced that the Arts Council have today launched *Arts 4 Everyone*, its attempt to divert some of the available Lottery funds from buildings to people. From what I gather, it seems to be heavy on the 'everyone', and light on the 'art'. I do think there's a potential danger here. I believe as strongly as anyone – stronger, perhaps – that art *is* for everyone. But you don't make art accessible by saying that whatever anyone does in their leisure time is art. (Although of course it *can* be.) You make art accessible by showing people what it is for, what it can do for them, how to recognise it. It's not about taking it down to the lowest common denominator. Art and self-expression are not necessarily the same thing. They serve different purposes. Self-expression is vital for good health, but should it be funded by the Arts Council? I ask this to the radio. It doesn't answer, so I turn it off and head for class at Barons Court.

There's a small crowd gathered in the corridor, and a press release pinned to the notice board which tells us, without any elaboration, that Genista McIntosh, Chief Executive of the Opera House, has resigned, due to 'ill health'. It doesn't seem possible; she has only been with us for four months, replacing Jeremy Isaacs who also left before the end of his term. Her sudden departure has come without any forewarning, and leaves us all speechless. Anthony Dowell, company Artistic Director, speaks to us later in the day, but he's unable to add anything of substance to the story. It's all such a mystery. Apparently, Genista's replacement is already lined up; the job is going to be taken by Mary Allen, the current Secretary-General at the Arts Council. I know Mary, and I have huge respect for her, but bearing in mind the Opera House's uneasy relationship with the Arts Council, it seems a bit like being taken over by the enemy. It's all too much for a Monday morning.

One question is on everyone's minds; did Jenny jump or was she pushed? And is she *really* ill? Whatever has happened, we'll all want to know the truth behind it. One thing is for certain, we're all feeling bereft. We know that with the oncoming 'closure' the House is in a tenuous position, and we all genuinely believed that Genista McIntosh was the right person to pilot us through the turbulence ahead. In her brief tenure, she established herself in the eyes of the dancers as someone we could trust, displaying an almost unprecedented interest in the ballet company. We've lost our House, now we've lost our Chief Executive. What other blows are in store?

A light note amidst the gloom; Darcey Bussell was on her way this afternoon to Madame Tussaud's for another session with the sculptor whose job it is to recreate her in wax. She told me she had asked at the last session how long waxworks remain on display, and was told that it generally depends on how long the subject remains in the limelight. So presumably they've already moved John Major into storage. We had to laugh. Not only do you see yourself replaced on the cast sheet by someone younger, better, more glamorous, but you are melted down, only to be recast in their image. That must be the ultimate indignity.

14th May 1997, London

I'm trying, without much success, to get ready to go on tour. I still don't know whether I'm going for two weeks or six, and I'm wondering how many pairs of knickers to pack. My original plan was to go to the US for a fortnight, come home for the next two weeks, finish the DK book, and then fly out to meet the company in Tokyo. Fourteen pairs should have done it. But the best laid plans, etc, etc. Darcey's troublesome ankle means that I am now on standby to dance Kitri after all. She definitely won't be dancing the role; after the two weeks in California, she will come home to rest her injury, and prepare for the New York season in July. Poor Darcey has a chequered past where *Don Q* is concerned. There are plenty of photographs of her as Kitri, as she did once get as far as a dress rehearsal, but so far, she hasn't got any further. Very good she was, too, especially when she managed to squeeze into Leanne Benjamin's tutu which had been laid out for Darcey by mistake. (Leanne is about half Darcey's height.) Unfortunately, she hasn't as yet *performed* it in front of a paying audience.

Today's papers are surprisingly restrained on the Genista issue, but at the Opera House, the rumour mill is churning out myriad theories. The favourite story at the moment is that Genista has been head-hunted for some sort of Labour think-tank. The official explanation, the illness theory, is not holding up. Staff at the theatre are up in arms, and seem to think she was pushed and didn't jump, but in any big organisation like ours, rumours can run riot at times like this, and I am trying to keep an open mind until we know the true facts.

I wonder if it's relevant that Genista's contract was for three years only? By the time it expired, we would barely be back in the Opera House, and she would have had precious little chance to influence and change any of the things she felt unhappy about in the way it's run. In fact, unless the Board re-appointed her, she would have had almost no *real* influence at all on the new Covent Garden. It was designed by a previous administration, and would be run by a future administration. I know I would find that an uncomfortable position.

I do feel sorry for Mary Allen in all this. At the moment, the whole scenario could be seen as 'the martyrdom of St Genista', and it's not easy to step into the sandals of a saint. There's an inevitable sense of unease afoot. It's perfectly normal in the arts world to bite back at the hand that feeds you funding, and in line with this, Opera House employees have never had a high regard for the Arts Council and its officials. Unfortunately for Mary, it will take time before we can forget that she was, until yesterday, one of them.

15th May 1997, London
The final show before the tour, and I'm dancing in *Amores* and *Symphony in C*. Afterwards, I have to pack up my boxes – make-up, hair pins, practice clothes, pointe shoes, dressing-gown, track suits and all the other essentials that get the show on the road. There's the added task of clearing out a locker, as over the next six weeks the ballet dressing-rooms will be used by the opera company who will commandeer one of my cupboards. Their rooms, at the back of the House, have already been sacrificed to the great rebuilding, and, in the new scheme, will be reincarnated as shops. Packing up takes me back to the early eighties, before the first phase of redevelopment, when sharing dressing-rooms with the opera company was the way things were. At that time, I used to change downstairs, in the big 'ballet room', a longer than wide room used by the *corps de ballet* and newest *coryphées*. It was bright and noisy, loud voices echoing without niceties, and bare bulbs around silvered mirrors. Between double shows it would turn into a much needed refuge, as dancers tried to snatch fragments of sleep on wicker baskets in dank corners. Every night after the performance we had to clear away our belongings to make room for the opera chorus, and then get them all out again next time the stage was ours. The opening of the new extension in 1982 meant we were no longer obliged to share. There were very smart new dressing-rooms, each one with its own shower. Not for us, oh no, but at least the old dressing-rooms, with their leaking sewage pipes

and vintage plumbing, were from that point ours alone, to enjoy to the full.

The locker clearing was a nostagia trip-and-a-half. I've worked at the Opera House since 1981, progressing from the ballet room to dressing-room five (Margot Fonteyn's old room, my dear). I've changed rooms four times in sixteen years, yet rather than throwing out the accumulated junk, I've simply taken it with me. Besides, there are some things you just can't throw away; special good luck cards, first pointe shoes ever to dance solo, odd bits of make-up that might just 'come in useful'. So my own personal dance museum has shifted rooms with me, thrust into the back of various lockers. Tonight I managed to defer the decision again, cramming it all into a spare blue box which will be stored across the road in 45 Floral Street until we come back into the new House. My foraging into the rear of the locker – a rubber glove affair if ever there was one – did bring forth evidence that this hoarding instinct is not unique to me. Wedged at the back of the shelf was a child's drawing – 'Good luck, Mummy' – and a yellowing piece of paper folded into a tight little square. I pulled it out and opened it up to discover a telegram to Antoinette Sibley from Kenneth MacMillan, dated 1986: 'Dear Antoinette STOP Welcome back to Manon STOP. Love Kenneth STOP'.

17th May 1997, London – Costa Mesa, California
Yesterday was the traditional pre-tour day off, except that I spent a long day at a photographic studio shooting pictures for the DK book. It was different, fun, but very tiring, and of course we didn't get nearly as much done as we hoped. Optimistically, I had thought we would be able to shoot the entire exercise section in one go, but in the event, I think we managed a couple of stretches and a portrait. Anyway, it was the first of several shoots spread around the company's upcoming touring schedule. At least it broke the ice.

Today we finally flew off on tour. It looks like I will be gone for six weeks rather than two (casting still isn't confirmed) so I have packed accordingly. As hard as it was to leave Torje at home, I am very glad he's there. Leaving a house for six weeks is logistically a nightmare. Bills have to be paid and mail has to be forwarded, and whereas in the old days you could probably explain to a bank manager that you'd be gone indefinitely, these days it's not so easy. You can't stop computers doing their job, and when the appropriate date flashes up in their little microchip memories, they send out their final demands regardless of your circumstances.

Besides, it's so much easier to leave than to be left behind. For the traveller, there is stimulus, novelty and adventure. For the person left, life essentially goes on in the same way, but with a very large gap. For an old timer like me, though, touring is not so much a matter of visiting new places as revisiting old ones. Last year I was under the surgeon's arthroscope, having my left ankle fixed (an interior impingement, if it helps to know) after two years of trying to pretend it might mend on its own. I missed the most novel tour schedule in years, which included some pretty sensational journeys, like Israel to Buenos Aires via London. For The Royal Ballet, more often than not, touring abroad means Japan and the United States, and I have stayed in this particular hotel, the Wyndham Garden in Costa Mesa, California, no less than three times. The staff now recognise me. 'Sure is great to have you back, Miss Bull.' There's no doubt that I'm in California. The people here are extraordinarily polite, in a formulaic sort of way. There are standard greetings for delivering room service, answering the phone, serving coffee and they never vary. It's like a record stuck in a groove, but still far, far preferable to the assortment of grunts that pass for service back at home. Costa Mesa is a dull place, numbed into inactivity by the burning Californian sun, but the shopping mall is great, and the theatre – run entirely on private endowments – is superb. And I have work to do. When I'm not dancing, I've got a book to write.

20th May 1997, Costa Mesa, California
I went over to the theatre for class and a dress rehearsal of *Sleeping Beauty*. It was the same old tour feeling, the mixture of the unfamiliar and the old hat. Same old Tchaikovsky melodies, same steps, but new surroundings and new faces in old costumes. The big ballets like *Sleeping Beauty* and *Swan Lake* require a certain number of 'extras', and whereas in London we have our regulars who crop up in every production, on tour we have to find local actors and dance students to fill the gaps. On occasion, in countries where language and cultural differences make this difficult, we have been known to recruit embassy staff, and I seem to recall that in East Germany we even used members of Her Majesty's Armed Services as 'guards' in *The Firebird*.

Because the company couldn't afford the luxury of getting us here a day earlier, the rehearsal and the opening performance are both on the

same day, and just hours apart. I am only in the prologue and the third
act of *Beauty*, so I have a long and useful gap where I am able to unpack
my boxes. We all have our own way of setting up a place in the dressing-
room. Some dancers like to lay everything out on a towel, others stick
photographs on to the mirror, and some (who shall remain nameless)
simply spread sideways as far as everyone else's good nature will allow.
I don't fuss too much about space for my make-up, but I am obsessive
about shoes. I have platoons of them, all neatly arranged in serried ranks;
usually a choice of about six pairs for a major role, and three for a solo.
Pointe shoes are the sharks of the footwear world, the least evolved of all
God's creatures. They have barely changed at all since 1770, when Anna
Heinel padded her slippers with cotton wool and danced on *pointe* for the
first time, on 'stilt-like tiptoe' as a critic said at the time. Pointe shoes
come in 'pairs', but in reality, both shoes are identical, with no
consideration at all for the fact that we are born with left and right feet.
No two pairs feel the same, and very rarely do they feel absolutely right.
The really bizarre thing about pointe shoes is that they can seem just
perfect the night before a show, and bloody awful once the overture
starts. I always have a stash of shoes on stand-by, in case the chosen pair
lets me down. On tour, where we do blocks of performances and I might
have two principal roles in three days, the shoes are lined up on alert, all
around the room. Woe betide anyone who moves them. They might look
the same, but they are all subtly different. Some dancers write little
comments on the sole – 'good turner', or 'feels weird' – and Christina
McDermott has an extremely complicated logging system (in her native
Swiss-German), but I line them up, in order of preference. The best
shall be first and the worst shall be last.

Between acts, I pop down to the wardrobe to try on some costumes
which have been altered, and ask 'Mother Brown' (Michael Brown, head
of wardrobe) if *he* knows anything about the revised casting for *Don Q*.
Sometimes the costume department is one step ahead of the dancers.
Not this time, though, so no joy there. Only one thing is certain – it
won't be Darcey.

But even with her problematic ankle, Darcey does a glorious
performance in *Beauty* this evening. She describes it afterwards as
'weird, you know, fluky', but in my experience of watching her perform
over the years, it would be weird if she didn't dance like that.

Overheard as I was leaving the stage door (read this with an American
accent): Little girl – 'Mommy, why is Darcee Boucelle such a good

dancer?' Mother – 'It's because she's pretty on the inside and she's doubly pretty on the outside.'

21st May 1997, Costa Mesa, California

Up early after too little sleep. Last night's reception for the sponsors went on longer than I had hoped. I woke up this morning at 7 a.m. and made the mistake of turning on my computer. I lose myself in writing, and at ten minutes to twelve I dash from my room and bump into Darcey who is also rushing across the road, late for a midday class.

The theatre has two windowless studios, one large and one small, which are pretty similar to dance studios all over the world. Today, the girls are crowded into the smaller room upstairs. Halfway through the barre, the door creaks open and a couple of the company staff come in and sit down. A few minutes later the same thing happens, and then again, more and more people until there isn't a single member of staff (ballet and administrative) who isn't present. I look around, trying to work out the reason for this unprecedented show of mass interest in something as mundane as class, and spot a young girl in the corner, a 'baby ballerina' whose reputation has so preceded her that everyone wants to take a look. The term 'baby ballerinas' was coined in the 1930s, as a collective noun for Irina Baronova, Tamara Toumanova and Tatiana Riabouchinska (respective ages 13, 14 and 15), stars of the Ballets Russes de Monte Carlo. It came back into use about ten years ago when Peter Schaufuss at Festival Ballet (now English National Ballet) introduced a group of pre-pubescent whizz kids, among them Trinidad Sevillano and Katherine Healy. I'm not certain of the wisdom of 'forcing' talent in the same way as you force tomatoes. There are too many examples in sports like tennis and gymnastics of young people burnt out before they've fulfilled their own potential. And dance is not only about youthful vigour; it's about artistry and the expressive portrayal of ideas, something that can only be achieved with maturity and experience. In truth, this young girl isn't really a baby ballerina, although rumour has it that she's been invited to dance at the World Ballet Gala in Japan this summer, a travelling circus of tricks and technique peopled only by dancers with a minimum *pirouette* capacity of at least four turns. She's a hardworking student who deserves a show of interest and she is obviously very talented. Unable to cope with such public display at this time of the day, I leave class early and pass two of the stage management team in the corridor. 'Oh, don't tell me you're going in, too?' 'Well, we thought we might . . .' Ah! The scent of fresh talent has obviously permeated the entire building.

In the evening, Philip Mosley, the Equity Deputy, came over to my hotel room to ask for my help in composing a farewell letter to Genista McIntosh. Various theories about her departure are still doing the rounds, and the press are now joining in the fun. One of the most far-fetched speculations I've heard mentioned centres around the alleged serving of 'stale and crunchy' sandwiches to the Princess of Wales. But whatever the truth, the dancers want to write and express their thanks to her for the positive work she did during her stay. She was refreshingly natural, business-like and extremely approachable. Especially appreciated were her low-profile appearances at several ballet performances. Of course, previous General Directors have also patronised The Royal Ballet, but more normally on the first night of each production, not on the fourth cast matinées. Yet Genista came to at least two of my performances of *Swan Lake* earlier in the year, and I only had three. For that reason alone, I am happy to have a hand in penning her a letter of thanks.

25th May 1997, Costa Mesa, California
Yesterday I set a new land speed record as the Bluebird in *Sleeping Beauty*. I do sometimes wonder what conductors are thinking of when they play around so much with the tempo. I don't mind a bit of variety – spice of life and all that – but there comes a point when the choreography and the tempo can't be reconciled, and the dancer, always at the mercy of the beat, is forced to compromise. Needless to say (but I'll say it anyway) this conductor wasn't one of ours.

Today I also broke new ground when I was applauded *in the middle* of a 45-second solo. The American audiences are much more vociferous about their feelings, and today they let it be known that they liked my *pas de chats* on to *pointe* in the 'Violente' solo. It cheered me up no end as I wasn't particularly looking forward to switching solos. I feel much more at home in my normal variation, 'Coulante', but then I have been doing it for about twelve years.

Tomorrow is a day off, signifying the end of week one, and the *corps de ballet* are desperate for a rest. Already dancers are dropping like flies. Performing night after night, as we do on tour, is definitely more of a strain, but I still wonder why so many of them have suffered injuries this week. There are basically two types of injury, traumatic and chronic. The latter happen over a period of time, starting as a minor twinge and developing into a constant source of real pain. They can often be traced back to a technical fault. Turning the feet out, *á la* Charlie Chaplin, beyond the 'ten to two' position is the classic origin of several injuries in the ankles and knees. Traumatic injuries, on the other hand, are the sudden twists and tumbles which happen without warning. Sometimes there's an obvious reason, like a hole in the stage or an unstable piece of scenery, but they often come about when dancers attempt to leap around before they are properly warm. Until muscles are warmed up, they are much less flexible, and the extremeties of classical ballet put them at risk. But most of this week's injuries happened during a show, so the usual rationale – insufficiently warm – doesn't apply. I worry that they may not be drinking enough water. It's much hotter here than it is at home, and consequently there will be a lot more sweat involved in an evening's work. If you don't replace the fluid you lose through perspiration, you can very quickly become dehydrated. Even a small amount of dehydration impairs co-ordination, and a decrease in co-ordination increases the risk of injury. Whatever the reason, I hope they recover before Japan, or *Don Q* could be seriously undermanned.

28th May 1997, Costa Mesa, California
Yesterday it was back to work, although it doesn't feel much like work. This week the company is dancing the Ravel triple bill, and I'm not involved. I'm obviously not a Ravel sort of dancer – don't ask me why – so I'm simply rehearsing, with Inaki, for the *Don Quixote* shows which may or may not happen. I still don't know. It feels strange to be out here on tour without performing. Even in California, there's only so much shopping a girl can do, and although I'm using the spare time to concentrate on writing, I can't help thinking I could be doing that at home. I find it quite difficult to focus when there is no end product. While I might be a week away from *Don Q*, I could also be several years away from it. Until I get the go-ahead for the performances in Japan, it's hard to know just where I am, physically. Today I felt less than 100 per cent, so I didn't rehearse at all. I've had a queasy stomach for quite a while now, and while shopping for a cure in Savon Drugs, I ran into William Tuckett who has been in bed for two days with a similar complaint. He persuaded me that what I need is not available without the say so of a doctor, so I went back to the hotel and called for one. It meant missing a half-hour rehearsal, but with the schedule that lies ahead (or does it?) I can't afford to be ill.

Now that dancing is occupying less of my available brain power, I have space to ponder the situation surrounding the House, back home. Ten days without any solid news, and my stomach starts to feel strange and queasy again as I re-run recent events in my head and wonder where we go from here.

29th May 1997, Costa Mesa, California

The treacle of the *Don Q* casting thickens. It appears now that I am definitely doing the performance on June 10th, in Takamatsu, but it is still unclear just who will be dancing the opening night on June 4th. Miyako Yoshida and Sylvie Guillem aren't here, Leanne Benjamin is going home in the morning, and Darcey Bussell is off. (A most inelegant euphemism to describe an injured dancer. It evokes images of rancid milk.) One could take an educated guess about the casting, but one refrains from doing so; even with such apparently incontrovertible logic, it might not be right.

And there is always the unexpected: I went in to the theatre to rehearse with Inaki, and discovered that he had to go to the dentist this afternoon to have his wisdom teeth removed. He was able to work a little, but he wasn't up to trying the trickier stuff, like throwing me around and holding me above his head on one hand. What is it about some performances? Why do they seem to be so jinxed?

This evening, with no performance to dance, I flick through the TV channels searching for something to entertain me – anything in all fifty-two channels – and come across a face I recognise. I can't quite place it; it has a kind of Inspector Dalgliesh familiarity. It takes me a few minutes before I realise the face belongs to Mike Morris, head of personnel at Covent Garden, and I am watching the American screening of *The House*, the documentary television series which went behind the scenes at the Royal Opera House and laid it bare to the nation. Despite having more stations than British Rail, American television is almost totally unwatchable, and feeling pretty certain that this is about as good as I will find, I continue to watch. Knowing what we know now about the House, I see the programme with different eyes, and it seems, in retrospect, to have been a clear harbinger of the chaos that lay ahead. Towards the end of this episode, the camera switches for a nano second to a full screen close-up of someone well known within the Opera House – it's so brief, it's almost a subliminal flash – and a shriek resounds throughout the Wyndham Garden Hotel. The rest of The Royal Ballet is watching too.

30th May 1997, Costa Mesa, California
The treacle clarifies. After class this morning I bumped into Inaki, toothless but standing, who asked me, in his best Argentinian accent, 'So, Deborah, you want to hear the good news? We're doing the opening night together.' Obviously the logic *was* incontrovertible. We started rehearsals two days ago, and we have five more days before the curtain goes up in Toyama. Somewhere during those five days we have to cross the Pacific.

Let's just be clear about this: Kitri is not an easy role. *Don Q* may not be the greatest ballet of all time, but it still involves some pretty tough dancing; three acts of leaping around which culminate in one of ballet's big 'show stoppers', the *'Don Q' pas de deux*, standard fare of every fund-raising gala in the world. It's the sort of role which would normally take at least a month's preparation, and here we are, the uncast and the novice, planning to do it next week. It's slightly ironic that from having no performances, I have been catapulted to the first night. Now I'm not stupid; I recognise that this is a result of circumstances and not an inexplicable revival in the fortunes of Deborah Bull, prima ballerina, nonpareil. But it is without doubt a test of resilience. Every time a dancer is uncast in a role we have previously performed, another little fragment is chipped from our already fragile self-esteem. It isn't easily replaced. In fact, I'm not sure it's ever replaced. Intellectually, I can rationalise the fact that I hadn't been given a performance of *Don Quixote* in Japan – after all, there are several casts and a limited number of shows. But that certainly doesn't stop the gradual diminution of my ego with a little nick here and a little nick there. In the end, rationality has no part to play in a dancer's self-image.

Nevertheless, ego bruised but still intact, there's a show to do next week in Japan, and only me to do it. One of the company asked if I have the letters MUG tattooed on my forehead, but I don't see it that way. Call me English, but I've never been one to expect the full-blown star treatment. I'm a Salieri not a Mozart, a Damon Hill not a Michael Schumacher. I wouldn't flounce away from the track muttering about the engine letting me down. Like Damon in his unreliable Arrows car, I'd stay and help the mechanics push it clear. Deep breath and some stern talking to myself and I'll be fine.

On the strength of the rehearsal this morning, we will definitely be fine. The clock struck twelve, and off we went, pausing only to change shoes between acts, and running the whole ballet with no problems at all.

I could feel the scar tissue start to form over the wound in my ego and I left the building an imperceptible millimetre taller. I only made one mistake: at the point where I'm supposed to revive my lover, Basilio/Inaki, I slapped him briskly on the cheeks. Or rather, I slapped him briskly on exactly the spot where he used to have two wisdom teeth.

Once I had floated down off my cloud, I felt tired and tearful. I often find that supreme physical effort has that effect. *Aerobic* exercise, long and sustained, releases endorphins which put you on a high. *Anaerobic* exercise, in my experience, makes me want to cry. I'm sure there is an emotional element at work here as well as something physical, but whatever the reason, I felt battered in both body and soul. I went back to my hotel room, locked the door, ordered room service and curled up with a plate of pasta.

Funny how life works out. I came out here thinking I would be back again in two weeks' time, with a fortnight at home to work on the DK book. As it turns out, I'm doing the first night of *Don Q* next week in Japan. The prospect of an easy tour has vanished.

June 1997

1st June 1997, Costa Mesa, California–Toyama, Japan

We're on the way to the airport as I write, the full company, plus some additions. Niccy Tranah has brought her new baby daughter, Octavia, on tour, and her parents have been staying here in Costa Mesa to act as babysitters. There's a moment of loaded sentiment as Dennis, Niccy's father, waves a temporary goodbye to Joan, his wife of fifty years, who is coming on to Japan with us. During their entire marriage, they haven't been separated for anything more than the odd day, and as we drive off, Dennis manoeuvres himself so that he keeps the coach in sight as long as he can. The windows are tinted, so he can't possibly be able to see the three generations of his family inside, but nevertheless, he keeps on waving until he is nothing more than a speck in the distance. I'm notoriously sentimental – I blub during the opening titles of *The Railway Children* – and there is something so touching about all this that I feel the familiar pricking behind the eyelids, and the give-away wobbly chin. (Why do we talk about stiff upper lips when it's invariably the lower one that starts to quiver?) I glance around me and realise I'm not alone. The rest of the company is either searching for tissues or hastily putting on dark glasses.

It is a nightmare trip. Today clearly demonstrates the worst aspects of touring, and although it's tempting to put it down to cost cutting, all the money in the world couldn't ameliorate the physical discomfort of crossing eight time zones as well as the date line. I've criss-crossed the skies in most directions, but the flight from the west coast of the US to Japan must be one of the worst there is.

We left the hotel at 10 a.m. on Saturday and finally reached our destination at midnight on Sunday. I was upgraded on the first and longest leg (LA to Tokyo) which definitely helped. I have very clear memories of a similar flight several years ago, when I was still a soloist. There was a chink in the Berlin Wall between business and cattle class and I could see row upon row of empty seats and the heads of the three principals who were dancing on the opening night. Back in steerage, every seat was full and my knees were up around my chin. When we arrived in

Tokyo, disaster struck and the entire cast for the first performance had to be changed. I prised my body out of the foetal position, danced Gamzatti in *La Bayadère*, and got promoted into the bargain.

This time, being the new, default, first cast, I was assigned one of the rare upgrades which travel agents earn when they block book a large part of the aircraft. Bliss. Had we been performing in Tokyo I would have been ready for the stage as soon as I disembarked. But unfortunately the fun didn't end when we reached Narita airport. We still had to cross Tokyo by coach and fly from the domestic airport to Toyama, a smallish town in the north of Japan. Hardly the centre of the *artistic* universe, but for the next few days it will be the centre of mine.

In a country which gave us the Walkman and the Game Boy, those two spurious contributions to world culture, the passport control officer struck a charmingly anachronistic note. Having satisfied himself that my work-permit was above board, he pulled out a neat little box of exquisite wood-block stamps of varying colours – presumably to differentiate between the numerous types of visas and permits – and gave me the all clear. It is precisely this co-existence of seemingly irreconcilable customs and culture which make Japan what it is, and this synthesis of tradition and technology, ancient and modern, is encapsulated in his little box of signs.

Somewhere in the rigmarole of passport control and baggage collection we managed to lose a body, although it wasn't until the interpreters had done a roll call by phone between the three coaches that we established it was Misha Messerer who had gone missing. Misha travels all over the world as a guest ballet teacher, and I felt sure he was the best person to be left behind; not only does he speak some Japanese, but he is famously unflappable, which makes him the perfect teacher for touring. Never mind that the stage isn't ready, that there's no piano, that the promoters have rented the local disco for us to use as a studio. Misha copes, and what's more, he makes light of it. He comes from a dynasty of Russian dancers; his mother, Sulamith (eighty-nine, and still going strong) holds the unique distinction of having been, in the 1920s, simultaneously ballerina at the Bolshoi Theatre and swimming champion of Moscow for five consecutive years. We're talking *seriously* unflappable genetics.

By the time we arrived at Haneda airport, Misha was safely there, having crossed Tokyo alone in a taxi. We took off for Toyama, not so much a flight as a flying bus ride, and to cap it all, when we landed we had another coach waiting to take us on the hour and a half journey to our final destination. By now I was suffering that familiar queasiness which comes with fatigue and defies you to touch coffee, knowing that while it will alleviate one condition, it will almost certainly aggravate the other. But it was quite interesting to be forced to stay awake at the time when I would normally be dozing. I have my most fascinating conversations with myself in the middle of the night, single-handedly resolving universal enigmas, but I'm usually too sleepy to get up and write down the answers. Now, while my head is still on Californian time but I'm physically in Japan, I'm full of lucid thoughts and awake enough to enjoy them. I view the surroundings through wide-open yet slightly spaced-out eyes, and find myself stimulated by everything I see.

Most other people were, by now, sound asleep, but Michael Nunn and I chatted all the way. Despite the rigours of the day, his customary wit was as sharp as ever. As we pulled into the hotel and the rest of the company started to stir, he asked, in a voice thick with innocence: 'Oh, are we here already?'

Well, not quite. We still had check-in to deal with, and just when comfort was most sorely needed, it seemed to be out of stock. The Japanese always look after us extremely well, but the hotel here in Toyama doesn't quite match the standards we've come to expect in Tokyo. My heart hit rock bottom when I opened the door to my room. It's basically an overnight business hotel which meets minimum requirements – no CNN, no dataport, no food available and cat swinging is definitely out. And it had one of those preformed bathrooms, constructed off-site from a single piece of plastic and dropped into position in the corner of the bedroom. Within the company they're known as 'pods' and I've only ever seen them here in Japan. There's absolutely nothing wrong with them, except for the fact that the taller men in the company can't stand up in them. Disgruntled and dishevelled, I sat down to eat the sandwiches that had been thoughtfully provided on arrival. They were made from that ultra-light, super-spongy white bread unique to Japan, the sort that Anthony Dowell says 'you can use to put on your make-up', and I felt this was not a high point in my life. The nightmare had gone from bad to worse. I hope it will all be over by the time I wake up.

I wonder why I feel so insecure when I change cities. Yet again I am gripped by a dreadful panic, a longing to have familiar things around me. I feel lost without words or language that I can understand. It doesn't help that I am exhausted beyond the limits of endurance, but I am already struck by the misogyny at work here in Japan – and I'm not particularly feminist, either. I don't like hostility dressed up to look like subservience. I prefer it to wear its own clothes.

2nd June1997, Toyama, Japan
Slept fairly well, although I was disappointed to be wide awake at 7.30 a.m. Still, I got seven and a half hours of sleep, which, compared to some of my colleagues, is pretty good going.

I spend the morning trying to log on to Compuserve, to send and retrieve my e-mail. I've come to rely totally on my daily messages from Torje to keep my spirits up, and to let me know what's going on back at the House. I'm determined not to be beaten by the rather bizarre phone system here. I haven't cracked it yet, but I do manage to locate some socket splitters which should help get me on-line. After the laid-back Californian experience of the last two weeks, I'm assaulted by something very different as I trek from shop to shop in Toyama. The obsequious-ness, the conformity, the rigidity, the constant noise. There are loud-speakers on every corner telling me I don't know what, and recorded birdsong which indicates when it's safe to cross the road. It's all a far cry from the US, and even further from Blighty.

Although the company have a day off to recover from yesterday's hellish journey, Inaki and I have to rehearse. We find the theatre. This isn't difficult in a town the size of Toyama, although getting to it without offending the traffic police is a different matter. It's a fantastic building. How can a small town in Japan boast a theatre which rivals even the best facilities in London? And why can we perform Western dance to packed houses in obscure Japanese towns which have at their heart the culture of the East? I know you have to leave home to be appreciated, but this seems to be taking things too far.

Our rehearsal isn't *too* bad, but we are both feeling the effects of twenty hours in transit and we'll have to do better on the opening night the day after tomorrow. In some ways, I would have been happy to trust to luck and leave the ballet at the level it was last Friday, in California. It was pretty good, all things considered, and I'm not sure there's time to improve. But on the positive side, our rehearsal today does iron out some technical hitches, and a little light exercise is not a bad idea when you're trying to reset the internal clock.

In the afternoon I have a radio interview, and I am surprised to be presented (on air) with a bag of tomatoes. Surreal. I can only hope they are the symbol of Toyama, and not a precursor of how the performance will be received on Wednesday. The interviewer insists on asking the questions herself, despite the fact that we are provided with an interpreter. Unfortunately, her grasp of English is not as great as her enthusiasm, and I have to keep asking whether she is speaking English or Japanese. The two languages sounded almost identical.

3rd June 1997, Toyama, Japan
The day before the first night of *Don Quixote*, and it's been long and tiring. We had two three-hour rehearsals, one in the underground studio and one on-stage in the evening. I walked through the first rehearsal, using as little energy as possible, and managed to get home for a nap before the second. The evening's call was supposedly the dress rehearsal, and I felt slightly cross that because there are no other casts available Inaki and I had to be there. By rights we should have been home with our feet up. I took it as easily as I could, but even so, just being on my feet was tiring. Afterwards I headed straight to the only Italian restaurant in town for potatoes, pasta and bread (the carbohydrates which will see me through tomorrow night's show) then home for about ten hours' sleep.

4th June 1997, Toyama, Japan
Wednesday. The big day. It's about 3 p.m., and I have just got out of bed from my afternoon nap to eat before the show. The phone rings. It's Inaki; he feels queasy. I summon him to my room and hand over the Pepto-Bismol. 'But I don't like that,' he protests. I tell him to stop whinging and get it down. I don't want to do the show on my own tonight. Come to think of it, I don't feel so great myself. The room is spinning, and the floor has a strange habit of undulating every few minutes. I recognise this disorientation as a familiar response to jet lag, but I wish it would go away – I feel like I'm on board ship. It could be that we are both just nervous, but I really do feel very unstable. Fingers crossed that a shower, some food and a bit of fresh air helps.

Hours later I'm back in my room, exhausted and exhilarated after the first performance of *Don Quixote*, to a packed house of appreciative Japanese.

Well, we did it, and how. The gods were definitely smiling on us tonight, queasy and dizzy though we might have been; it all worked in an

'I don't know where *that* came from' sort of way. But boy, was I tired. The first act of *Don Q* is all about jumping and because of last year's injured foot, I have only recently started jumping again. So combined with the jet lag, all that leaping around was quite a shock for these 34-year-old legs. I didn't know how I was going to stay upright in Act Two, but somehow, I did. By the time we got to Act Three, the big number with all the flashy bits (Petipa with knobs on), Inaki and I stood limply in the wings and groaned to each other: 'I'm dead. I can't do it.' I was seriously worried that the whole thing would fall apart, as we both had left-over licorice limbs in place of legs. My only option was to try to relax and, in true stalwart spirit, do the best I could. The music dragged us on and with nervous smiles we took the stage for the fireworks of the last act. Then one of those miracles happened. I found a hidden reserve of energy, like the old boiled sweet that you dig out of your handbag when you're absolutely starving. The *pas de deux* went like a dream. My legs and I were reunited in the nick of time and I danced away like my better self, the me that believes I can do it, not the me that doubts my every move. This time, every balance, every spin was spot on. I know that in retrospect this is going to read like pure conceit, but right now, floating as I am, I can report that we both agreed it *could not have been better*. And it's a *great* feeling, knowing that you've done your very best, a mixture of pride in your own achievements and humility that a plethora of external elements should have chosen to combine, in your favour, at *precisely* the right time. It's akin to Halley's comet. Don't expect it too often in a single lifetime. The last time I felt like this was at White Lodge, twenty years ago, in an end-of-term demonstration class.

Now it's 1.20 a.m. and I've just packed, ready for today's early start. Our bags have to be outside our rooms by 9.30 a.m. and we catch the train to Nagoya soon afterwards. A slightly larger town, and as it's a regular date on the Japanese touring circuit, Nagoya will feel a little more familiar. After all the excitement, I don't feel much like sleeping, but I guess I should try. What a night. After all the toing and froing over casting, all the self-doubt, all the trauma of getting here, I never imagined it could all go so well. I hug the unexpected success to myself, and basking in the comfort this strange bedfellow provides, I finally fall asleep.

5th June 1997, Nagoya, Japan
Baggage outside rooms at 9.30 a.m. I didn't sleep very well – much too hyper – and I hauled myself out of bed at about 9.25 a.m. I parked my

case outside the door in a suspiciously empty corridor. After breakfast
my solitary bag was still there, and eventually I dragged it down to the
lobby myself. For the next two days I won't see it; we are travelling to
Nagoya with overnight bags only, packed, in my case, with a toothbrush,
clean underwear and several pairs of pointe shoes. I never trust shoes to
arrive on their own, and whereas you can always go on with a makeshift
costume, substituting pointe shoes is never quite so easy. I remember all
too well the time the blue boxes were delayed, in Palermo, and I did a
dress rehearsal of *Swan Lake* in a pair of shoes donated by Darcey
Bussell. It was a kind and generous gesture, but I wouldn't like to repeat
the experience.

At 11 a.m. we all gathered downstairs, laden like pack horses, and
trudged across the road to the station. This may not sound like a lot to
ask, but it epitomised a trip totally devoid of glamour and, in my case,
short on humour. At one point, the train inexplicably reversed its
direction and we even had to turn our own seats to face the opposite way.
The question 'Do I have to do *everything* myself?' sprang to mind. The
tour already feels less like an artistic experience and more like an obstacle
course. I know that art is supposed to spring forth out of adversity, as it
did last night, but a *little* comfort from time to time wouldn't go amiss.

The train arrrived late in Nagoya (yes, a Japanese train was late) and I
went straight out to buy a wheelie bag. Forget fashion, forget chic. We're
on the move. With several day trips and more overnight stays to look
forward to, I'm entering the comfort zone. I shall wheel my way around
Japan.

Another city, the same impressions. It all seems a bit like a blurred film;
there is nothing to rest my eyes on. There are no words I understand, no
buildings I understand, no faces or people I understand. I desperately
want to adjust the lens and bring it all into focus. Still, with my penchant
for familiarity, everything has a more favourable outlook now that we are
in Nagoya. We were here on our last tour, but only for a day trip. I
remember the theatre very well. We had a one night stand, just a few days
after I'd stepped in for Leanne Benjamin and danced Aurora, with two
days' notice, in Osaka. That was two years ago, when my ankle was at its
worst, and I always found that when the foot was really bad, the shoes felt
impossible. Pointe shoes are a nightmare at the best of times. There are a
few of us in the company who are real shoe fetishists – Belinda Hatley,
Christina McDermott and myself in particular. We will spend hours
selecting shoes and generally have several dozen at the ready for a major

performance. Miyako Yoshida, on the other hand, would have one or two. Does it improve our performance? Do our feet look any better? No, of course not. Is it all in our heads? Probably.

On this particular occasion, I had my usual complement of shoes, although stock may have been slightly depleted by the show in Osaka. But even Cinderella's glass slipper wasn't going to feel good on that left foot, and I had one of my (fairly) infrequent paddys, throwing all the shoes on the floor and declaring that I couldn't possibly go on. I did, of course, but this theatre, with its bamboo-matted dressing-rooms, reminds me of how long I struggled to ignore that injury before I finally bowed out and succumbed to the inevitability of the surgeon's expertise.

6th June 1997, Nagoya, Japan

An interesting rehearsal of *Romeo and Juliet*. Over the years I have danced several roles in *Romeo*, starting out as a minor peasant and moving on to dance the harlots who entertain Romeo, Mercutio and Benvolio. Sadly, there's no longer a role for me, so I wasn't there to witness today's call, but apparently Monica Mason and Anthony Dowell stepped in for Leanne and Bruce Sansom (who have their show tonight) and danced the lead roles *full out*. Every gesture, every mime scene, double *sauts de basques*, and, allegedly, the balcony scene kiss thrown in. I can't believe I missed it. The episode will undoubtedly pass into company history. It made me laugh because I can see myself in twenty years, like Mon, never having danced Juliet, with a stage call on a day trip to some obscure city my one opportunity to do so. And I would do exactly the same thing as she did. I'm not the only person in the company to have made that particular comparison today.

7th June 1997, Osaka, Japan

We have arrived in Osaka for a one night stop-over and a single performance of *Don Q*. Osaka is the starting point for visits to Kyoto, and I really didn't want to come within striking distance without going there. So once I had dropped off my bags and eaten another of those cotton wool sandwiches I bravely headed for the train station and the 'Limited Express'. I had no more than two or three hours, as I still find it impossible to break that hard and fast rule of the theatre – check in at 6.55 p.m., 'the half' – but it was better to go briefly to Kyoto than not to go at all. I decided I would have to limit the number of temples I could see, and narrowed it down to Ginkaku-Ji, the 'Silver' Pavilion, and the

Philosopher's Walk back towards the station.

The guide books are full of beautiful images of Kyoto, but arriving there on the train you could be forgiven for thinking you'd come to the wrong place. It looks like every other bit of Japan; more off-white buildings, more noise, more chaos, more traffic fumes. I found a taxi and told the driver where I wanted to go. I needn't have bothered. Everyone who comes to Kyoto is visiting either the Gold or the Silver Pavilion.

I was dropped off at the bottom of a narrow, sloping passageway, lined on either side with kiosks selling film, souvenirs, postcards, ice-cream and other, indigenous, foodstuffs. I fell in with the crowds who swept me up the hill towards the temple. Inside its gates, everything was perfect, the light, the weather, the *peace*, and I gradually felt the spirit of Kyoto begin to wash over me. As I wandered around the garden, I grew less aware of the big picture and focused more on the details, small things which seem to me to contain the essence of the place. Texture and sound became paramount and I wanted to touch everything, to feel the smooth heat of the bamboo, hear the cool of the water. After a while I stopped noticing the crowds of school children – it is, after all, Saturday – and I was able to concentrate on myself. It's been a week of stress (external, not internal) and it was wonderful to feel it drain away and be replaced by a sense of calm, a rare experience indeed for me. The sun was a little too intense, but in the shaded light of the Japanese foliage it felt cool and perfectly pleasant. The machine gun chatter of the tour guides faded into the background. I was with myself. Modern Japan receded and the afternoon was magical.

Down from the temple and past the souvenir shops, I joined the Philosopher's Walk. An elderly Japanese couple were picking the tiny, bitter-sweet cherries from the overhanging trees and handed one to me. It was an uncommon expression of spontaneous welcome; in formal circumstances, the welcome is elaborately gracious. Out in the street, there is sometimes – not always – an air of suspicion, especially towards a single, unaccompanied female. I diverted briefly to visit Honen-In, a garden famous for the twin mounds of sand just inside its gate, and I watched the gardener decide on the motifs he would rake into their surface today. I looked on in total fascination, aware that he was working within a discipline every bit as codified as my own, yet I was unable to fathom the rules which were dictating his decisions. As intellect takes over from instinct, my mind goes back to business. They'll be calling 'the half' in Osaka. I'd better go.

10th June 1997, Takamatsu, Japan
Arrived yesterday in Takamatsu, a seaside resort on Shikoku island, in
the south of Japan, for my second performance of *Don Quixote*. The rest
of the company made the trip from Osaka this morning, but I didn't
fancy following four hours on a train with three hours of jumping
around, so a small group of us dancing the principal roles made up an
advance party and came here a day early. First there was the shinkansen
– the bullet train – and then a 'local' for the final leg of the trip, crossing
a wide stretch of water before arriving at this Brighton of the East. We
checked into what seemed like yet another standard business hotel, but
it concealed the most diverse collection of rooms behind its dull façade.
Mine had sliding doors of paper which opened to reveal a tiny Japanese
sitting-room with tatami matting and ankle-high tables.

Performance days are always a bit tense, but the stress of the day was
relieved for me by a comment, downstairs at breakfast, from a dancer
who will remain anonymous. The more conventional elements of
breakfast, toast, cereal and so on, were served alongside a tiny green salad
with a very dubious-looking dressing, a slick of pale-coloured, viscous-
textured fluid. I didn't say a word, merely looked aghast, and a
porcelain-perfect ballerina piped up, 'yeah, there's a man out the back
with a magazine.' The incongruity of the source of the comment has kept
me laughing all day. Face like an angel, mind like a sewer.

But it's hardly surprising. Dancers are completely relaxed about sex
and sexuality. We walk around half-naked, we touch each other
constantly for a living and we refer to body parts as nothing more than
tools of the trade. I, for instance, am an expert on bottoms, having spent
several years wishing I'd been born with something other than the one I
have been given. Of course there are boundaries which are never crossed
– it's usually a case of all talk and no trousers – but the boundaries are as
flexible as we are and inoffensive sexual banter is common currency
amongst us.

This evening's performance of *Don Q* with Inaki should have been my
last, but rumour is rife that Darcey (who arrives tomorrow) will not do
the third of her three scheduled performances. Her ankle is much better,
but it's not good enough yet. The show went well, but afterwards I
missed the feeling of relief which followed our surprise success on the
opening night in Toyama. I am fast falling in love with my latest partner,
in a totally professional sense, of course. He's a real darling, and calm as
a walking valium, which helps me no end. There's nothing unusual,

though, in this amorous inclination towards Inaki. Over my seventeen years in the company, I must have danced with at least twenty-five different male partners, and I've fallen in love with most, although not all of them. I've been partnered by men who tower above me, and men who can't reach my outstretched arm when I'm up on *pointe*. Men who are frightfully famous and men who are just starting out. Men who are absolute sweethearts, and men who are absolute sods. But none of this matters. What matters is that I can trust them when we work together. The rehearsal process which precedes performance is always intimate, and often embarrassing, and I need to know that they won't laugh at my weird ideas and peculiar working practices, at least not until they're outside the studio. Inaki has been wonderful.

12th June 1997, Yokohama, Japan
We're in Yokohama, or Oklahoma as Inaki calls it. I always thought of Yokohama as nothing more than a suburb of Tokyo, probably because we normally perform here on a day trip from the capital. In fact, it's a large city in its own right. Our hotel is perched on the top of a hill, and it's a ten-minute walk to the nearest shop. From the tenth floor, I look down at a huge, bustling dockyard, but I still feel as if I'm stuck in the middle of nowhere. Last night, after we arrived, I ordered dinner in my unusually spacious room. There didn't seem to be any reason to leave it, unless I intended to get in a cab and go wherever it's at in Yokohama. As nice as this place is, 'it' ain't here.

I've finally got to the stage where I don't know where I am. I think I'm actually writing this in Yokosuka, on a day trip from Yokohama. It may sound like a very 'Englishwoman abroad' type of comment, but Japanese cities really do look the same. Even in the very beautiful ones like Kyoto, the lovely bits are pretty much tucked away, hidden. All the cities tend to look identical, especially to a Western eye that can't differentiate between name plates and street signs. My overriding impression is of a mass of fragile constructions, mostly in shades of 'chino-off-white'. Very GAP. It's really interesting that in a country where conformity seems to be a prized quality, the buildings make no attempt at all to fit in. They just exist, higgledy-piggledy, each one independent of the others. Don't they have town planners here? The skyline seems very nineties, each building striving to make an individual impression rather than subjugating itself to the whole. Strange, in a nation where the whole is still revered in a way that died at home long ago. If anything, in England it's the other way around. We're all hung up on whether or not the buildings fit in, but the individual and his right to be unique is considered sacrosanct.

We're now a month into the tour. The company's bearing up but homesickness is beginning to set in. Philip Cornfield, one of the pianists, made the mistake of playing 'Londonderry Air' for the *fondu* exercise at the barre, and a dancer from the Emerald Isle dissolved into tears and rushed out. Perhaps the endless travelling has made this month seem even longer.

Darcey Bussell arrived yesterday, in good form, her ankle greatly improved after a couple of weeks off. She bears no news of the House, and I'm finding this lengthy silence without fresh information un-settling. I long to be back on the inside, rather than trapped in this far-flung exile which keeps me away from Torje and English newspapers. I'm hungry for news.

I'm waiting to hear, for certain, whether or not Darcey will do the last performance of *Don Q* in Tokyo. The next question is, of course, if she doesn't do it, who will? You would think that having done two performances already with Inaki, the answer to that would be obvious. But I've been around for much too long to risk holding my breath.

13th June 1997, Yokohama, Japan
Well, I got my answer to yesterday's final question when the call sheet for next week appeared. There, in black and white, was a *Don Q* rehearsal for Inaki and me. Just one, mind you, but it was all I needed to know.

15th June 1997, Yokohama–Sapporo, Japan
On the move again, this time to Sapporo. I travelled on the bus with Oliver Symons, a veteran of touring and an expert at making the per diem stretch right to the last day. He has a wealth of old stories about the company, and a sharp eye for a new one. This morning, prior to our departure, he had been watching a wedding in the Yokohama hotel. Japanese weddings generally take place in big Western hotels, and they cost breathtaking, mind-blowing sums. The hotels vie with each other to offer bigger and better packages with titles like 'Your Perfect Day' or 'British Wedding'. The quirk that surely drags them all to Yokohama is the possibility of getting married by an indoor lake in the lobby while a steady stream of guests check in and out in the background. The priest on this special occasion had held Olly captivated, throwing in a few words in English (probably for the amazed onlookers) and gesticulating

wildly, like a traffic policeman. I asked him if he had picked up any tips for his role as Friar Laurence in *Romeo and Juliet*. 'Oh no, dear,' he replied. 'It was *much* too much for the stage.'

The plane journey was marred by tragedy. Just after take-off, one of the interpreters was on her feet and running to the back of the plane. She returned with Lucy Haith and Angela Coia, the two company physiotherapists, and I could see from where I was sitting that there was a medical emergency up front. An old Japanese lady had suffered a heart attack, and the captain announced over the speaker system that we would be returning to Tokyo. The plane turned back and forty minutes later we landed. Throughout this entire time, Angie and Lucy were practising CPR (cardiopulmonary resuscitation) on the patient, trying to keep her alive until the paramedics could take over on the ground. Unfortunately there was no hope and she was dead by the time we touched down. Luke Heydon, a company soloist sitting next to me, said that these things always happen in threes. This death, for him, was the third. The first was an old school friend who died recently in a tragic accident, the second a member of the opera chorus for whom redundancy piled just too much on an already overburdened plate. She killed herself last week.

18th June 1997, Sapporo, Japan
It's lovely to be back in Hokkaido island in the north. It's so different from the rest of Japan, so much greener and much less densely populated. Although there is an indigenous population, the island wasn't really settled until halfway through the last century. It is wonderfully spacious, and I love seeing the mountains so close to Sapporo. It's been a beautiful day, cooler and fresher, and this evening the sun is still bright and strong, even at six o'clock. After the chaos of the last two weeks I feel I can breathe again and relax, if only for a moment. We're here for just four days.

Life back at home isn't quite so peaceful. Gossiping with the stage crew during a break in rehearsals, I learn that two days ago the *Independent* in London carried the hot news that the Opera House has been using Lottery money to fund its redundancy programme. Well, it would be hot, if it were news. The necessity for funding to carry us through the closure period (including the unfortunate laying off of several staff) was clearly and openly declared in the original application. But in their unshakeable belief that there's no story like an old story, the other papers have rushed to join in this particular bout of Opera House bashing. The *Mirror* has even set up a telephone hotline so that the public can vote on whether or not they think redundancy payments are a fair use of Lottery cash. There's a general sense of outrage that the Lottery, bringer only of joy, should be tainted by its association with something as unpleasant (or realistic) as the loss of a job. Of course, it would have been wonderful if the entire staff of the House could have remained on the payroll throughout closure, but without a House to clean, or staff to feed, several jobs simply disappeared. Imagine the fury that would have ensued if the House had been discovered paying staff to continue in jobs which no longer exist. Why the *Independent* should have chosen to drag the matter up at this particular juncture I can't imagine.

19th June 1997, Sapporo—Tokyo, Japan
On the move again, this time from Sapporo back to Tokyo. Amanda Jones, our press officer, managed to pin me down on the coach from the airport to discuss my July reading in a Barnes and Noble bookstore in New York. I'm supposed to read *Cinderella* to a room full of children, and then judge the ones who have turned up in fancy dress. We've both avoided thinking about it, as we know that the store will be expecting me, too, to come kitted out in full regalia: tutu, toe shoes and tiara. In fact, whoever organises these things has already registered their disappoint- ment at Amanda's reluctance, on my behalf, to do anything quite so tasteless and tacky. It doesn't help that an American ballerina was more than willing to oblige just a few months ago. But we're British, dammit, and I do believe there are times when dressing up simply isn't appropriate. We are not clowns. Amanda and I agree that public humiliation is best avoided. I'll do the judging in Armani.

We've arrived in Tokyo in time to meet Hurricane Opal, brewing for some time out in the ocean and now making its presence felt on the south island. The north island, from whence we came, is still bathed in glorious sunshine. Typical. It doesn't matter what time of the year we come here, it's always the rainy season and we invariably manage to whip up a storm.

I must admit, it's great to be back in Tokyo. I've stayed here in the Shinagawa district so many times now that I regard it as my second home, and, most importantly, I know exactly where to lay my hands on the bare neccessities of life, namely a bunch of bananas and a couple of litres of water. It's a lively little district, due mostly to the presence of a major train station where overground and underground lines merge, the Clapham Junction of Japan. From my larger than usual room I have a terrific view of some of the longest trains I've ever seen in my life.

The company is holding out pretty well, except that having come all this way to dance Juliet, Darcey has lost her Romeo. She was to have danced with Michael (Stuart) Cassidy, but he's nursing an injured knee and he doesn't feel that he can make it through *Romeo and Juliet* without jeopardising the rest of his season. There's an awful lot of work still ahead, both in London and at the Met in New York. So poor Darcey finds herself asking, in the great tradition of all Juliets, 'where is my Romeo?' She's still waiting for an answer.

Being taller than your average ballerina, Darcey needs a partner of stature so options are few and far between. It's rumoured that it might even be Adam Cooper, super-Cooper, ex-principal of the company and the man who hit the headlines last year dancing the lead role in choreographer Matthew Bourne's all-male *Swan Lake*.

The House news from home continues to sound ominous. A couple of days after the *Independent* ran its 'exclusive', I'm told the Opera House was in the headlines again. Chris Smith, Secretary of State for National Heritage, gave a warning two days ago that the House's status as a publicly funded institution might now be under threat. At an informal lunch with journalists – is there such a thing? – he openly announced that he had something to say to the Opera House management: 'You have a choice. If you want to carry on being in receipt of public money, you have to show the public responsibilities that go with that. I do have the power to sit down with the Arts Council and talk about their funding responsibilities . . .' A simple sentence hiding a strong statement of power. In an interview with *The Times* the same day, he puts it even more bluntly: 'The Opera House must not be an exclusive place that only the toffs can go to.' The toffs? Whenever I hear about these 'toffs' that supposedly frequent the House, I think about the small crowd of regulars who gathered, nightly, outside the stage door after each show; David, a Tower Hamlets schools inspector, and Martin, who takes the train every night from Ipswich (and back again) and has seen every cast of *Sleeping Beauty*, stretching right back to Fonteyn. They are neither toffee nor, for that matter, humbug. They're pure gold and they make up the House's core audience.

Chris Smith's uncompromising remarks come a week after he ordered an Arts Council internal inquiry into the goings-on that led to Genista McIntosh's departure and her speedy replacement by Mary Allen, the Arts Council's Secretary-General. 'I want to get to the bottom of the conflicting interests,' he warned.

20th June 1997, Tokyo, Japan
It seems that everyone wants to know about the internal wranglings at
the Opera House. From the latest staff bulletin, I've had news of *another*
inquiry to be held later this year. Last week's article in the *Independent*
mentioned, in passing, that Gerald Kaufman, the erstwhile script writer
for the sixties satirical TV show, 'That Was the Week That Was' and
former Labour minister, is tipped to chair the new Commons Select
Committee on National Heritage. Kaufman said then that he expected
the committee to 'investigate what is happening at the Opera House'.
The staff bulletin confirms that a Select Committee investigation will
indeed take place, looking into the running of both the Opera House and
English National Opera at the Coliseum. It all seems a bit premature to
me, as Kaufman hasn't actually got the job yet.

22nd June 1997, Tokyo, Japan
My final *Don Q.* I had a good feeling about it and I was right. There were
moments of purely personal triumph; not moments for the public to
savour (although I hope they enjoyed them too) but little demons that I
privately knocked on the head. No matter how secure and confident you
feel in the studio, when you get on stage and the curtain goes up, there's
a 50 per cent chance that all that solidity will go liquid. What seemed, in
rehearsal, like a walk in the park turns into a tiptoe through a minefield.
On a good night like tonight, the confidence and the security don't desert
you as the overture strikes up. You find yourself dancing with a
heightened awareness, and with more time than usual to enjoy it. The
tempi and the steps are the same as always, but rather than battling to
reconcile them there seems to be time to indulge and the courage to dare.
Tonight, for some reason, I had that courage. I dared and it worked. It
was a goody. At least, I think it was, but for once in my life, I'll have a
chance to find out.

At home, in accordance with the rules of the Musicians Union, we're
allowed to film one orchestral rehearsal of each production. This means
that while the company have a clear and useful record of the first cast in
action, the other casts very rarely get an opportunity to see themselves
on film. Despite the fact that I'm a child of the Sony age, I have no record
of myself on stage. (Unless you count my television appearance in the
corps de ballet in *The Nutcracker* and two brief solos in *Sleeping Beauty*.)
For me, seeing myself dance is just like hearing my own voice; an
enormous shock and a deep disappointment. It's proof, yet again, that

the way I see myself bears little relationship to the way everyone else sees me.

Here in Japan there's no such union rule, and Sylvie Guillem wanted to exploit that fact by videoing her performance of *Don Q* last night. Now it wouldn't have crossed my mind to suggest that if one cast was being filmed, then all three casts could be filmed, but Inaki, my younger (and technologically sophisticated) partner worked this out, and lo and behold, a film has been made. I guess it could solve my Christmas present problems, but I know that my image of this show as a 'goody' is going to be cruelly shattered by one click of the remote control, and the steady improvement which rose-tinted retrospectacles would inevitably bestow will be forever denied me by the existence of this incriminating evidence. I know. I could just refrain from looking at it, or even refuse to accept the tape which will find its way to me in due course. Yeah, sure. Course I could.

24th June 1997, Tokyo, Japan
My last day in Japan. I had breakfast with Ted Pursey, one of the most familiar faces around the Opera House. He's worked there since 1961. Theatre runs in the Pursey family blood, and he has several relatives, all across London, getting various curtains up on time. Like me he rose through the ranks, starting out on the crew and progressing over the years to the post of Assistant Technical Director. He'll be retiring soon, and I suggested to him that he should write a history of the theatre from behind the scenes. He's seen it all, triumphs and tantrums, and his account of what goes on would come from a different perspective indeed. Like me, he regrets the gradual disintegration of the 'old school' approach, the feeling that the theatre and what we do there is more important than any single personality who passes through it. And he agreed that if anything brings down the Opera House it won't be governments or lack of finance, it will be the absence of the personal goodwill that ultimately makes the place tick. He gave me some harrowing figures on the recent redundancies; the opera chorus has gone down from 80 to 36, and the stage crew, which used to number 103, has dropped to 48. Overall, 320 of the 820 strong work-force are facing redundancy. Jobs will be reoffered when the House reopens, but what are all these people supposed to do during three years of lay-off?

It reminded me how fortunate we've been in the ballet company, where the redundancies have been in single figures. For this we can be grateful to Anthony Dowell, Anthony Russell-Roberts and to the nature of the work we do. You simply can't have a major classical ballet company with fewer than the eighty dancers we currently employ, and as the next couple of years will depend on selling out larger theatres, we'll have no option but to stage the sort of works which are most capable of attracting larger audiences – the big classical ballets. And there is the other argument, mercifully unproven (as yet) that you cannot disband a *corps de ballet* and expect it to reconvene two years later without a serious drop in standards as well as numbers. Listening to Ted, and with no more performances of *Don Q* to distract me, I realise that this leg of the tour is coming to a close and tomorrow I'll be back in London, in the thick of it all again.

25th June 1997, Tokyo–London
A small group of us, those not involved in *Romeo and Juliet*, head home today. The rest of the company, and Adam Cooper, guest artist, have two more shows before they fly back. In the end, Adam *was* prevailed upon to fly out and partner Darcey in *Romeo*, and I guess he's stepped into the breach so many times that it still feels natural, even though he's no longer a member of The Royal Ballet.

I was certainly glad not to have to don ballet shoes today. The combination of intense heat, humidity and too many hours on *pointe* is a potent one. The feet swell, making the shoes rub, which in turn leads to agonisingly sore toes. Nowadays, we have some very advanced remedies, a gelatinous matter familiarly called 'squidge' being foremost amongst them. When I was a gal, the popular answer to skinned toes was raw steak. I guess raw flank is probably the least abrasive substance to put against raw flesh, but I always felt there was something particularly unsavoury about the whole idea, so I never tried it. In my book, raw steak represents the dancer's all-time greatest double myth: slap it on your feet to protect your toes, and the heat transferred during the show will cook it up into the perfect post-performance protein fix. Apocryphal, all of it.

The journey home was uneventful, long and tedious, and this time I wasn't upgraded. I'm yesterday's news; I've done my *Don Q* and I'm flying home in steerage.

In the skies over West London, we were locked into a holding pattern, a great circling aviation waltz, before they let us back on to English soil. It feels naughty but nice to be home when everyone else is still hard at work dancing away on the other side of the globe.

July 1997

Back home, with a few days of freedom to get over the jet lag, do my laundry and deal with the pile of mail. The company reassembled at Barons Court on Monday for a day of gentle rehearsals, walking through things for memory rather than running them for stamina. It's pouring with rain, and has been for several days, but then it *is* Wimbledon fortnight, so I guess that's to be expected when the tennis comes to town.

Yesterday we worked up at the Opera House. Its closure is drawing closer day by day, and the place seems as if it is being dismantled around us. Familiar pieces are going missing, and the noise of the demolition is excruciating. It goes on all day, drilling, banging, bashing and the building work is whipping up layers of dust which have lain, undisturbed, for decades. The place is an asthmatic's nightmare.

We were there, rather than at Barons Court, to take part in the annual school performance, a special celebration this year to mark both the Golden Jubilee of the school and Dame Ninette de Valois' hundredth birthday. (This one was a little early – 'Madam' completes her personal century in June 1998.) In honour of this virtual double whammy, Peter Wright, ex-director of the Birmingham Royal Ballet, and an integral part of Madam's companies since 1949, had agreed to stage a *grand defilé*, a procession of the entire school and both companies, from the toddlers at White Lodge to veteran dancers like Donald MacLeary and Monica Mason, who have gone through the system and stayed on to give something back. This sort of parade takes place annually at the Opéra in Paris, but for us it was a bit of a novelty, and it took several tries and a lot of laughter before we got it right. Jolly chaos ensued. With so many senior managers and distinguished figures in the room, it was hard to know just who to take orders from.

We returned later for a 7.30 p.m. performance, but as the *defilé* was taking place at the end of the show, I was able to go out front and watch the first two acts. To mark the jubilee, the show involved contributions from principal dancers of both Dame Ninette's companies. The students provided the *corps de ballet*, and I really was impressed – *corps de ballet* dancing is not easy, especially when every nerve in your body is screaming 'Stand out! this is your only chance!', as it would be at a graduation performance. Good dancers don't automatically make a good *corps de ballet*, and dancers who are trying to be good, on their own terms, make a dreadful *corps de ballet*. I spent five years in the *corps*, and the hardest thing about it was learning not to try and shine. The next hardest thing was learning not to move until I heard the beat, whereas my instincts were (and still are) to move a fraction in advance so that the beat and I arrive at the same instant. Musicality is not an absolute; each dancer hears music slightly differently. Leanne Benjamin and I, for instance, are at opposite ends of the spectrum on this, as I want to hit the beat bang on the nose and she wants to stretch each movement to last out its entire resonance. In recent years we've danced as a pair in *Mr Worldly Wise* as well as *Amores*, and have learnt to laugh about our differences rather than tear each other's eyes out.

After the dancing was over, we lined up in the wings, a queue of over two hundred and fifty artists ranging from seven to seventy stretching back to Floral Street. To the strains of Tchaikovsky's *Eugene Onegin*, we processed on. At a similar occasion last year, the fiftieth anniversary performance of *Sleeping Beauty* at the Opera House, Madam made it on to the stage. We had altered the patterns of the final tableau to incorporate members of the original 1946 cast, and create a gap, centre stage, for the woman who, with enormous single- and probably bloody-mindedness made all this happen. The final chords died out and there was a moment's panic as it seemed that Madam wouldn't appear, when the insistent tap-tapping of her Zimmer frame announced her arrival. On she came, flanked by two of the best-looking and strongest men in the company, impervious to the absence of music, but responsive, even at 99, to the spotlight. Tap, tap, tap, a step at a time, and then she stood there, soaking up the applause and waving to the audience, who, as one, had risen to their feet to acknowledge her unique contribution to this century. It was an unforgettable moment and I felt so very proud to be involved.

This time, though, she didn't make it. Instead she stayed in her stalls circle seat, from where she had watched the show, commenting loudly throughout. (The years haven't dulled her vocal cords; I remember hearing, loud and clear, during a performance of *La Bayadère*, 'Who is that? I wish she'd come forward so I could see her face.' No one had the heart to tell her it was Derek Rencher.) Tonight, as the spotlight swept round to highlight her presence in the theatre, she rose to her feet and accepted the applause. Doctor Theatre is a potent physician, and the adulation of the audience obviously added a little extra tonic.

It has been sad to watch her decline over the last decade. For me, Madam has always been old, so the idea of her getting older wasn't a problem. But the physical manifestations of reaching such a very advanced age are particularly disturbing for a dancer to witness. My first memories of her are from a summer school at White Lodge, the junior school of The Royal Ballet, in 1978, when she came to teach a master class. I remember being vaguely disappointed that after about fifteen minutes she was so frustrated with our lack of co-ordination that she made us all sit cross-legged and follow imaginary birds across the room. It wasn't exactly what I'd had in mind – more like some sort of fantasy scenario whereby she spotted me, age 13, and said, 'Who is that girl? I must have her in the company right away.' By the time I did make it into the company, twelve years later, her presence was felt less frequently, but nevertheless she appeared from time to time. Only eight years ago she came to rehearse *Les Sylphides* and, armed with a single stick, spent the best part of an hour's call correcting my first entrance, a tiny hop and a run downstage. Then she turned her attention to the *jetés* across the stage which open the 'mazurka', her eagle eye spotting right away that I was taking off a hair's breadth too late. Somewhere there is a marvellous photograph of her, stick raised offensively as if she really can't bear to watch me do it wrong once more.

I have never been completely certain if Madam knows who I am. It seems, however, that she does. Whilst watching a performance from the wings last year, she asked another dancer, 'Who is that dancing the Bluebird? Is it Collier?' 'No,' came the reply, 'it's Deborah Bull.' 'Who?' 'Deborah Bull.' 'Oh yes. Lovely dancer. Dreadful name.'

4th July 1997, London
Heavily into rehearsals for *Steptext*, the ballet which Anthony Dowell calls my 'signature piece'. It came into the repertoire in 1995 and I had the unusual and unforgettable luxury of a six-week rehearsal period with its choreographer, Bill Forsythe, director of the Frankfurt Ballet. In some ways, it is the toughest piece I dance; a series of *pas de deux* with three different partners, each one more exhausting and exhilarating than the last. Danced to a taped version of a Bach chaconne, it is no more than fifteen minutes long, but at least fourteen of those minutes are spent

on-stage in constant motion. *Steptext* arouses extreme passions in people who come to see it. Half of them adore the physicality, the musicality and the way it transgresses almost every convention of the theatre. The curtain goes up on an unlit stage five minutes before the show begins, and dancers stroll on and off, seemingly as they please. From the outset, the audience's preconceptions about a 'night at the ballet' are overturned. Once it seems to be safely under way, the music stops abruptly, choreographicus-rudely-interruptus, and the dancers just walk off. As you can imagine, the other half of the audience absolutely hate it.

Anyway, next week, after back-and-forth negotiations over costing and casting, *Steptext* will be filmed along with *Symphony in C*. I'm keeping my fingers crossed; I've put in the hard work, my side of the bargain, and I'm hoping that good fortune puts in the rest. And I've had the *Steptext* full body wax, in preparation for my rather revealing red leotard.

12th July 1997, London
It's been oppressively hot in London this week, and we have been trapped inside the non-air-conditioned Opera House for most of it. Roll on the new building, I say, with its 'comfort-cooling' temperature system.

Last Wednesday we had a double show; I danced *Steptext* in the afternoon and *Symphony in C* in the evening. The camera crews were at work during both performances, but unfortunately, so were the builders. So in addition to the stops and starts in the Bach chaconne, there were the sounds of the building work to upset the purists. I guess you could call it a truly site-specific work.

Mercifully (thank you, thank you) it was a really good show, although I know that when I see it played back I will hate every minute of it. It's very strange, having danced un-recorded for seventeen years, to have now been captured on celluloid twice in three weeks. And there's one more to come. The Opera House closing gala on Monday is being broadcast live on the Beeb, so if I can manage to set the video recorder correctly for the first time in my life, I'll have that too.

At work we have been trying to pull out *Prince of the Pagodas* and dust it down in time for next week's opening in New York. The rest of the company danced it at the beginning of this season, but I was in the final stages of recuperation from my foot operation and it came a little too

soon for safety. I went to the initial rehearsals, full of optimism, but
when it became apparent that I wouldn't make the shows, I backed off
and stayed away. When you're forced by injury to miss out on roles you
particularly enjoy, it's difficult to strike a balance between the urge to
help the second cast and the need to preserve your sanity. It's hard to
watch someone else step into your dancing shoes. As we hadn't danced
Pagodas for several years I didn't feel I had much advice to offer anyway,
so in the interests of mental stability I stayed away. Now, with only a
sketchy knowledge of the piece, I am having to do extra homework so
that I don't hold everyone else up. In fact I'm not alone; there are quite
a few new faces in the ballet since it was performed last autumn as bodies
on the injury list mount, as they always do at the end of the season. We
had a particularly tetchy rehearsal for one number, and as tempers
became increasingly frayed, the problems got worse. Faced with a
nervous partner, the best course of action is to assume the calm and
patience of an abbess. With every tut and tsk the nerves coil tighter until
the rehearsal may just as well be abandoned before everyone loses it
completely. I sure hope the comfort-cooling system promised for the
new House works on tempers as well as temperatures.

Yesterday I appeared on live breakfast TV (starting at 8.15 a.m.) to
talk about the closing of the House in three days' time. Instead of
focusing on the future House and how wonderful it will be for Britain to
have a theatre worthy of the level of performance that goes on in this
country, the emphasis of the interviewer, Nick Hyam, was relentlessly
negative; the 'much criticised' Lottery grant, critics say this,
commentators say that, blah, blah. Oh, come on Nick. Can't anyone be
bold enough to suggest there might be good reason for excitement? The
British Museum was built on the proceeds of a lottery. I wonder how the
public in 1759 responded to the use of lottery money for such a lofty
purpose?

Afterwards I went straight back home to bed. Yesterday evening we
had the final ballet performance in the House as we know it, with
Symphony in C filmed for the second time, and I didn't want to be caught
on tape yawning. It was an emotional event, with curtain calls extending
into the night and three enormous bouquets, veritable euphoria of
floribunda, two from the Ballet Association and one from the American
choreographer Twyla Tharp. There was so much love drifting back and
forth through the proscenium arch that I wished Nick Hyam had been
there to record it for the breakfasting public.

Today, Saturday, I'm exhausted, and glad of the chance to take it easy for a day and a half. I had a quick run-through with Ashley Page of the *pas de deux* we're dancing on Monday at the Farewell Gala and then home to enjoy the sunshine on my terrace. I'm starting to feel a sense of panic that I won't have said goodbye to all the relevant bits of the theatre when we're finally locked out after the gala. It's already a different House from the one I entered in 1981, when I first joined the *corps de ballet*. That was before the first phase of the redevelopment was completed, when there were still shared dressing-rooms and one tiny studio, next to the canteen, where the principals and soloists did barre before stage calls. The rest of us warmed up in the crush bar, on carpet. It was hardly the best preparation, but it sure made you work to hold your turn out. That claustrophobic studio disappeared when the 1982 extension, with its Olympic-sized studios opened, but you can still catch a glimpse of it in Michael Powell's 1948 film *The Red Shoes*. What a maze of a place the House is. Endless doors and miles of underground corridors which lead I don't know where. Even after seventeen years in the building, I'm sure there are hidden corners that I have yet to discover. Well it's nearly too late now. Fifty-five hours to go and then it will all disappear as the men in hard hats and fluorescent jackets take over.

14th July 1997, London
I am just back home from Covent Garden's Farewell Gala, my final foray on to the stage which has been home to British ballet since 1946 and host to almost every famous dancer who has ever lived. Now the doors to the theatre are locked and the builders have the key. We have closure although, in the American sense of the word, I'm not sure I have closure at all. I can't believe I won't touch it, see it, or smell it again. It wasn't a perfect place; the paint was peeling and the plumbing leaked, but it was home, the House, *our* House, and the ghosts that will be disturbed by the builders, as they raze it to the ground, seem in some way to be part of my past. It hurts; I'm dreadfully, painfully nostalgic, but I know it has to happen.

It was chaos backstage tonight. The whole point of the evening (aside from raising a tidy sum for the redevelopment fund) was to get everyone on the stage at the same event; all the people who are currently involved with the opera and ballet companies, and lots of others who have made a significant contribution to the life of Covent Garden over the decades. There must have been over a hundred and sixty people on the bill tonight; all the usual suspects from the ballet company, and such luminaries as Felicity Lott, Robert Tear, Elizabeth Bainbridge, Anna Tomowa-Sintow and Placido Domingo from the opera. With half the dressing-rooms out of commission, we had to make do with the old ballet rooms and any other space that stage management could conjure up. The MacMillan Studio upstairs was fitted out with tables, mirrors and lights, and pressed into service as a temporary dressing-room for the opera chorus. With people crammed into every available niche, and clothing strewn from wall to wall, it looked more like a London underground station during the blitz.

Down at stage level (and we were the lucky ones) Miyako Yoshida and I had to vacate dressing-room number five and lodge next door with Sylvie Guillem and Viviana Durante (making her return to the stage after a year out) in a room designed for two. As I struggled to find a sliver of mirror and a seat to sit on, it became obvious that the evening backstage was lacking the glamour which the audience was displaying out front. I was a bit sad not to be in number five for this last performance, but I've been in so many dressing-rooms over the years that I can hardly start claiming one room as my own. Demonstrating my own spirit of the blitz, I shut up and got on with it. The stage managers had enough to do without dealing with my emotional trauma. But moving rooms was not as easy as transferring a make-up bag across the corridor. Oh no. I thought I'd done most of my clearing out before the tour in May, but delving into my remaining locker I found I still had years of nostalgic plaque to deal with, and I divided it into three separate standard-issue shoe bags; home, tour (we leave tomorrow) and long-term storage. God knows where it will all end up. I guess at some point during the next year I will arrive at a theatre, retrieve my shoe bag from the skip and discover it contains absolutely nothing of any use, just a heap of mouldy good luck cards, a tutu signed by Jennifer Penney, ex-principal, and my first ever make-up sticks that for some reason I still can't bear to part with.

On-stage, the gala was an alternating mixture of opera and ballet, with ensemble pieces couching various duets and solos from the great names of music and dance. Most of the repertoire was rooted in the last hundred years, and it was left to Ashley Page and me to represent the twentieth century in his *pas de deux*, *Walk and Talk*. He made it years ago for a summer tour and it has proved to have amazing staying power. I was thrilled when Anthony Dowell decided to include it tonight. It is probably appropriate that Ash and I should be the 'here and now', him in his Doc Martens and me in a slinky black trouser suit. He has earned his place in the records as a serious creative force of the last decade, and I seem to have become 'the one who does the modern works'. The reception was excellent, and I heard afterwards that the duet went down particularly well with the audience watching on the big screen in the piazza outside the Opera House.

Once we had danced I had a mad rush to be ready in time for *Symphony in C*; change of hair, new shoes and into my tutu. The first half of the evening closed with its last movement, a wonderful opportunity to get as many dancers as possible on to the stage for one last time. During the interval, we had to remain on-stage while Vivien Duffield and Lord Chadlington, of the Opera House Board, gave speeches of thanks to those people who had paid prodigious sums of money to attend the gala and support the fund-raising appeal. The ex-Prime Minister, John Major, in the audience with his wife, Norma, received special praise for helping to instigate the National Lottery, the largesse of which underpins the House's redevelopment. The greater British public, watching the gala at home on TV, didn't get the speeches. They had this week's episode of *The Vicar of Dibley* instead.

I watched some of the second half, but spent most of the time running around saying my goodbyes to the building. I felt like a woman condemned as the final hour ticked away. At the end of the evening we all regrouped on the stage, and Darcey Bussell, dressed in the costume of the Lilac Fairy, put us to sleep. Actually that isn't true. That's what we thought she was going to do. Instead, she bestowed her blessing on the House and all who serve in it. I guess having her put us to sleep would have provided some easy jokes for the papers; I know all building contracts run over time, but surely a hundred years is pushing it, even for the Opera House.

I had my own version of a dramatic ending in mind. As the builders had already worked their way up to the backstage wall, and were probably standing there, having a quick cigarette and waiting for us all to push off, impatient for the midnight hand over, I thought it would be really neat if we turned and gestured to the backcloth just as a deadly demolition ball came crashing through. What a way to go that would be.

I was surprised that didn't happen at the drinks party which followed. The curtain came down at about 11 p.m., and an hour later we were supposed to leave, the last revellers turning out the lights. By the time

I'd finally changed and packed up for the last time, it was already pushing the witching hour. No one seemed to mind that we partied on a bit longer than we were meant to. Good job really; it took about an hour to get a drink. The crush bar was truly heaving and the air was thick with genuine goodwill. Famous faces mingled with long-time supporters (occasionally they were both one and the same) and I bumped into Opposition leader William Hague, with his fiancée Ffion Jenkins, who impressed me enormously by remembering precisely when and where he had last seen me. (October last year, at the Prudential Awards. I was sitting next to him for dinner, and when I went back to my table after presenting the awards, he was gone. As he was Welsh Secretary at the time, I thought he might have taken offence at some of my digs at the Conservative administration. Apparently not.) Throughout the foyers, people hugged as if we were saying goodbye to each other as well as to the building. There was no pomp and ceremony, just a warm send-off to a grand but tired old lady who was about to get her face smashed in, and not just lifted. Outside, bags overflowing with sentimental souvenirs (I confess: I took a sign – BALLET DRESSING ROOMS ☞ – off the wall) and serious things like pointe shoes for the shows in New York, we looked more like a collection of bag ladies than the ballerinas who had sparkled their way through *Symphony in C* a few hours earlier.

All in all, the day has been so much of an obstacle course that the performing element, when it finally happened, felt curiously muted. It almost got in the way of everything else that had to be done. I know that I will wake up in the morning and wish that I had taken in more of this historic occasion, but for now, I feel too exhausted to care.

15th July 1997, London – New York
Up early for a midday flight to New York, followed by a drive through heavy traffic into Manhattan. For as long as anyone can remember, the company, when in New York, has stayed at the Mayflower, a large, solid hotel on the west side of Central Park. On my first tour, as a student in 1981, I thought it was the height of chic. Since then, my standards have risen as the hotel's have fallen, and it has finally been decided to break with tradition and put us somewhere else. A classic case of better the devil you know; the Mayflower might have been a bit run down, but it felt like home. The chain hotel on 57th Street where we are staying this time is not really much better and it feels completely alien. It's further downtown from the Metropolitan Opera House at Lincoln Center, in a

rather dubious area. All in all my heart is in my boots and, what's more, I'm such a snob that I'm embarrassed to give out the phone number.

Yesterday's gala is still running through my head like a video on a loop. Different scenes keep coming to mind. It seems to me that the whole event was weighted in the wrong political direction; too much old and not enough new. The country at large is still high on New Labour and yet there was too distinct a whiff of Old Tory in the air. Almost every member of the freshly unemployed previous administration was there, and although Heritage Secretary Chris Smith was on hand to represent the new government, he didn't get a mention, and he was definitely outnumbered, politically, by the likes of John Major, Virginia Bottomley and William Hague. Tony and Cherie were notable by their absence. I'm not sure this imbalance augurs well for us.

In the newspapers I read on the plane, I find another pointer towards the future; the Department of National Heritage is to be rechristened. Perhaps 'heritage' harks back to a past of ancient monuments and old aristocratic houses. Perhaps it's rather vague about just what that heritage might be. But at least the word heritage implies that it's something of which we can be proud, and the lack of precision leaves room for a charitable interpretation. The Department for Culture, Media and Sport, on the other hand, seems to have something missing from an otherwise very precise list; art, perhaps. It's a strange threesome to yoke together: two extremes of public taste sandwiching a manipulator of public opinion. I hope Chris Smith is up to the yoking.

17th July 1997, New York
After a day to get over the jet lag, we were all back to work with a full run-through of *Prince of the Pagodas* in the underground studio at the Met. It was chaotic; *Pagodas* requires a lot of 'extras', or, as they used to be called, 'supers'; not an abbreviation for superfluous, although sometimes you do wonder. Once again, I realise how difficult it is to pick up extras abroad, as you never know what you're going to get. You would think that New York would be full of out of work actors able to make a decent job of spear carrying, but if it is, we haven't found them. Instead, we have a collection of wannabees, who see this as their opportunity to make it big. Some turn up armed with full CV, photographs and an 'audition number' at the ready, presumably in case Darcey Bussell or Jonathan Cope happen to be off. Sadly, what they don't realise is that the main criterion for selection is whether or not they fit the costume. At

least they're more entertaining than the ones in California. I'm reminded of that hilarious scene in Mel Brooks' *The Producers* when wannabee Adolfs are auditioning for the part of Hitler.

Back at the hotel, I had a call from Auberon Waugh of London's *Literary Review*. I haven't heard from him since he asked me to review *Nigel Lawson's Diet Book* last year, an exercise which led directly to a suggestion that I write my own. Seeing me on TV, dancing at Monday's gala, must have jogged his memory and he called to find out if I would review John Drummond's new book on Diaghilev. It will keep me busy between my first show, tomorrow, and my second, ten days later.

On the subject of reviews, it seems I had an excellent notice in the *Evening Standard* (probably the best of my career) for Monday's *Talking Tate* programme, which preceded the gala. The very funny and very acerbic Victor Lewis-Smith said, 'Just as I was about to dismiss joined-up dancing as a load of Fokine nonsense, along comes Deborah Bull to make me want to try again.' I got a whole page, and a photograph, for a thirty-second programme. Watching the gala on video, I so much preferred seeing myself in Ashley's piece to the classical formalities of *Symphony in C* that I resolved to give up on tutus and stick to what I do best, the modern stuff. Victor Lewis-Smith makes me wonder if I should give up on the dancing altogether and just talk about it instead, like a former footballer turned commentator.

While I'm away, Torje is charged with keeping me in touch with the news at home via e-mail, and the first of his bulletins makes it clear that the Opera House, despite the good feelings engendered by the gala, hasn't been getting such a good press. In a continuation of what is starting to look like a campaign against Covent Garden, the *Guardian* ran a piece calling for the House to be privatised. In a naïve moment, I catch myself asking just what did we do wrong? Two years ago, when the Lottery Board accepted the House's application for funding to redevelop the theatre, there was an unspoken but widespread feeling that people might actually be pleased. After all, the scheme has been on the drawing boards for about a quarter of a century. Phase one was finished fifteen years ago, and it looked as if it would take a miracle before funds were available to carry the development through to its conclusion. The 'miracle' came in the form of the Lottery, but we were totally unprepared for the deluge of criticism that came with it and now seems likely to continue.

20th July 1997, New York
Well, it's official. Gerald Kaufman, back–bench MP, has been elected to
chair the National Heritage Committee, the body which exists to
monitor the Department for Culture, Media and Sport. (Surely some
mistake? A lack of communication over the revised title? *Ed.*) The first
press release announces that the committee will undertake three
inquiries, with the Royal Opera House at the top of the list. Despite
Kaufman's premature announcement last month, in which he promised
to investigate the two London opera companies, English National Opera
seems to have been spared his attentions for the moment. The first
session will be held before Parliament's summer recess, in a week's time,
although it's unclear as yet who will be called to give evidence. I'm not
exactly sure how worried we should be; as far as I can gather, select
committee reports are not binding, so it may just turn out to be yet
another sheaf of papers to clog up Whitehall's filing cabinets and create
sound bites for the evening news.

24th July 1997, New York
It has been a long, hot and torpid week in New York. I would love to be
able to write something really interesting about it, but frankly, the whole
trip has been totally flat. The only *frisson* of excitement was provided by
an infestation of rats in our chain hotel which forced Niccy Tranah out
of her room and into my (very large) bed for the night. The opening
night of *Pagodas* went pretty well, and the audience seemed very happy
with it, but there followed a long and steamy hiatus where I had no work
at all, and I'm afraid I'm in a slump. Normally there would be rehearsals
for the next programme to focus on, but as we're within spitting distance
of the end of the season there is nothing left to rehearse. It should have
been a great opportunity to let my hair down and have fun, but I can't
switch on and off like that. I want to be either working or playing, and I
feel uncomfortably wedged between the two at the moment. On top of
that, New York is in the midst of a heat wave, and a sweltering city like
this just isn't the place to be when the temperature is nudging triple
figures. It's too damn hot. So I'm a bit miserable, and the creeping guilt
that I haven't taken advantage of the city's riches has made me feel even
worse.

    While I've been slumping the company has been working really hard,
with performances of *Cinderella* and the Ravel programme, both of
which don't involve me. In the midst of all this the dancers have their

annual interviews, a chance to talk to their director, Anthony Dowell, and assess the way the year has gone. Principals aren't automatically included but we can ask for a slot, if we want one. I didn't. This is the time when promotions are awarded and contracts (occasionally) terminated, so it's a week of bubbling and extreme emotions. The tears are usually in response to promotions; joy that it happened, or painful frustration and disappointment that it didn't. I remember all too clearly the real physical pain of not being promoted when I felt that I was ready for it and several other people had also been convinced that it was on the cards. It all happened right at the close of the 1990–91 season and I lived with that disappointment through a very long summer holiday, assessing it, turning it over and over and finally converting it into renewed determination. But whenever I see a little face swollen and red-eyed with crying, I go straight back to that end-of-season party where even at dusk I didn't remove my dark glasses. I finally achieved the promotion to principal, the last rung on the company ladder, in 1992. Now I guess the only way is down, or out, or both.

I went to see Twyla Tharp's new company, 'Tharp!' up in Harlem. I met Twyla last year when she came over to London for three months to choreograph a full-length ballet for the company, *Mr Worldly Wise*. Twyla is probably best known for *Push Comes to Shove*, a piece she choreographed in the eighties for Mikhail Baryshnikov which exemplifies her unique style, a blend of dance techniques crossing all the boundaries. Her unstoppable energy swept through the company and carried most of us along with it. I loved working with her; she was tough and uncompromising, to herself as much as to anyone else, and I thrived on it. We still scheme together from time to time to try and repeat the experience, so far without success. But I have a suspicion that one day we'll work together again. Her company was rehearsing in a theatre which formed part of a college campus at a street with an unmentionably high number. It seemed out of place, this little hive of artistic energy way uptown, and the too, too chic Shelley Washington, one of my dearest friends and the company rehearsal director, had shed the Prada and turned up in an old pair of baggy dungarees. I barely recognised her. I realised yet again how lucky I have been during my career. I've done my share of schools, hospitals and church halls, but always as an extra to normality, not as normality itself. My normality is proper studios, with sprung floors and changing-rooms nearby. The majority of the dancing world, apart from large companies like ours, would expect to take class in a freezing cold, hard-floored environment, without changing facilities or food and drink on site. I frequently feel guilty about our vast studios, fully plumbed changing-rooms and on-site canteen, but sack cloth and ashes don't really help anyone. If the bigger companies didn't have adequate facilities there would be no basis for an argument. But there is too wide a gulf between what we have and others don't, and whenever I come up against it, I'm shocked by the incongruities.

On Tuesday I had the much discussed book reading in Barnes and Noble, set up for me by our press office back in May. A lot of my friends would say I was the worst possible choice for an event where children are involved, as they have me down as a bit of a child-free zone. It isn't really fair comment. I have armfuls of nephews and nieces whom I love to pieces, and both Niccy and Nicky (Tranah and Roberts) have offspring whom I adore. But I don't go ga-ga over every baby who crawls across my path the way that some women do. This absence of overt maternal response is enough to convince people that I'd prefer not to be in the same room as a bunch of half-metre tykes. It's not quite true. I'd prefer not to be left in a room with a bunch of half-metre tykes with no way out, but if I can hand them back as soon as they start becoming grisly then I'm fine. Which is how it was today. So the whole experience was not unpleasant, although I learnt round about page two of the *Cinderella* saga just how short a child's attention span is. It's about two pages' worth. I carried on regardless, and made my way to the end of the shortest version of *Cinderella* I could find in the store. Afterwards I had to judge the *Cinderella* look-alike contest, which, despite the obvious objections, was open to the boys as well as the girls – well, this is America. It suddenly dawned on me that I would need a security escort to get me past the mothers of all the kids who hadn't been placed. To be honest, it was an impossible decision to make, and I might as well have just used the 'pin the tail on the princess' method of selection – close my eyes and point. How do you choose between one child in frills, tiara and mommy's high heels and another in exactly the same get-up? In the end, I chose a brother and sister act who had really gone to town, and then wished I hadn't. It soon became clear that it was mommy who was the driving force behind the duo and they would rather have been at home watching *The Simpsons*. Second place went to a girl who, in true *Cinderella* style, lost her slipper on the way to the stage.

I had tea with Alison Devlin, of DK Inc, who will be publishing the still untitled diet and fitness book in the US. She wants me to come over in the New Year for a publicity tour, the prospect of which made me laugh out loud. That's not at all the sort of thing that Deborah Bull does. But just to be on the safe side, I rush out to buy three new suits from a Broadway shop opposite the Lincoln Center. Better to be prepared.

27th July 1997, New York
Another enthusiastic audience for the last night of the season. The show felt a bit dull to me – too many 'last nights' in recent weeks, or could it just be that I'm still feeling as flat as Denmark? The dancers applauded the final curtain, as we always do at the end of the season, but the response owed more to habit than spontaneous joy. Beforehand we had said goodbye to Neil Skidmore, who is leaving after twelve years with The Royal Ballet. His wife, Michelle, is staying on, but even with such a strong remaining link I know that we will lose touch. Neil has been a unique presence in the company, the only person as yet to combine life as a DJ with a full-time career as a dancer, earning himself the soubriquet of Boogie. I will miss having him around.

Despite my ongoing depression, this week I had to pull myself out of the doldrums and rev up again for the final show. I have been going in to class every morning, and over the last few days I've had a few rehearsals in the airless studio, three floors down, at the Met, with the Marc Chagall canvas on the wall. But none of this has kept me nearly busy enough. I used the time off to finally get myself to various New York exhibitions, including the 'Lost World' at the Natural History Museum, with Nicky Roberts' three-year-old son, Jordan (my second child-friendly experience of the week). I spent a wonderful afternoon in the Guggenheim, at an exhibition of drawings, an experience which made me realise yet again how little I know about everything. (I comfort myself with the idea that this realisation is in itself the beginning of knowledge.) It was fascinating to see how in art, as well as in dance, process has become an end product in itself. Historically, drawings were never meant for public consumption – they were merely a preparatory step on the way to a painting. Now, like us dancers on the stage, painters are showing their underwear.

The rest of my down time is spent finding out what's going on at home. With his superior grasp of technology, Torje has scanned various newspaper cuttings into his computer and sent them to me via e-mail. It's a spicy collection. The inaugural meeting of Kaufman's Select Committee investigating the Royal Opera House took place on the 24th, with three of the key figures in the ongoing drama giving evidence. Now, perhaps, we might get to the bottom of all this brouhaha.

First in front of the committee were Jeremy Isaacs, recently departed General Director, Lord Gowrie, Chairman of the Arts Council, and Genista McIntosh, an even more recently departed Chief Executive. Isaacs stood up well under Gerald Kaufman's fire, even though he was forced to argue Lord Gowrie's expressed opinion, in a letter to the *Sunday Times*, that the plans for the opera and ballet companies to perform during the closure period were 'a shambles'. Faced with a building project that would close the House for two years, Isaacs had held out to the very last for a new theatre to be built at London's Tower Bridge alongside the Thames. When this plan eventually (some say inevitably) collapsed, he was left to piece together two performing seasons from scratch. Hence our upcoming exile at the Labatt's Apollo in Hammersmith, one of the capital's major rock venues. But some interesting details emerged from Isaacs' testimony – for instance, that he would continue to receive a salary for *not* working at the Opera House (reported to be £120,000) between his departure last December and the expiry of his contract in September this year.

By all accounts, Genista stood up even better. The press, determined to extract the maximum amount of scandal from the whole affair, have pulled out quotable fragments from her evidence to clear up the question surrounding her health. She concedes, after repeated interrogation, that she had not, in fact, been ill, but she added that 'had I continued in my job I might have become ill'. The full transcripts should be available by the time we go back to work in the autumn, and I can't wait to read what lies behind the headlines.

28th July 1997, London
A full day in New York before the flight home this evening, and I spend some of it enjoying the end-of-tour ritual of trying to fit all the shopping into an already overstuffed suitcase. (As usual, I brought far too many clothes with me in the first place, and now, amongst other things, there are three new suits to squeeze in.) After two days of thunderous rain, New York is once again balmy and warm. Stepping outside is like stepping into a hot bath.

I wonder why it has all felt so spiritless here – I guess it could be the heat, but it feels also as if the city is empty, as if the entire population of New York has gone to the Hamptons, or somewhere like that. No one in their right minds would stay here in these temperatures. But I suspect my slump has something to do with the sudden change of pace. The days in London leading up to the gala were total madness, but at least I was *doing* something. Life felt vital, important. After starting out here on full power, I have been left to slowly simmer for ten days and then brought suddenly back to the boil for the last night. No dancer likes to work that way.

We flew back home to the prospect of a month off. Ah, holidays! Our summer holiday would normally last for five weeks, but we open the autumn season a little earlier than normal at the Hammersmith Apollo (nice and local for the rehearsal studios at Barons Court) and dates have had to be shifted so that we are ready in time. It might sound like the most generous of vacations, but in reality, it's the thirty-five days that the majority of the work-force get. It's just all rolled into one, and apart from a mid-season break sometime after Christmas, that's it for the year. In practical terms, it's the only way to do it; imagine the chaos if we all took our holidays as and when we felt like it. But it isn't ideal; a couple of weeks away from it all is wonderful, but after that, batteries recharged, I'm generally ready to leap back into the fray. And it's much too long to go without exercise, unless you're willing to watch your fitness reduced to zero and pay the price of struggling to win it back again.

In my early years in the company, I solved this by spending the entire summer in class, either here in London, or at Marika Besobrasova's school in Monte Carlo, an extraordinary place perched on the Monaco hillside and packed full of dedicated young girls (me included) who would throw themselves willingly into the twice-daily two-and-a-half-hour classes. Since I discovered Torje, I've learnt there are ways to stay in shape which don't involve leotards and pointe shoes. Nowadays, I take a couple of weeks off and spend the remaining time trekking through the mountains with my knapsack on my back. I come back to work as fit as when I left.

The plane lands at Heathrow and after a few goodbyes, we all go our separate ways. No mountains for me this year. As Torje has already left London for pre-tour rehearsals with the Rolling Stones in Toronto, I will go home briefly to unpack and repack. Then I'll catch a plane to Canada and join him. I just can't wait.

August 1997

25th August 1997, London
It's the night before I go back to work, the sunset on my summer vacation. I wasn't going to write anything during the holidays, as being away from dancing didn't seem to figure in *Dancing Away*. But I'm breaking my rule to report that Chris Smith, Secretary of State for Culture, Media and Sport, has announced to the Arts Council that the government intends to cap the amount of Lottery money available to the arts. The Lottery was set up to give five equal slices of the cake to charity, sport, the arts, heritage and the millennium celebrations. Despite this being made perfectly clear from the outset, the proportion of money going to the arts (unsurprisingly, a fifth) and the places to which it has gone (particularly the Opera House) seem to have taken people by surprise. Now, in a gesture towards public opinion, the government has taken it upon itself to limit the money available to the arts, leaving more available for a sixth 'good cause', health and education. Funny, I thought that's what our taxes were for. The dark clouds that I sensed behind the blazing sunshine of May 1st begin to reform. Is the party over? Traditionally the arts have prospered under Labour but, as we are finding out, New Labour has a very different agenda from the Labour of old. It's hard to reconcile this lot with the Labour administration of 1945, who, in creating the Arts Council, effectively purchased the best of the nation's art for the nation.

26th August 1997, London
Back to work on a new season after a holiday which seemed far too short. Every year the same feelings, the same dread of walking down the Talgarth Road in West London to The Royal Ballet's headquarters at Barons Court. It's like being a kid again, trying without success to think of a way of dragging out the summer holidays and delaying the inevitable return to school. ('But I really *don't* feel well, mum, my tummy hurts . . .') Every year it gets worse, and I know that there'll come a time when I find myself saying 'I can't do this again'. Anthony Dowell has talked about the knot that tightened in his stomach whenever he went through the

gates into White Lodge, saying that even now, several decades later and having scaled every height there is in classical ballet, he still gets the same nervous feeling. I know what he means, as I head back to the same building, the same faces, the same exercises, the same music. I have been walking the 400 metres between Barons Court station and the school for the last nineteen years, and I still don't understand what the knot is about. It's not that I don't like the faces, the building or the exercises. Nor am I unhappy there. I'm simply scared. Perhaps it's just another manifestation of the insecurity that most dancers have built into them from an early age.

That insecurity – and various other aspects of a dancer's training – have been splashed across the press over the last few weeks. It all started last month with a claim from Linda Goss, an ex-teacher at White Lodge, that her attempts to expose unfair treatment of the pupils at the school had led to her dismissal. I don't know Linda Goss – by the time she arrived at White Lodge I was long gone. I can only say that I don't recognise the regime she describes. I look back on my time at the school as five years of unfolding knowledge, with one ballet teacher in particular, Patricia Linton, a major influence on my life. Without her guiding inspiration, my unfocused and disordered talents might never have been shaped into a coherent whole. I was pushed, yes, challenged, certainly, but ultimately no one ever issued a greater challenge than those I set myself. The industrial tribunal failed to uphold Goss's claims, but the press have got hold of her story and are spinning it out for all it's worth: 'Beware the Ballet School Bullies', shrieked the *Daily Mail*. Back in New York last month, I had a call from Grace Bradbury who was writing a piece about it in *The Times*; weeks later, the stories are still appearing.

Flicking through a sheaf of press cuttings on the notice board, I discovered a small snippet from the second sitting of the Kaufman inquiry. Lord Chadlington, Chairman of the Opera House Board, and, as Peter Gummer, public relations guru to the Conservative Party, was called in to give evidence at the end of July. He revealed that while the ballet company was enjoying a successful season in New York, he was saving the House from insolvency by touching two long-term supporters of Covent Garden for a loan. Jeremy Isaacs' claims, in the previous sitting, that the House is in 'reasonably good shape' would seem to be a little far-fetched.

31st August 1997, London
I still seem to be on Toronto time, as I had a devil of a job getting to sleep
last night. I turned on the TV and finally drifted off sometime after
midnight in the middle of the American hospital series *St Elsewhere*, an
unacknowledged forerunner of *ER* (without George Clooney) and an
excellent soporific.

I was woken at about 4 a.m. by the telephone. It was Torje, in
Toronto. He had just returned from dinner and turned on CNN. 'I
thought you'd want to know; there's been a car crash in Paris. They're
saying that Dodi Al Fayed is dead, and Princess Diana is injured.' In my
semi-conscious state, I turned on the television. For about half an hour
I watched the coverage, saw the wreckage of the Mercedes in that Paris
tunnel, and wondered at Diana's luck, to have survived what must have
been an enormous impact. My God! Eventually I dozed back to sleep
and the television turned itself off.

About five hours later the phone woke me again. It was my friend
David. We agreed that it was all dreadful, and asked how it could have
happened. I didn't know we were talking at cross-purposes. After he
hung up, I turned on the TV to see newscaster Peter Sissons alongside a
portrait of Diana, with the fateful legend '1961–1997'. The earlier
reports weren't true. It wasn't just a broken arm, slashed thigh and
concussion. She's dead. Like the rest of the nation, I can't quite take it
in. It's not just the loss, both to her family and to the country, although
that goes without saying. There's something more, something deeper,
something harder to define. We always think that these things 'won't
happen to us'. Yet if they can happen to a member of the Royal Family,
a family which should be cocooned in the cotton wool of invincibility,
safe and untouchable, it most certainly *can* happen to any of us. Her life
hasn't quite been the fairytale she was promised – it's been closer to a
movie script, with its outrageous extremes of tragedy, melodrama and
glamour. Until now, I've never seen her as real, just a face on the news-
stands. But in her horrific and pointless death, she's at last become
vulnerable and real to me and to everyone else. How sadly ironic that it's
only when she's robbed of her life that I can finally think of her as
human.

One commentator has already made the inevitable comparison with
the death of John F. Kennedy: 'We'll always remember where we were
when we heard Diana had died.' He's right, although in some ways the
comparison is not really an obvious one. Unlike Kennedy, it's not as if

we ever expected Diana to change the world in a big way. But as George Eliot said in *Middlemarch*, there's no knowing which of our actions, or lack of action, will have consequences hanging on it for ever. With Diana, we all knew that every one of her actions, touches, smiles and gestures were, for someone, a defining moment in commonplace lives. Did she change the world? Probably in small ways. But for people directly affected by those changes, the difference was all-encompassing.

Needless to say, throughout the day the tributes have flowed ceaselessly from around the globe. It suddenly strikes me that she seems eerily still amongst us.

September 1997

1st September 1997, London
The first Monday morning of the season. I go off to Barons Court and, predictably, the talk is all of Diana. After class we had the yearly company meeting where we try to persuade some unsuspecting, public-spirited dancer to offer themselves up as Equity Deputy, the poor sod who has to galvanise us into making practical decisions, to liaise between dancers and management, and to formulate and present annual pay claims. It's got to be done, but as usual, no takers so names were drawn from a hat to form a committee. The problem, of course, is that the Equity Dep inevitably has to face up to the management, on occasion, with news that the dancers won't do this, don't like that or can't accept the other. Quite understandably, we all shy away from the role, thinking that our careers will be put in jeopardy by the exposure. But as I cowered in a corner (it was a very crowded corner) desperately praying that my name would remain in the hat and I would be spared for another year, I realised that actually, victimisation isn't what happens at all. The management level of the ballet world is populated almost entirely by ex-Equity Deps: Monica Mason, the Assistant Director here, Stephen Jefferies, Director of the Hong Kong Ballet, Wayne Eagling, Director at Dutch National Ballet in Amsterdam, and others. So perhaps it isn't such a bad career move after all. In the end, dancer David Pickering was thrust into the front line for the coming year as the committee formed by this impromptu raffle voted him to be its Chair.

4th September 1997, London
As if writing books and ballet dancing for a living weren't enough, over the past couple of years I've taken on other jobs, too. (All unpaid, unfortunately.) One is at London's South Bank Centre, where I have recently been appointed to the Board of Governors, and another is at the Arts Council, where I serve on the Dance Advisory Panel. This group of unbiased, independent 'experts' scrutinise funding applications and advise on their approval or rejection. It's a hugely responsible position, requiring breadth of knowledge and endless amounts of time. The

current mechanisms of public arts funding require that *pro bono* positions like this remain 'advisory'; hence additional to a day job. It's hard work, and hard for a working girl to fit in, but the Advisory Panels give artistic credibility to the Council, which could never hope to claim expertise in *every* area of the arts for which it doles out funds. Today we had a meeting to discuss the Dance Department's annual 'Plan'; basically its bid for finance from the Arts Council itself. Each of the departments within the Arts Council must submit a similar document, and based on these, Council decides on the allocation of the total monies they have received from the Treasury, £185 million in 1997/8. As individual departments aren't allowed to submit a budget which doesn't balance, there isn't the option of simply saying 'dance cannot survive, let alone expand, with any sort of cut whatsoever'. Which is, of course, what we should be saying. And when there is the very distinct possibility of a cut in the overall arts bursary from the government (who probably have other designs on our dosh) the Council's departments are squeezed between the rock and the hard place. Today the dance panel faced that squeeze.

These are very difficult times for ballet. When money is short, you might think it would be the small and the new that suffer the sharp blade of the cuts. But at the moment, with charges of élitism (that old chestnut) still being fired regularly at ballet by both media and government, and political correctness clouding clear judgement – somehow, ballet and the established wings of the dance world have fallen foul of the populace – we find ourselves increasingly at risk. Perhaps, in the past, we've been guilty of imagining ourselves to be immortal and above it all, but I don't think any of us make that mistake now.

The public clamour after Diana's death is increasing. Newpapers have devoted whole issues, the television last Sunday was devoted to her entirely, and Kensington Palace and its surrounding park have become a sea of flowers as never-ending waves of devotees turn it into a shrine in her honour. The lighted candles, photographs, and messages pinned to the trees take me back to Kyoto and its Shinto shrines, but the open emotions are more South Asian and belie the Englishness of Kensington Gardens. It seems that we live in a topsy-turvy world; a woman who was often mocked and belittled in her life is now praised and beatified in her death. Most of the papers, particularly the tabloids, managed to sanitise their Sunday editions before they hit news-stands, but one or two of the old-style items slipped through the net, reminding us that until a few days ago, Diana was a woman in the midst of a headline-grabbing love affair, and not the saintly icon she has now become. Alone amongst the papers, the street-vendored *Big Issue*, run, as it presumably is, on a shoestring, could not afford to scrap its print run and remove a tongue in cheek, sniping article, written before Sunday morning's tragedy. Instead, they were obliged to insert an apology slip and cross their fingers in the hope that their readers wouldn't take offence. It would be too sadly ironic if a charity devoted to one of her 'causes', the homeless, were to suffer deficits through her death.

But what has shocked me more than anything this week – and this week's headline news was shocking enough – is the unprecedented volume of 'the people's' voice and the power of its influence. This week, the people have managed to dictate the terms of Diana's funeral, alter the route of the funeral cortège from Kensington Palace to Westminster Abbey, and actually force the Queen out of mournful isolation – probably the only type which seems real and appropriate to her and her breed – to make a public statement and, tomorrow, a televised public address on the subject of her grief.

I'm all for the public having a say – that, surely, marks a democracy – but should those who wail loudest have most effect? Today, in the *Evening Standard*, for instance, the mandarin art critic Brian Sewell told us, as only he could, 'the public is an ass.' This may be too strong a condemnation of people power, but back in 1681, John Dryden noticed something similar: 'Nor is the People's Judgment always true; The Most may err as grossly as the Few.' In times like this, acerbic observations are shouted out of court, and seeing this mass spectacle of grief unfolding over the week, I, like others, feel an encroaching republicanism in the air.

6th September 1997, London
The morning of Diana's funeral, and my friend David and I joined several thousand people in Hyde Park to watch her cortège pass by. It has been the most extraordinary occasion, the most comprehensive and controlled display of public grief I am ever likely to witness. It was a bright and sparkling day, and the simplicity of the horse-drawn gun carriage contrasted sharply with the glamour of Diana's life. But I am sensing a mood here in the country which I find unsettling, a mood which verges on anarchy. I hope 'the people' have thought about where this will take them; the funeral demonstrated the need for formality and tradition to hold us together in times of tragedy, and yet I'm strongly

aware of a potentially destructive element in the emotions on display. Charles, Earl Spencer, Diana's brother, brought the house down at Westminster Abbey with his bold and emotional condemnation of the gross intrusions which plagued his sister's life, in particular her difficult relationship with the media and the Royal Family. As much as I admire him for saying so eloquently what he did, I cannot help feeling that this is not a time for division, unless his intention was revenge and the downfall of the monarchy. If those were his aims, he did very well indeed. If not, then he only achieved personal catharsis and a familial defence of Diana and her sons. There was something ancestral, almost Shakespearean about it. The 'people' applauded as one, and I know what the headlines will be in the morning. The broadsheets will ask serious questions about the future of monarchy. The tabloids will probably herald the arrival on the scene of the people's choice of a new King Charles – except this one will be a Spencer, not a Windsor.

9th September 1997, London
Week three of the new season, and I'm gradually getting back into the rhythm of rehearsals for *The Sleeping Beauty* at Labatt's Apollo. I have a single performance of Aurora on October 15th. I took only two short weeks off this summer, and in those two weeks I went almost daily to the gym at the Four Seasons Hotel in Toronto. Yet I feel as if I haven't danced for about six months. I swear it's psychological – if I *had* to dance the whole of *Sleeping Beauty* tomorrow, I would do it. But as it is, I'm like an ill cat, tentatively tipping from toe to toe across the studio floor. Today, I took bolder steps, and did most of the first act, the toughest bit. It wasn't so difficult. This cat will be back on the prowl within two shakes of its tail. I'm rehearsing with Monica Mason again, which is a joy. Back in the seventies Monica, a young prodigy from South Africa, was one of a vintage bunch of principal dancers nurtured in the Commonwealth; Merle Park and Vergie Derman (both Rhodesian), Jennifer Penney (Canadian), Deanne Bergsma (South African). As a student I used to love to watch Monica dance; strong, dramatic, and with an intelligence exemplified in every step. She taught solo classes to the Royal Ballet School's graduates, me included, while she was still performing, and eventually retired from dancing to become *répétiteur* to choreographer Kenneth MacMillan. When I joined the company in 1981 her main responsibility was preparing dancers for his works, and as my first major roles were in Kenneth's ballets (*Mayerling* and then *Manon*),

I have rehearsed with Mon from the very beginning. She knows my work better than anyone else, and often much better than me. Now she is the company's Assistant Director, but a major part of her work is to give rehabilitation classes to dancers who have been injured. Over the years she and I have spent hours together in the small studio at Barons Court in the aftermath of my various ankle traumas, literally my Achilles heels. She knows my weaknesses and my strengths – the last she could probably take much of the credit for enhancing.

To really benefit from her coaching classes, a dancer has to leave her ego outside the door. Whilst we would all freely admit we are nowhere near perfect, none of us likes to believe that we're guilty of fundamental errors, like rolling ankles or weak abdomens. Yet 90 per cent of injuries are directly related to faulty technique and blind errors, and eradicating the injury necessarily involves hunting out and correcting the fault. To do that you have to acknowledge that it exists. Mon is an excellent diagnostician with X-ray eyes, and she sees straight through track pants and leg warmers to the underlying muscles, tendons and ligaments. Once she has penetrated to the core and gleaned what's wrong, there's no point in trying to offer excuses. It's best just to let resistance fall away, and set about correcting it. You'll have to, eventually, if you want to keep dancing away.

Even though I haven't been in 'rehab' for over a year now, and have missed out on Mon's daily coaching sessions, I'm still mindful of the problems she identified as the cause of my ankle injuries, in particular the need to hold the turn-out from the top of the leg, and not to rely on the foot alone to maintain line. It's often a good idea to look above the site of an injury to find its root. Today I was feeling really smug, as I had done a step from the Act Two solo *exactly* in accordance with Mon's corrections. Or so I thought. For after I'd finished, she gently reminded me to be quite certain that I was holding the turn-out in my supporting leg as I prepared for a *pirouette*. And smug me thought I'd cracked it. It was exactly the thing I'd been congratulating myself on just moments before. In ballet dancing, pride always comes before a correction.

14th September 1997, London
Had dinner last night with Sarah Stacey and Clive Syddall. I first met Sarah and Clive as yet another consequence of my 1996 appearance in an Oxford Union debate where I seemed to surprise lots of people with an 'eloquent' defence of the proposition that Lottery money should fund

the arts. My 'team' comprised Lord Gowrie, Chairman of the Arts Council, and Jeremy Isaacs, my boss at the Opera House, but for some reason I attracted the most attention. I think what really shocked everyone was the idea that a dancer could think on her feet as well as dance on them. It seems that all the non-dance happenings in the last year – writing, talking, board memberships – can be traced directly back to that evening in Oxford. *Country Life* ran a profile soon afterwards which included the presumptuous forecast that it wouldn't be long before the world of television and Deborah Bull made contact. Clive, who has a television production company, called me up, fulfilling the prophecy.

I'm working with Clive's company, Paladin, on an idea for a television series designed to take the lid off dancing. I'm a passionate believer in the value of dance above and beyond a 'good night out'; I think it goes on around us all the time, playing a part in people's lives without their even realising it. Dance, especially the type I do, has had such a bad press over the last few years that our popular image has taken what could conservatively be described as a nosedive. There are several connected and unconnected factors at work here; Lottery awards, the shortfalls of the education system, the cut in grant aid to dance students, and a general unwillingness by newspapers and commentators to speak up for dance and the arts at a time when their stars seem to be in the descendant. Affairs back at the House haven't helped much either.

Television is without a doubt a huge and powerful influence on mass opinion, the ultimate tool for opening eyes and broadening minds when used correctly. But television seems to be bifurcating into two separate strands; BBC 2 and Channel 4 broadcast mainly balanced, informed and 'quality' programmes to a minority audience who have the working knowledge to understand them, while BBC 1 (to a lesser extent) and ITV feed, in the words of Richard Hoggart, 'crap to the masses'. (It's rather difficult to know exactly where the Channel 5 lies in this, as I have never yet met anyone who can actually receive it without some interference.) I'm not criticising the 'masses' here. We can only know what we've learnt, and without an education system which gives children the ability to appreciate something more than *The National Lottery Live*, it's not surprising that the weekly ratings read like they do. *EastEnders*, *EastEnders*, *Neighbours*, *Neighbours*, etc, etc.

So as two of the channels focus their beams ever more sharply on increasingly specialised and esoteric subject matter, the other two sweep back and forth across the vast and widening spectrum of 'popular culture', illuminating everything in their path but never pausing long enough to really throw any revealing light on what they pick out. Everything becomes a quixotic jumble of bright colour and loud noise.

Unfortunately, dance, as one of the so-called 'élitist' arts, has fallen into the first category; gratifying for those of us who wish to study such specialised subjects as the weight and intent of the single gesture, but a distinct turn-off (and confirmation) for those who think dance is an expensive form of navel gazing. And as we professionals advance and innovate with our work, we leave behind a populace who are unable, through no fault of their own, to join us. I want to open up dance so that people can see it, enjoy it, and celebrate it with me. After all, they fund it, each and every tax payer forking out 63 pence per year towards the Opera House's subsidy.

Sarah and Clive and I spend a long and enjoyable evening talking this through, and maybe one day, something will come of it.

Reading the *Sunday Times* this morning, I saw that my earlier speculations on Earl Spencer were not far off the mark, although the call didn't, in the end, come from the tabloids. It came in a letter to *The Times*: 'How about President Earl Spencer' – did they really think Earl is his Christian name? – 'to be succeeded by President William Windsor?' Ah! The People's Republic of Great Britain.

The *Sunday Times* also included an excellent article about the actor Simon Russell Beale, or Simon Beale as I used to know him. I met Simon through a mutual friend almost eighteen years ago, and had some wonderful and hilarious lunches with him and Alessandra Ferri, a contemporary of mine at the Royal Ballet School. Our separate ambitions were, on Simon's part to join the Royal Shakespeare Company, and, on ours to become principals of The Royal Ballet. Our combined success rate was 100 per cent.

Reading the profile of Simon led me to reflect again on the disparity between the status of actors and dancers and on the differences in how our training prepares us for the stage. Why can Simon effortlessly spill out endless thoughts on characters he's portraying? Why can he plumb the fertile soil of a broad and general artistic fluency which can inform and enrich the way he discusses his performances? He can talk about Shakespeare and Anthony Powell in the same breath and I can't. I know that these are the intellectual tools of both his trade and his current repertoire, and not of mine. Dancing develops physical, not intellectual

agility, and a dance education didn't, in itself, furnish me with the ability
to discuss the finer points of Petipa and Diaghilev in any constructive
way. And though Shakespeare's plays form the basis of several
cornerstones of the ballet repertoire, what depths can I draw on to
inform my interpretation of Juliet, should I ever be lucky enough to be
cast?

It's as if it is considered enough to equip dancers with the technique
necessary only to 'do the steps' and no more, a sad diminution of what
they may be capable of, and a sad impoverishment of the art form itself.
If ballet is to reaffirm its position as a creative art, then its artists must be
educated as true creators rather than simple re-creators. To that end,
they need to be exposed to the full richness of artistic endeavour in the
same way that Simon has been. I cannot think of any other performing
art where students are taught gesture alone, without full and proper
reference to the history and tradition which underlies that gesture, and
to the whole world of art out there which has connected and cross-
referenced roots. Dance demands that its performers be prepared and
gift-wrapped at a very tender age for a career which will be over before
they reach their forties. Simon Beale, at 36, is even now breaking new
ground for himself and entering new mediums. He will be able to
continue doing so into his dotage. There's no such luxury for a dancer.
With fewer miles than Simon on the clock, I am having to start
considering a future beyond dance, at exactly a time when I feel I have
the most to offer on the stage.

17th September 1997, London
Had a late night yesterday. It was the opening performance of Les Ballets
Trockadero de Monte Carlo, a troupe of ballerinas who haven't been in
London for several years. They have something I could never, ever
aspire to: they're all men who dance *en travesti*.

Despite the fact that it's been around for years, I've never seen the
company as a whole, although I have seen one of their founder members,
Larry. He's a permanent feature at the Met in New York. His 'day' job
is dressing the principal artists who perform there, and he occupies a seat
in the corridor between the dressing-rooms and the stage. He has seen
generations of dancers come and go, always with the same inscrutable
smile and biting, camp humour. About four years ago, after one of our
New York performances, we all headed off to a club where Larry –
whose stage name is Ekaterina Sobechanskaya – and Co. were due to

perform. As a cabaret act, and helped along by numerous drinks and general high spirits, they seemed perfect. As a complete evening's theatre, it wore a bit thin.

The present company (Larry, sadly, is no longer an active member) were performing at the Peacock Theatre off Kingsway, the temporary home-in-exile of Sadler's Wells. It's rather a nice place, and very central. It seems a shame that it should remain dark for much of the time. The evening consisted of several well-worn excerpts from the classical repertoire, and it all started off well, with an announcement over the public address system in an accent thick with vodka and Russian cigarettes: 'In accordance with the traditions of the great Russian Ballet' – a pause for effect – 'there will be changes to this evening's programme.' The voice proceeded to regale us with a list of some of the funnier pseudonyms: Margeaux Mundeyn, Maya Thickenthighya, Margaret Lowin-Octeyn, DBE. You have to say them aloud. Unfortunately, things didn't really get much better than this, and the most I could say to my guest at the end of the evening was that at least he hadn't paid for his ticket. Now, to be fair, I have to add that quite a large chunk of the audience seemed to be having one hell of a time, and I was left with the feeling that perhaps I wasn't watching the same show. I could clearly identify the hysteria of several of my fellow dancers – you don't work with people for fifteen years without knowing what they sound like when they laugh, and when they cry. Not for the first time, I wondered if I exist separately from them in some sort of parallel universe. Fortunately, I did run into some like-minded friends in the interval, and worryingly, some very good friends who thought it was all marvellous. I don't want to sound like a killjoy. I can laugh at ballet, and I promise you, I often do, but only when it's very funny. Besides, the best ballet jokes are often unintentional, and they certainly don't stretch out for three long hours. I've also seen this type of parody done better. The finest example I've ever seen – sorry, Larry – was a re-creation of the nineteenth-century *Pas de Quatre*, which Jules Perrot originally staged for Fanny Cerrito, Lucile Grahn, Marie Taglioni and Carlotta Grisi, the absolute dance darlings of their time, the Spice Girls of 1854. It was an impresario's coup of the same magnitude as getting the Three Tenors on stage together. At a 'Friends Christmas Party', a now sadly defunct annual expression of thanks to the Friends of Covent Garden who support the Opera House through thick and thin, four of the men in the company performed their own *Pas de Quatre*, prepared and rehearsed in strictest secrecy. They did it absolutely straight, and this of course was the difference. Les Ballets Trockadero take note: You don't need to *tell* us its funny. If it is, we'll know.

Today, the South Bank was expecting some firm news from the Arts Council on its Lottery application. We are keenly waiting to hear whether there will be money available to build Richard Rogers' now infamous 'glass wave', the canopy which tops off his design for the proposed redevelopment of the centre. Good news or bad, it would be nice to know for sure, but once again, the decision has been deferred. The statement from the Arts Council in Great Peter Street points to 'unresolved' questions about the bid, and makes reference to the predicted reduction in Lottery money available to the arts. All is not lost yet, but despite its healthy financial profile and matching funds to the tune of £17 million, a pledge from publisher and philanthropist Paul Hamlyn, it seems as if the South Bank may turn out, indirectly, to be the first victim of last month's Lottery capping. We wait to hear.

18th September 1997, London
A very full day. I am still suffering from the most extraordinary bout of insomnia, a sure sign that stress is building up in some area of my life. I finally got to sleep at 4 a.m., and this morning I had to be up before 8 a.m. I can't usually function on so little sleep, but I've coped pretty well today. They do say that you need less sleep as you get older. Perhaps this is one more sign that I'm making the transition from 'promising young thing' to 'mature and interesting'.

At 10 a.m. I meet Amanda Jones, company press officer, at News Direct in the Gray's Inn Road. It's the third interview I've done in three days – part of the ongoing campaign to sell the 3,500 seats at the Labatt's Apollo. It's a big space to fill, and tickets are moving slowly. Afterwards, I make my way to my next date, the opening of the Koestler Awards Exhibition. It's a beautiful, late summer day, marred only by the fact that my new shoes are rubbing with increasing force right where my ballet shoes will be tomorrow morning. I enjoy the walk along Queensway, but make an unscheduled stop at Boots to buy a box of plasters.

I first learnt about the Koestler Awards by chance, when I was wandering around Whiteleys, the shopping and cinema complex in Bayswater, killing time before the start of a film. There was a stark banner on the wall, announcing an art sale in the top floor exhibition area. I went up to have a peek and discovered that this was no ordinary art but the work of inmates from various prisons, young offender institutions and special hospitals throughout the country. During the Spanish Civil War, the Hungarian-born writer and intellectual, Arthur Koestler, was imprisoned in Seville. As a result of his experience, he came to believe that lone prisoners, more than anyone, need the self-respect that comes with expressive creativity. So, in 1960, he came up with the idea of an art competition, expressly for prisoners, where the winning entries would be exhibited publicly and sold. The sums involved are negligible; typically, the prizes are worth twenty to thirty pounds, and most of the work sells for small change. But this is inconsequential. The real point is to give people held in institutions the experience of what Sir Stephen Tumin, Chairman of the Koestler Trust, calls the 'practice of daily work, the matching of mind to skill, the process of art or craft'. On that first visit last year, I was surprised to find a painting of myself dancing, copied from a photograph in the *Mail on Sunday*. I wrote my name down in the visitors book, and was subsequently invited to attend the opening today.

I arrive early, but I go right up with a view to snapping up a bargain or two before the masses arrive. Unfortunately, the rest of the invited crowd had the same idea, and someone has already pledged the asking price of £28.00 for two bowls, entitled 'Male and Female Dancer (after Bakst)'. They are so beautiful, and I would love to take them home. This year, as last, the impact of the work on show goes beyond the intellectual. It hits me, physically, somewhere in the region of the solar plexus. Some of the paintings are 'better' than others, but that is so far from the point as to be hardly worth mentioning. As Tumin says in his introductory speech, 'You probably won't think some of these paintings are worth much, but think of the value to the people who did them.' That value leaps out of the pictures and makes me want to grab hold of all those people who think incarceration should be punishment rather than rehabilitation, and forcibly drag them here to have a look. *Newsnight* presenter Jeremy Paxman officially opens the event and like the man standing alongside me, he compares the exhibition to the one currently making headlines at the Royal Academy, *Sensations*. He says that he was struck by how violence, especially sexual violence, appeared to obsess each of the artists on show in *Sensations*. At Whiteleys, in this show by artists who presumably have a greater working knowledge of one or both of those things, it doesn't really play any part at all.

In the evening, I drive across to Turtle Key Arts Centre, in Fulham, close to Barons Court, to see another exhibition. The journey from home should take about twenty minutes, but this is one of the occasions when, for no apparent reason, all movement on the roads around West London stops, and drivers struggle to retain their cool while their engines overheat. Eventually I arrive, an hour later than I intend, but in time for the first 'performance'. As I park the car, I hear a roar from Chelsea's football ground, a few streets away. Ah! The snarl-up is explained.

Louise Mizen is an artist who paints horses and dancers, two subjects without an obvious connection, although Degas also made both those subjects the focus of his life's work. Louise originally began with horse studies, but presumably through her husband, Andrew Ferguson, one of the best osteopaths I know, has moved on to work increasingly with the image of the dancer. This evening, she attempted to bring together dancer and horse in painting, music, movement and the spoken word. Not an easy task, but it worked well and, sometimes, powerfully. The performance started with a still projection of a horse on the back wall of the performing area. With a jolt, it sprang into life and became a film of the most beautiful creature – and it was dancing! I swear that horse was dancing. I have never seen anything quite like it. After a while, the American dancer Antonia Franchesci entered, a single figure clad in piebald tights, head tossing, nostrils flared and prancing across the stage in step with the film and then on her own. There are very few occasions in any theatre which have the 'uplift' factor for me – if I catch my breath once, it's good going. And here I really did catch my breath.

That was the second time today. A good day for art.

19th September 1997
At last I have a copy of the transcripts of July's sittings of the Kaufman inquiry; Jeremy Isaacs' clever deployment of facts and figures to defend his tenure and the House in general, and Genista McIntosh's evidence.

I learnt a little more about the real reasons behind Genista McIntosh's abrupt resignation; I learnt a lot more about just what we are missing out on. In a sublime example of integrity combined with grace under fire, Genista took the stand with dignity, honesty and kind diplomacy. After repeated questioning, she does concede that it was stress rather than illness which forced her resignation, but she resolutely refuses to apportion blame for the cause of that stress, saying only that there was a 'mismatch' between her and the organisation. 'There are certain difficulties in the way the Opera House is structured that I found particularly hard to deal with, yes, I accept that, and that is something to do with me as much as it is with them.'

Reading through the transcripts, it is hard not to agree (for the first time) with Gerald Kaufman's closing remarks, that he 'cannot understand how any organisation that was lucky enough to have you did not go out of its way to keep you'. Genista, quick as a flash, responds in a manner which only serves to underline his sentiments: 'I cannot leave the stand,' she replies, 'without saying that there is no suggestion from me or anybody that that effort was not made.'

Was she really the wrong person? And, if so, shouldn't we have changed the job?

27th September 1997, London
I am finally able to turn on the computer again after a week from hell. It all started last Saturday, when very early in the morning, my mum picked me up and drove me north to Lincolnshire. We were off to visit my second eldest sister, who has recently remarried. When I was at the Royal Ballet School in Richmond Park, we lived in Ingoldmells, a seaside village on the Lincolnshire coast, just north of Skegness. The rest of the family moved away in 1980 but one sister remained. I only spent about four years in Lincolnshire, but my first ballet classes were at the Janice Sutton School of Dance on Skegness High Street. In fact, if it weren't for Janice my dance career might have stopped on the High Street. It was she who suggested I audition for the Royal Ballet School, at the age of eleven. I'd certainly never heard of the place, but I already knew I was going to be a dancer. No question.

So the long drive up the A1 is one I came to know very well. In the early days I felt out of place, a northerner amongst sophisticated southerners, and so that I didn't feel left out when the majority of my friends went home for the weekend, my parents made a valiant effort to ferry me back and forth home once in every half term. We weren't permitted to leave White Lodge until four o'clock on Fridays, so it meant arriving home after midnight and leaving again after lunch on Sunday. Perhaps that's where I learnt the value of the short break, a precious commodity in the ballet world since it's usually the only type of break you get. When people talk to me about 'long weekends' I invariably assume they mean the sort that doesn't have a show on Saturday night. To a dancer, a weekend that begins on Saturday rather than on Sunday morning is a terrific bonus.

This particular Saturday the drive up the A1 was to celebrate my sister's recent wedding at a pretty restaurant in the Lincolnshire countryside. The next morning, twelve hours after the meal, I woke up feeling very strange. My stomach was churning and I couldn't seem to get warm. I curled up under a duvet by a raging fire and still shook like a washing machine on its spin cycle. Mum gamely managed the five-hour drive back to London, with me feeling worse and worse beside her, only to come down with the same symptoms later that evening. Oblivious to this, I fell straight into bed and slept through the night, waking only to make high-speed visits to the bathroom.

Being a dancer I immediately take the blame for everything that goes wrong with me, both inside and out, and this time I assumed that my recent and persistent insomnia had weakened my immune system and I'd picked up some sort of gastroenteritis. The next day, when my temperature reached 104 degrees Fahrenheit, I decided I'd better go and consult my doctor. Since there was no possibility of getting there under my own steam, however much heat I was churning out, David, my long-suffering and very best friend, came by to chauffeur me. It wasn't until I learnt later that day that six of the party at Saturday's meal were now out of action that I changed my diagnosis to food poisoning. On Friday evening the call came through from the Environmental Health people; the Olde English restaurant had obviously specialised in even older English hygiene. Six of the party of eight had cases of salmonella.

Unlike most of the odd and un-named viruses that come my way, salmonella seems such an important thing to catch. I feel terribly grown up and curiously blameless about it all. For once, there is nothing I could have done to prevent myself falling ill, other than eating at a different restaurant, of course. I can usually find some way to shoulder the blame for every cold, cough or injury I suffer. But this time, *it wasn't my fault*. I couldn't help it. If I didn't feel so awful, I would feel elated that my conscience is clear.

Now, of course, I face the uphill climb back to where I was a week ago on the snakes and ladders game of fitness. Contrary to what many dancers believe (much of it wrapped in guilt inculcated from youth), you don't lose every ounce of stamina you've built up by leaving class early once in a while. There is the dancer's oft repeated but seriously fallacious mantra: 'one day without class and you notice, two days without class and your teacher notices, three days without class and the whole world notices.' In the dance world, the value of rest is entirely overlooked, and the idea that you can't survive more than twenty-four hours without a quick *tendu* fix becomes a good excuse for not giving dancers time off. In reality, of course, we can survive for a couple of days without class, and sometimes it's a jolly good idea to do so. This afternoon I spoke to the choreographer Mark Baldwin, who called to ask if I would dance for him at a charity event he's involved with in November. He's in Berlin for the première of his new work and he's terribly worried that the theatre management there have scheduled a rest day on the eve of the opening. (In England, that would always be the day of the dress rehearsal, unless of course you're an opera singer.) I asked him if the work was very strenuous. 'Yes, and it's part of a triple bill that keeps most of the dancers busy all evening.' 'Mark,' I replied, 'can you imagine an athlete running a marathon the day *before* a marathon?' We've been so brainwashed into believing that the way to build 'stamina' is to flog ourselves right up to the evening before the performance, that it takes a blind leap of faith to try it any other way. But 'tapering' training in the week leading up to competition is established practice for athletes, and it's based on sound physiological thinking. One day, dance will catch up.

But missing a week of classes because you have salmonella food poisoning is something quite different, and goodness knows how long it will take before I'm back on top form. Judging by the way I feel after today's short walk, it could be quite some time. Having said that, the body is remarkably resilient and, once I have a few days of solid food back inside me, the mood may change.

October 1997

I'm still trying to recover something of my strength after seven days without food. I went in to work at Barons Court on Tuesday and did fifteen minutes alone with Monica Mason; on Wednesday I did twenty, and on Thursday I attempted barre with the rest of the company. It's incredible just how weak I feel. I managed two exercises, then sat down and missed the third while I recovered from the effort. Today I did considerably better, surviving about forty minutes in all, and actually climbing up on to *pointe*. But it looks as if my performance of *Sleeping Beauty* in two weeks' time is out of the question. I won't make a decision until next week, but while I can contemplate doing *Beauty* without a build-up when I'm at full strength, the idea of doing it now, when I'm running on empty, is something I don't even want to think about. It's particularly galling as it's my one major show between now and Christmas.

I have a chequered history with *The Sleeping Beauty*. Although I've danced the ballet three or four times in the past, it's always been as a replacement, in times of crisis. This would have been my first ever *scheduled* performance and now I'm the one in crisis. I first danced it just after an ankle injury, in December 1994. I'd been off for a few months and was working my way back into smaller, less demanding roles. At the same time, Anthony Dowell was having nightmares because all of his principal ladies were injured – as far as I can remember, only Viviana Durante was dancing. He called me into his dressing-room at the Opera House and asked if I thought I could manage a *Beauty* in ten days' time. Always up for a challenge, and desperate to dance Aurora ever since I was a gal at White Lodge, I said yes. It was the most extraordinary experience; the only time I had been 'off' previously was two or three years earlier, with an Achilles injury. That had put me out of action for six months, and during the entire time, no one ever suggested that I could be doing some other kind of exercise to keep myself fit. Dancers don't run, cycle, go to the gym – it 'builds up the wrong muscles', or so we dancers have always been told. With this injury, I went about it differently. Armed with the benefit of Torje's knowledge of physiology, rather than second-hand and suspect beliefs, I was in the gym every day, exercising solidly for at least an hour and a half, and towards the end of the six month lay-off, running about five miles a day. In the end, I literally bounded back into the studio, ready and able to take on Aurora. I was, without a doubt, the fittest I have ever been in my life, totally giving lie to the idea that being 'off' means getting out of shape.

For my second *Beauty*, I had even less warning. It was about six months later, and we were on tour in Japan. I was scheduled to dance Myrthe, Queen of the Wilis in *Giselle*, a man's role if ever there was one, and I will openly admit I was not looking forward to it. Although I was officially 'back' from the injury, the role of Myrthe involves twenty minutes of continuous jumping, and I was worried about how my ankle would cope. There are several casts for the role, and on the morning of my performance they were teasing me mercilessly as they all knew it was absolutely the last thing I wanted to be doing. But the day had dawned, and it seemed there really was no way out. By four o'clock I was in the theatre, preparing shoes and about to do class. A knock on the door. Anthony Dowell. Leanne Benjamin had finally decided that she couldn't do any more work on a troublesome foot, and she was flying home. Could I manage a *Beauty* in two day's time? And if I could, would I mind missing the evening's performance in order to rehearse? Talk about a last-minute reprieve from the cold-hearted Myrthe. Never mind that I was swapping one act of jumping for three acts of what is probably the most technically challenging female role there is. To me, it felt like a royal pardon. With all this in mind, it's even more galling that I'll most likely miss the first performance of *Sleeping Beauty* for which I've actually had time to prepare.

Over at the Apollo, where efforts are still continuing to keep audience levels up, the week has been full of real 'Stories from the Ballet', and I can't believe that I'm missing it all. On Tuesday evening, Irek Mukhamedov injured his toe, limped – literally – through the balcony scene of *Romeo*, and was replaced in the following acts by Michael (Stuart) Cassidy. Michael had been at home, presumably with his feet up, tucking into a nice dinner and settling down for a night in front of the television when the phone rang. On Wednesday evening, Donald (Anthony) Twiner, every dancer's favourite conductor, succumbed to a serious bout of flu halfway through *Romeo and Juliet*. Paul Stobart, a company pianist, bravely took up the baton and led the orchestra through Act Three. These 'show must go on' stories are what make live theatre so unique, and so wonderful. I have seen dancers leap on-stage in the wrong costume, and in roles they barely know, to keep the curtain up. I've done it myself, most memorably in *Beauty*, when I glanced across the stage and noticed a suspicious gap in the Florestan quartet. Where there should be four, there were three. I simply dropped my Bluebird tutu, and stood nearly naked in the wings until wardrobe brought me a costume and I took to the stage in a solo I'd never even rehearsed. The performer's goodwill has always been the oil that helps keep the Opera House wheels turning, and management abuses it at their peril.

In the mortal world outside the Apollo the arts have suffered yet another blow. Unexpectedly, Lord Gowrie has resigned his post as Chairman of the Arts Council. He will leave in April, a year before his term of office expires. As always, the papers say that it is for 'personal reasons'. But the rumours abound, and speculation runs high. Gowrie is without doubt a Tory man through and through. Although an appointment such as this should be apolitical, it has long been feared that he and the Labour administration would not see eye to eye. Lately they've been looking very askance at one another.

It does seem that Gowrie's departure may mark the end of an era in the arts. The government has hinted that there is no reason why the post of Arts Council Chairman should remain 'non-executive', a euphemism for unpaid. Stand aside what writer Valerie Grove calls the 'languid, well-connected patron of the arts'. Make way for the business manager who, with his market surveys and eye on the balance sheet, will make sure that the 'people's money is spent on the people's priorities', to quote Tony Blair. Clear the stages of *Giselle* and *Swan Lake*, and make way for a new production starring Anthea Turner and a lot of coloured balls. As we all compose our own personal obituary for the arts in this country, we should bear in mind the chilling words of Culture Minister Chris Smith: 'Enough of the Churchill papers. It's ordinary people who play the Lottery, and it's ordinary people who should gain.' So the fifty-two thousand people who have seen The Royal Ballet at Hammersmith's Labatt's Apollo are not 'ordinary', Mr Smith? The twenty million people who visited art galleries and museums last year, are they, too, not 'ordinary'? Just what are they, then?

6th October 1997, London
In bed early last night in an effort to do everything within my power to

hasten my recovery from the bloody salmonella, I watched a fascinating
TV programme on the actor Antony Sher. Watching him prepare for his
leading role in *Cyrano de Bergerac*, I felt the same sort of envy that I
experienced while reading his book *Year of the King*, in which he writes
about preparing for the role of Richard the Third. I envied him his place
in the creative team – to some extent, a ballet dancer is only an
instrument who channels the choroegrapher's creativity and ideas.
Moreover, I envied the sense of commitment and exploration as the
assembled cast experimented with different approaches to their roles.
And I envied the time Sher and his director allowed themselves to play
with ideas and notions of character, like shifting from chair to chair as
different thoughts were expressed and weekending in Paris to look for
the face of Cyrano and the theatre where Rostand's play was first
performed. Always restlessly searching for the context in which their art
can thrive. How wonderful it would be if there was time in the ballet
world to explore familiar territory in an unfamiliar and prolonged way.
Sher spent much of the programme working on the shape of his nose.
We rarely get asked for our thoughts on costume and make-up. It does
make you think. Both of us stage performers, but in very different
spheres and with very different ways of working.

Despite my best endeavours, today I had to face up to reality. After a
week of pretending that it might, somehow, be possible, I have had to be
very adult and make the decision to bale out of my single performance of
The Sleeping Beauty. Actually, I wasn't adult about it at all. I had to go
and find my conscience, Monica Mason, and get her to make the
decision for me. It feels totally wrong to give up on the ballet when it is
still ten days away, especially as ten days is the most preparation I've ever
had in the past. But the difference is that if I was fit, they could throw it
at me with a couple of days' notice and I'd leap at the chance. The
problem this time is that I'm still not well. In fitness terms, I'm barely
out of bed. I did barre this morning, and it was as much as I could do to
resist the temptation to lie down on the floor between exercises. In some
ways, I feel weaker than I did last Saturday. I know, in my head, that I
won't be up to doing it, and I certainly won't be up to doing it well. But
it hurts. It is so painful for me to give up on anything at all, ever. Most
of my lucky breaks have come from subjugating weakness – injury,
illness, depression – to a will that relentlessly drives me on, regardless of
the obstacles. But this time I know I have to give in. My tanks are empty,
so to speak, and it would be dangerous to try and push myself beyond the

bounds. Again feelings of guilt bubble to the surface; perhaps if I'd tried harder, taken it a bit easier, slept more, slept less, taken more time off, come back sooner, eaten different food . . . I thought I could walk away from this illness without blaming myself, but old recriminations die hard. It seems I'll never convince myself that a Lincolnshire chef's failure to wash his hands before he served my dinner *isn't my fault*.

I'm certainly road testing all the advice in the *still* untitled book for DK: 'Dramatic weight loss through dieting alone depletes muscle mass'. It most certainly does. 'The body has an instinct for survival and will combine all its forces, psychological and otherwise, to persuade you to eat and restore the body mass.' I'll say. I'm eating for England this week. The book goes to print in less than a month, and I'm frantically making changes to the proofs. My head is full of prescriptions and descriptions of physical ideals, and I don't match up to any of them.

In the midst of a depressing day I found something in London's *Evening Standard* to lift my spirits; a positive voice for the arts! And from a politician! In his campaign for election to the post of London's Lord Mayor, Ken Livingstone, formerly Red Ken, is advocating free admission to all the capital's galleries and museums, paid for by a tax on flights in and out of Heathrow Airport. Hurrah. A voice in the wilderness, bravery indeed. Does he know how unpopular this might make him? Or perhaps Livingstone is the one person who has no fear of unpopularity and can carry it off. As head of the Greater London Council in the 1980s, I guess he's been there before. He sure has my vote. Come to think of it, I wonder if he wants Lord Gowrie's job at the Arts Council?

8th October 1997, London

Two consecutive nights at the ballet: First, the Royal's opening of *Giselle* down at the Labatt's Apollo in Hammersmith. Thanks to the continuing effects of the salmonella, it looks like this may be my first and only trip west. It was an interesting experience being on the other side of the curtain amongst the audience. I can't deny that as an evening out the Apollo doesn't quite match the splendours of the old Covent Garden Opera House, but the Apollo's management has definitely pulled out all the stops to transform it into a pleasant place to spend an evening. The foyer areas are much more spacious than Covent Garden and, architecturally, they are rather splendid. It was built as a cinema in the days when cinema-going was a glamorous event and not just the shoe box experience it is now. And the foyer is certainly a dramatic place, with swirling lines and an early atrium effect at its centre. Inside the auditorium the sightlines are exceptionally good; it was built so that patrons could see the action on the wide screen, unlike the nineteenth-century opera houses, whose horseshoe crescents were designed to give patrons a clear view of the action in the boxes and stalls. What transpired on stage was definitely not the main event. My seat was up in the Apollo's balcony, at some distance from the stage, but I had an uninterrupted view of what was going on. Apparently the theatre boasts the widest proscenium arch in the country, perfect for the long line of Riverdancers who play here to packed audiences for months at a time. Unfortunately it doesn't have the depth to match, and although the dancers coped remarkably well, it must feel a bit like dancing in an Egyptian frieze. Perhaps next time we visit we could revive Nijinsky's *L'Après-midi d'un faune*.

I find it so difficult to watch dancing. I never quite know which bit to look at. I get obsessed with feet, arms or necks, and then realise I have seen a whole variation without once looking at the face. And there is the added difficulty that I know most ballets inside out and backwards. Objectivity and unadulterated enjoyment are denied me by virtue of that knowledge. I can rarely see ballet or hear its music with fresh eyes or ears. But perhaps my biggest problem is that I know the dancers so well; their idiosyncrasies, their quirks and habits, the way they speak and move. It was so hard for me this evening to lose Viviana Durante within the character of Giselle. However exquisite she was I kept seeing the person I know as well as the ballerina.

Act Two had its own special problems. Nicola Tranah was dancing Myrthe, Queen of the Wilis. She started out very smoothly, a ghostly apparition skimming across the stage in ballet's longest sequence of *bourrées*. Unfortunately, it didn't last too long. Just a few minutes in and she had one major skid, although she did somehow manage to stay upright. The next time she wasn't so lucky. Her feet went from underneath her and she rose into the air before crashing down, flat on her back. The audience gasped. When a dancer falls on stage there is always a sharp intake of breath. It's not only concern for the poor soul beached on the boards. It's also the shattering of illusion, the abrupt return from fantasy to reality. For some reason certain dancers hit the deck more often than others and falling down is not especially prominent in my repertoire of tricks. But there's a saying in the theatre, that you will always return to a stage on which you have a fall, so the prospect of a return to the Hammersmith Apollo should cheer up Niccy no end.

There are two distinct recoveries from a fall; the unbelievably quick, and the unbelievably slow. Sometimes dancers spring up so fast that you aren't really certain they fell at all. Other times, they seem to spend an age collecting themselves and climbing back to their feet. Tonight, Niccy fell into the second category. But there was more to come. About five seconds later, another foot which refused to make permanent contact with the floor, and another skid. It was all she could do to keep from shaking her head in disbelief. She finished the solo to massive applause, almost an ovation. That's the funny thing about the English. We do appreciate effort, almost more so when it doesn't quite hit the mark. The English love their underdogs.

At an appropriate break in the action, Johanna Adams, the company's stage manager, brought the curtain down and came on stage to make an announcement: 'You may have noticed that we are having a little trouble with the dry ice machine . . .' So that was the problem. The 'mist' at the opening of the second act had turned to liquid, leaving small puddles all over the stage. Poor Niccy would have been better off in flippers and a snorkel than pointe shoes and wings.

My second evening at the ballet this week was at the Piccadilly Theatre in the West End, for the première of Adventures in Motion Pictures' new production of *Cinderella*. Matthew Bourne created a storm last year when he transmogrified the character of Odette/Odile in *Swan Lake* into a man. This time he's taken on the Perrault fairy story and Prokofiev's score. Actually, he hasn't taken on much of the fairytale. The action has been uprooted and relocated to World War II London during the blitz. Prince Charming is recast as a wounded pilot and Cinderella becomes the abused victim of a hard-drinking, hard-hearted stepmother. The shift works with only a small suspension of belief. Matthew is a great producer and he is helped by terrific performances from Sarah Wildor and Adam Cooper (a couple off-stage as well as on), the first on leave from The Royal Ballet, and the second, sadly, an ex-member of the company. Sarah is a wonderful actress as well as a beautiful dancer. I first noticed her years ago when she was cast as the original Clara in a new version of *The Nutcracker* at the Opera House. She was about thirteen at the time, a 'White Lodger', and I was amazed even then by the sheer beauty of her technique. As a professional, she has distinguished herself not by virtuosity but by her dramatic skills, in roles like Juliet, Manon and Giselle. As most of these ballerina roles are tragic parts, she has never had much of a chance to turn her hand to comedy. But anyone who knows Sarah knows she has a wicked, and not always repeatable, sense of humour, and I loved seeing some of that come across on stage.

Bourne seems to have identified very precisely a formula by which dance can be taken out of the margins of the experimental and relocated, literally, centre stage of the mainstream. It's not always possible to judge a new work on the strength of the first-night audience's response; this evening's reaction would seem to predict a triumph for his *Cinderella* on pretty much the same scale as Bourne had with *Swan Lake* last year. But although it's a wonderful evening's theatre, and a witty and clever re-working of a familiar tale, I'm not convinced it has the same magic ingredients. *Swan Lake* was a surprise hit – Matthew made it because he wanted to, and it just happened to hit the right spot and reach a huge popular audience. This time, with a West End opening and big investments riding on the show, it must have been very difficult for him not to aim, even subconsciously, for the same sort of success.

Watching Act Two, I came across an interesting dilemma. In *Cinderella* we get the big, classic love duet, complete with short, sequinned tunic, passionate partnering and Prokofiev's luscious score. Not the sort of emotional coupling we're used to seeing in 'contemporary' dance. In Bourne's *Swan Lake* there were no 'big' duets, at least not between a man and a woman. Passion was either suggested or suppressed, and the question didn't come up. Here in *Cinderella* I struggled to reconcile the conflicts of style and content. It was almost musical theatre. It was a minor quibble and unnecessary if categorisation isn't important. For the vast majority of the audience, it's simply dancing. I'll leave it to the dance historians to judge this further.

The performance was followed by an extraordinary first-night party at the Savoy – a definite cut above the usual, and a clear indication of where the money is coming from. This is commercial, not subsidised, theatre. Theatre for the masses. The party was themed to tie in with the show, and included a band and some obviously planted jive dancers to get things going. I had a bit of a twirl myself, but I still don't feel up to anything energetic.

12th October 1997, London
A rainy day in London, one of those days where the drizzle is relentless and the raindrops even thicker than usual. I'm still not feeling up to

going to work, although I do try to avoid working on Saturdays even when I'm in the best of health. It wasn't always thus; the first half of my career with the company saw me at work every day of the week, without fail and, whenever possible, squeezing in extra classes. Those were the *corps de ballet* days when I never got a chance to go on the stage, at least not in the sort of roles I was interested in doing. There were always plenty of opportunities to be one of the crowd, but I wanted to show what I could really do on my own and the technical challenges of class seemed like the only chance. Nowadays the same need isn't there and, besides, I'm hellishly busy doing everything else. Free Saturdays are a wonderful chance to catch up on real life, to get away, to go shopping. If there's no performance then class can wait until Monday.

Today I wasn't up to working anyway. I did go out in the evening, to the Roundhouse in Chalk Farm. I was there earlier this year to see Billy Forsythe and Dana Caspersen's art installation which was quickly dubbed the Bouncy Castle. It's real title was *Tight Roaring Circle*, but I think it will go down in history as the Bouncy Castle. The company which sponsored it, Artangel, are now supporting *Bernadetje*, a venture by a Dutch theatre company. Unlike my last visit, we, the audience, were not called upon tonight to become the show. This disused tram turning house has been reincarnated from adventure playground to something approaching a theatre – at least seats were installed – although the atmosphere and the temperature were not quite up to standard. We were allowed to sit and spectate. The performance itself was, well, difficult to describe. There were Dutch actors and several children who had never acted before speaking heavily accented English, with an impressive grasp of the local swear-words. There were dodgem cars and a lot of dancing which had its roots firmly in club culture. It all seemed very trippy and I did wonder whether my sheltered childhood (and adulthood, come to think of it) was limiting my ability to grasp what exactly was going on, or its point. I tried imagining that I had to do an overnight review of the show, and searched for a few pegs on to which I could hang my thoughts. None were forthcoming, so I shall have to await the critics' reports in tomorrow's papers.

I have a sneaking suspicion that the power of art to 'move' has little to do with the art itself but with something inside us. It's not so much the power to move as the ability to be moved. Tonight I remained resolutely *en place*.

15th October 1997, London
Tonight I should have been at my own palace, as Aurora, celebrating my sixteenth birthday, but thanks to the lingering salmonella this fantasy made flesh was not to be. Instead I went to Buckingham Palace, along with about five hundred other people, for a dinner given by the Association for Business Sponsorship of the Arts (ABSA). I was escorted by my friend David (looking splendid in black tie) who had been generously 'loaned' to me for the evening by his girlfriend. Far too overdressed for the tube, we used my normal car service to take us there, and felt guilty that what the driver thought was a run of the mill 'Little Venice to Westminster' would put him through the auto equivalent of a full body search. He wanted to drop us off outside the gates, but I forced him to drive us, me in my vast Neil Cunningham frock, through the august portico. We must have looked fairly suspicious as they examined the Cortina minicab from every possible angle, boot open, bonnet up, before they finally let us pass through. It was fascinating to go behind the façade of what I thought was a fairly two-dimensional building and find it is nothing of the sort.

The evening was hosted by Prince Charles. He explained that his mother had very kindly allowed him to hold this event at the palace while she was away, an interesting variant on the more usual illicit parties that countless teenagers have held in their parents' empty houses. There was a short performance of music and dance extracts, all taking love as their theme, followed by a wonderful address (without notes) by the writer, actor and comedian Stephen Fry. For the first time ever I heard someone else make the link between nature and the arts, something I have often talked about, in private, with Torje. Torje comes from a society where there is little tradition of 'art'. There is music, painting and dancing, but it has never really been formalised into high art the way it has throughout much of Europe. I maintain that the Norwegians don't need it, as they already have something bigger than they are – nature – to tame and inspire them. I've never said this in public, as I've learnt to keep my more romantic notions to myself ever since an English Literature essay came back with 'this sounds like waffle' written in the margin. So I was much relieved to hear Stephen Fry voice my own thoughts, although with much greater panache. He used the wit of Oscar Wilde to help him say it: 'The Americans are so violent because they have such ugly wallpaper.' In our overcrowded societies, we have lost contact with nature, sacrificing green fields and forests to the need for housing. We have taken away the attractive wallpaper and we need something to replace it. That something should be art.

20th October 1997, Boston
The next morning, Thursday, I put the evening gown and tiara back in storage, and dug out the black lycra and the old faithful denim jacket. Reincarnated as 'rock chick', I set off to New York to see Torje and catch up with the Stones tour again.

I saw two shows there (a bit of a celebrity circus, starring Brad Pitt and a glamorous supporting cast) at the Giants Stadium in New Jersey and then, on Saturday, flew up to Boston for the Stones' next gig. Torje had a rare night off and we went to see the Boston Ballet dance *Romeo and Juliet*. The company perform in the Wang Theatre, an historic building which has been adopted and renovated by Dr Wang, computer manufacturer and philanthropist, and his wife. It isn't quite finished, and if anyone has a roll or two of carpet to spare, there was a bare patch by my seat where it could be put to good use. But the Wangs are doing a tremendous job and I keep my fingers crossed that the good doctor might one day relocate to England and transfer his energies to the Royal Opera House instead. At this stage, the House is probably in need of a lot of carpet as well as the means to pay for it.

But for all the gilt and glamour, it's another of those steeply tiered auditoriums where you feel like you're sitting on a supermarket shelf and peering down towards the stage, looking past the dancers' heads to see their feet. It's a most uncomfortable angle from which to watch dance. For all the complaints about seeing the stage sideways in Covent Garden's familiar horseshoe configuration, I would much prefer to turn my head and look out of the centre of my eye sockets than peer down over my lower lashes with my own nose, distorted to Cyrano-like proportions, ever in the forefront.

This was a new production by Daniel Pelzig, the Boston Ballet's new director, and we were seeing its third or fourth performance. I find it really difficult to watch other versions of *Romeo* when I have Kenneth MacMillan's so deeply ingrained in my imagination. Call me biased but I think his interpretation of the story is pretty near definitive. Seamlessly blending Juliet's *pointe* work with the grounded, earthy dancing of the harlots and townspeople is the work of a master; you can't even notice the joins. It feels totally appropriate and utterly true to Prokofiev's music. When the curtain went up in the Wang Theatre and I saw the townspeople of Verona skipping around on *pointe*, my heart sank. The performance improved as it went on, but I did find myself fantasising a bit to really get involved. I could only share Lady Capulet's grief, for instance, by closing my eyes and thinking of Kenneth's Lady Capulet, beating herself in an effort to numb the pain of Tybalt's death.

23rd October 1997, London
Back home after my quick weekend away, and the full company is called to a meeting with Anthony Russell-Roberts, our Administrative Director. AR-R works up at Covent Garden, and I suspect it must be serious news he has for him to have made an unscheduled trip across London to Barons Court. In fact he has a mixed bag of messages, and he starts off with something positive: the Opera House redevelopment is on schedule and on budget, which, in the light of what followed, led me to wonder whether we should get the builders involved in the overall running of the House as well.

He also confirmed that the total attendance at Hammersmith was fifty-two thousand over three weeks. Fourteen thousand people a week is rather more than most theatres in the capital attract, but the press have begun to write off the Apollo season as a complete failure, based on what they call low attendance. I'm angry enough to write a letter to *The Times* asking why they insist on describing the place as half-empty when it was, in fact, well over half-full, attracting greater numbers than we could have played to in a similar run of performances at the Garden. But will they listen?

Anthony's bad news is rather more extensive: the Arts Council has received a standstill grant from the Treasury, which means we can expect the same, or worse, to be passed on to The Royal Ballet. The plans for next year have been altered accordingly, he tells us, with the repertoire reworked in an effort to cut costs. (More revivals, no new works.) He reiterates that there will be no loss of jobs. I hope he is right, but methinks he doth protest too much, and although the messenger brings a comforting tune we've heard this one before.

Anthony always allows time in these 'information sessions' for our questions, and, as usual, dancer and choreographer William Tuckett kicked off. Will has an incisive intelligence, a suspicious mind and a fluid tongue. He was not alone in querying the marketing of the company during the closure period. Several other dancers had strong views on the issue, and anecdotal evidence of neighbours and friends who hadn't a clue where (or even whether) The Royal Ballet is performing this season. I felt rather sorry for Anthony as he tried valiantly to make a defence. Being a member of management he obviously has to toe the line and can't always say what he really feels or divulge what he truly knows. Even if he had wanted to engage with the mood in the studio, he's part of a team which includes the marketing department and can't be seen to disparage them publicly.

The age-old division between the opera and ballet companies resurfaced, with dancers suggesting that for the next two years we should follow Scotland's example and devolve into a separate state. Because the Arts Council grant is awarded to the Opera House as a collective body, rather than to the individual companies which inhabit it, there is a feeling that our budget is adversely affected by the losses opera is making. In its plans for closure, the opera company took the opposite tack from the ballet. Rather than trying to maintain the company as a whole, they cut the numbers and, as a result, will spend the next two years performing smaller works. That of course involves doing *new* works, as most of the opera's repertoire is designed for a full-sized troupe. As it turns out, they have done some very interesting productions (such as Deborah Warner's version of Benjamin Britten's *The Turn of the Screw*) which have been critically acclaimed but haven't necessarily attracted large audiences. Depending on how you do the sums, it could be argued that they are losing money. As both companies are funded from the same Opera House purse, there is a feeling in some quarters that we have taken the brunt in two ways: artistically, in that we have two years of standard yet big-selling repertoire ahead, and financially, in that we are sharing their losses at the box-office.

Out of all of this there seems to be emerging evidence of a link between audience and venue rather than between audience and company. We may find this to be slightly less marked for the ballet, as audiences are used to seeing dance in a number of different theatres, and are more likely to travel around to see it. There's also a popular tradition of ballets like *Sleeping Beauty* and *Cinderella*, particularly around Christmas, which will draw audiences to productions rather than buildings. But most people wanting to see opera in the capital would think straight away of two theatres, Covent Garden and the Coliseum. Without the whole package, the environment as well as the music, it doesn't appear to have as much of a pull unless the forces of marketing do the tugging.

31st October 1997, London

A busy week. The first batch of pages for the DK book went to print. It has finally been christened *The Vitality Plan*, which retains an element of my original title which I'll hold back and use later. For a woman who can't make decisions, signing off on the final version of the book has been really tough. I keep wanting to snatch the pages back for yet one more read-through and more changes; a comma here, a full stop there and lots of adjectives elsewhere. But I have had to learn to let it go. It's been like the full sweep of parenthood condensed into six months.

At work I have started to rehearse a new piece, for this spring's 'Dance Bites' tour, with Cathy Marston. Cathy trained at the Royal Ballet School and dances with the Luzerner Ballet in Switzerland. She's a talented choreographer and this is the second time Anthony Dowell has asked her to make a ballet for us. Despite initial doubts about working with someone almost half my age, it has, so far, been great fun, and a huge relief to win back that feeling of involvement which disappears all too quickly when you're out of action for more than a couple of days. I'm beginning, too, at long last to recover some of my strength after the salmonella incident in September. God, it's taken a long time, well over a month.

I spent yesterday evening at the Prudential Awards for the Arts, at the Tate Gallery. Within the arts world, the Prudential Awards are extremely prestigious and fairly unique in that they dole out money with absolutely no strings attached. Over the nine years of their existence, the arts have benefited to the phenomenal tune of over £3 million. Last year I was a judge in the dance category, and it turned out to be one of the toughest jobs I have ever done. I had a real dilemma deciding where the money would be most useful. Was it more important to continue advancing the art itself and award experimentation or to take time out from the forward thrust of new work and think about bringing the public along too? It does seem to me that the further art develops at the 'top' end, the more we move away from a body of people who have absolutely no mechanisms to move with it. Is £50,000 (the amount of each individual award) better spent in artistic development or perhaps audience development? This year I'm just a guest at the proceedings, and I don't have to worry myself over such issues. But they'll come up again soon, I'm sure. In the light of last year's musings, it was interesting to see that in twelve short months attitudes had flipped around, and most of the money tonight went to companies involved in increasing access.

Despite Prudential's largesse, it was in some ways a gloomy event. I went with Nicholas Snowman, Chief Executive of the South Bank, who spent much of the evening fielding questions from journalists about the continuing saga of the South Bank's application to the Lottery fund for redevelopment. Despite the fact that the South Bank is in excellent shape, both financially and artistically, the Lottery application is grinding a laborious path through the various channels of the Arts Council and government funding mills. It seems that there is real fear about making another big award to a London project. The Opera House, on the other hand, despite its Lottery money, is not doing so well. Yesterday's *Guardian* carried an article alleging that cheques were bouncing, and over two hundred casual workers hadn't been paid, a claim denied by the House, yet printed anyway. For the record, it wasn't true. Gerald Kaufman's Select Committee sat again yesterday after its summer recess, with Mary Allen up before it to answer questions about the Opera House. I think he gave her a pretty tough time, producing, no doubt with a flourish, a letter from Genista McIntosh in which she said that she had not left voluntarily but had been asked to go. I suppose it is his self-appointed task to get to the bottom of it all but I do wonder whether this report, when it appears, will be more Kaufman rhetoric than solid evidence of misconduct. He seems to allow more time for his own public reflections on the answers than he does for the answers themselves.

Mary was at the Tate this evening and looked grey with exhaustion. The House's finances appear to be in worse shape than ever and there had been an Opera House Board meeting this afternoon at which she put forward a plan for survival. The Board gave her authority to 'investigate that plan further'. She told me that although she had been obliged to look at the question of redundancies, she had come to the conclusion that losing a handful of positions was not the solution to a £4.5 million deficit, and besides, if we lose many more people we will no longer be in a position to do the job we're here to do. We in the ballet are operating on the very minimum level of swans as it is. There's only so far you can stretch the feathers to cover up a threadbare *corps de ballet*. In the absence of any better ideas, I shall cross my fingers and wish her the very best of luck. She may need it.

All in all, I left the Tate feeling rather down. But there was a moment of pure joy as Max Stafford-Clark took the podium to accept the award for Out of Joint Theatre Company. In the great tradition of all awards ceremonies, he used the occasion to register his disappointment at the government's performance so far. (Last year, in my speech, I had a go at both the government and the opposition, just in case, berating the Conservatives for their attitude towards the arts, and questioning Blair's obsession, even then, with the judgement of 'the people'.) This year, Stafford-Clark made his point by telling us the story of the beleaguered arts, starved by eighteen years of a Conservative administration. Sometime around the beginning of May, they see the cavalry coming over the horizon. They welcome them with outstretched arms, crying 'Food? Water?' The cavalry pull to a halt and proudly announce, 'We're going to give you a dome.' With parched and cracked lips, the artists try once more: 'Food? Water?' Irritated now, the cavalry's patience snaps: 'What's the matter? Don't you like our dome?' I had a fine view of Peter Mandelson, the Minister Without, as he sat, impassive and unmoved amidst gales of laughter and thunderous applause.

November 1997

5th November 1997, London

The last few days wouldn't pass muster as an *EastEnders* script, so thick and fast have different strands of the drama unfolded. On Monday evening I was on the telephone to Judith Mackrell, dance critic of the *Guardian*, discussing a piece she would like me to write for the paper. The *Guardian* has been attacking the Opera House relentlessly ever since it called for its privatisation last July, building up to a crescendo of staggering intensity over the last week. Judith thought it might be interesting to hear from an artist on the inside what it feels like to be virtually under siege. We chatted for a while, then halfway through the conversation, she stopped. 'You haven't heard the news, have you?' 'Heard what?' 'English National Opera are moving into the Royal Opera House.'

I instantly put down the phone and tracked down Amanda Jones, press officer to The Royal Ballet. It seems that Judith had somewhat overstated the case: Culture Secretary Chris Smith has commissioned a report from Sir Richard Eyre, former Director of the Royal National Theatre, to look at the feasibility of Covent Garden operating as a receiving house for all three companies, The Royal Opera, The Royal Ballet and ENO. Eyre is brave indeed to have agreed to accept the thorniest mantle of them all. But he is one of the few people who could take on such a task. Widely respected and genuinely passionate about art, if anyone can assess the state of lyric theatre and come up with a sensible route forwards then it is him. Nevertheless, the arts world is in a storm, and I have to admit that it does seem a bit of a cheek to suggest requisitioning the House after all the work that has been done to get the place just right for the people who own it. Both the Opera House and ENO have announced their opposition to the plan, fearing, amongst other things, that it would lead inevitably to a merger, particularly in the light of Smith's comments to Tuesday's Kaufman inquiry that London can't support two opera companies. Funny, every other capital in Europe can.

On Tuesday *The Times* ran the banner headline 'People's opera to move in with toffs'. What is a respected broadsheet doing running a headline like that? I know it derives from the Murdoch stable, home of the most populist rag in the newsagent, but it usually keeps up some pretence of objectivity. The Queen Mother might have said, twenty years ago, that *The Times* 'isn't a newspaper – it's a national institution', but I'm not sure she'd be saying that now. In common with all other newspapers, it ran this latest story as a *fait accompli*, rather than the conjectural proposal it is.

But for the Opera House there was worse to come. Less than twenty-four hours after Smith dropped his bombshell, the Chairman of the Board of the Royal Opera House, Lord Chadlington, admitted to the Kaufman inquiry that unless the House can find £3 million by 12 November, it faces insolvency. Presumably it was the early warnings of this financial crisis that lay behind Mary Allen's obvious air of harassment at the Prudential Awards, and prompted Anthony Russell-Roberts' unscheduled visit to Barons Court last week. We've been in trouble before: only four months ago, just prior to his last appearance in front of the Select Committee, Chadlington delivered a rescue package of £2 million. It's tempting to bury my head in the sand and wait, once again, for the all clear but this time I'm not convinced it will come. I have never before felt quite so nervous about the future of the House. This time they may just let us sink.

After class today, Wednesday, Anthony Russell-Roberts talked to the company once again, explaining the predicament that we face, and trying to allay our ever-increasing fears that by next week we will all be out of a job. The November 12th deadline has come about because this is the date by which we have to put forward 'viable' closure plans to the Arts Council in order to secure the continuation of our grant. He also confirmed what I suspected, that the Opera House freehold is not owned outright by the government, and it cannot therefore be 'taken over' by force. It was a tense meeting, the company understandably edgy and nervous about its future.

I spent all afternoon at Dorling Kindersley in Covent Garden, finalising the second batch of proofs for *The Vitality Plan*, and then rushed back to Barons Court in time to hear Mary Allen address the company at 5.45 p.m. She rushed in and rushed out, a woman on a mission, and went straight to the point, confirming that her survival plan (presumably the one she told me about last Friday) has now been put into action. A new donor has been found and the continued existence of the House is guaranteed (God willing) without redundancies. She was wonderfully optimistic about the future, but she admitted there is a lot of work still to be done. Her endless efforts to balance the unbalanceable budget have uncovered some very strange management procedures whereby mistakes can be made and losses incurred yet not come to light for several months. To rectify this she has put into place draconian measures; no money will leave the House without her knowledge, and every cheque has to be personally monitored by her.

One of the dancers – probably William Tuckett – asked Mary for her thoughts on the Chris Smith proposal and she said that more than anything, she was 'saddened' by it. She feels it has come at a time when we desperately need the breathing space to get ourselves back on our feet rather than face more upheaval.

We left the building with a little more optimism than we brought to work this morning. Mary headed for the underground, alone, to deliver the same news to the opera chorus at the Shaftesbury Theatre where they're performing at the moment. It seemed an inauspicious exit for the person who had just delivered salvation. I headed off to deliver a lecture about four major choreographers and their influence on The Royal Ballet, a topic that seems woefully unimportant at this particular juncture. I had been chased for months to talk at the Roehampton Institute, and I finally chose a date when I felt sure the DK book would be long gone and I would be enjoying a period of calm. Instead it's been the culmination of the maddest week of my life – book proofs to be corrected and finalised, lectures written and delivered, and on top of that, an article for the *Guardian* to be completed by the day after tomorrow – and possibly the most turbulent week in the Opera House's history. How appropriate that today should be November 5th, Guy Fawkes night, and all around me, sparks were flying into the early hours. Let's hope there's not a new gunpowder plot afoot to blow up what remains of the Opera House.

7th November 1997, London
Yesterday evening, in the four hours between leaving work and going to bed, I risked a nervous breakdown to supply the *Guardian* with an article which they had press-ganged me into writing for today's paper. I opened my copy this morning to find it wasn't there. Just a bit of context for you: they wanted the reaction of a dancer to the week's turbulent events in Covent Garden. But I don't really think like a dancer any more. I can't

deliver the 'where am I going to hang my pointe shoes' type of article, as that is the least of my worries at the moment. There are much bigger questions occupying my grey matter nowadays, questions about funding, access and education. Am I becoming politicised?

Just so all my efforts don't go to waste, I'll run it here instead:

It's been a good week for rabbits; the government finally passed a bill outlawing their use in the testing of cosmetics. Unfortunately, their intervention in the arts world has not been so positive, destroying with a single proposal the 'arm's length' principle of funding.

At the beginning of this century, dance in Britain was in a sorry state, reduced to grabbing performances where it could between the variety acts in music halls. Sounds familiar? Less than a hundred years later, Dame Ninette de Valois, the woman who dragged ballet out of these artistic slums and gave it a home celebrates her own centenary by watching the company to which she has devoted her life rescued from the brink of insolvency.

How did we reach this point? Seventeen years ago, when I joined The Royal Ballet, the first phase of what is now the controversial redevelopment was under construction. When it opened its doors, it provided a tantalising foretaste of what we could expect: A permanent home, and increased public access to a theatre designed originally to open only when the fruit and vegetable traders had gone home.

Now, so close, there is a possibility that all of this may be engulfed by the current wave of populism. What always seemed like a dream may remain just that. For the dancers who devoted a quarter of a century of unpaid extra time to ensuring that the new theatre fulfilled our requirements, it must feel a bit like being shot on the last day of the war.

Thanks to the recent 'proposal' from the Culture Secretary (which sounded to most people suspiciously like a commandment), the Opera House may be requisitioned as a receiving house, providing a permanent base for not two companies, but three. It is a proposal that should be treated with the suspicion it deserves. For a start, it pays scant regard to the position of The Royal Ballet within the theatre, and to the fact that the architects had a hard enough time accommodating us all as things stood. It is also awash with inconsistencies: suggesting that while one company performs, the others tour is, on the face of it, a grand idea. Nothing would make us happier than taking ballet out to the people who help to pay for it. But adding a rider that there will be no increase in funding to make this possible rather puts a damper on the suggestion. Touring is not cheap.

Most of the newspapers, in their extensive coverage of the crisis, have also skimmed over the existence of The Royal Ballet. It is fascinating to read detailed accounts of the Opera House's future which contain no more than a nod towards 50 per cent of the performing that goes on there. And fascinating, too, to contrast the bullish confidence of the press, even when their stories are completely inaccurate, with the nervous uncertainty in our rehearsal studios over the last ten days.

Despite all the furore, it has been business as usual in West London. We have been trying to get on with what we do best, but whichever way we turn, it seems we cannot get it right. 'Access', says the government, as if they invented the word. So we perform at the Labatt's Apollo, a venue large enough to accommodate far greater numbers than the Opera House, and with seat prices low enough for more people to afford. Audiences came, saw the show, and whooped and whistled at the final curtain. I don't know if we attracted a different crowd from the Opera House regulars, but they certainly behaved differently, and the dancers loved it. We entertained 52,000 people in three weeks – the equivalent of 25 sold-out performances at most London theatres. We danced the most accessible ballets in the repertoire, gave as many shows as we would normally give in three months and dropped ticket prices into the bargain. If that wasn't access, I don't know what is. But access costs, and in a climate where success is measured purely in financial terms, the season has received an unwarranted amount of criticism.

'Access' is not new. It is something we already do. We are not élitist, and the reason the public think we are is because people who should know better describe us that way. If possessing a skill is a criterion for élitism, then it is a label that doctors, scientists and journalists should also wear. There are no grounds on which people are excluded from the Opera House, with the unfortunate exception of the cost of a ticket – a matter of concern for all of us, and one which is tackled with initiatives like the Hamlyn Week, when no seat costs more than £7.00. But unless subsidies are increased, seat prices have to remain high. It is a little known fact that we are obliged to earn 62 per cent of our budget from sponsorship and the box-office. It all comes down to mathematics; running costs minus revenue grant equals ticket prices.

In contrast to the way we are portrayed, the work we do at The Royal Ballet is not all gala performances and fashionable first nights. I have performed in hospitals all over the country, the 'Chance to Dance' scheme opens doors to children in two inner-city areas, and dancers regularly visit schools in an attempt to fill the gap in the education system where dance should be. Because, in the end, that void represents probably the greatest bar of all to the idea of access. If dance isn't encountered by young people while they are at school, how can they be expected, as adults, to consider it an asset worth paying for?

Despite all our best efforts, unless funding is increased to realistic levels and the arts re-established within education, we will remain on a downward spiral which won't be halted by squeezing three great companies into The People's Theatre, Covent Garden. Nice try, but it's going to take more than that.

I felt better once I'd got that little lot out of my system.

8th November 1997, London
At work, on the last day of a very long week, choreographer Cathy Marston, Jonathan Cope and I concocted more 'shouldn't be feasible' choreography. We spent the best part of two hours on one entrance alone, but Jonny won't rest until he's squeezed every ounce of potential out of an idea. It's always worth the effort, and today we came up with a one-handed lift which is based on a punch in the stomach. Beautifully Herculean. Apart from being every ballerina's dream partner, to a choreographer Jonny must seem like a gift from God. He is indefatigable, however exhausted he claims to be, and fearless to the point of folly. When he's in creative mode I just close my eyes, say a quick prayer, and allow him to sweep me along. In the event of a disaster I know I'm in safe hands.

We're giving an early preview of this *pas de deux* next Sunday at another fund raiser, this one at Her Majesty's Theatre in the Haymarket, in aid of The Royal Academy of Dancing. As the official première is not until February, there are no costumes as yet. So I went with Cathy and the designer, Paul Andrews, to High Street Kensington where we scoured the chain stores for cheap alternatives. After we had found something suitable, we sat in the local Prêt à Manger sandwich shop, drinking coffee and discussing fabric samples for Paul's eventual designs. For the first time in my dancing life, I felt totally involved in the creative process. Paul was interested in hearing my opinion on things like colour, texture and shape, issues which would normally be none of a performer's business. Collaboration like this is a novel experience and so much more rewarding than simply doing the steps.

I suppose it helps that Cathy and Paul feel like 'one of us', one of my generation. In fact, they are both at least ten years younger than me. But there's none of that 'them and us' feeling which comes when you work with someone of whom you're in awe. This must have been what it was like in the early days of, say, Kenneth MacMillan, Lynn Seymour and Nicholas Georgiadis – a group of contemporaries working, laughing, and shopping together. I think that this kind of close professional relationship is essential if you are to break new ground. You have to feel able to fail to take the art off in new directions.

9th November 1997, London
Today I was back at the Roehampton Institute, for the *Politics of Preservation* dance conference. Like all conferences it was running late. It seemed that the delegates had a stronger union than the dancers, as when I suggested running straight from one lecture to the next in order to catch up (I had a date afterwards) I was shouted down with cries of 'but we must have our tea'. And here I was thinking we were all there for the discussion and debate rather than the tea and biscuits.

I was there with Ricardo Cervera and Monica Mason to demonstrate a role she created in 1962, the Chosen One from the *Rite of Spring*. When The Royal Ballet last performed *Rite*, ten years ago, choreographer Kenneth MacMillan decided to break with tradition and had this solo danced at certain performances by a man rather than a woman. The chosen male was Simon Rice. As he has since left the company, Monica asked Ricardo to learn *Rite* for today's demonstration. Because most of the audience hadn't seen the ballet, she decided I should 'perform' the role in its entirety, probably the most exhausting solo ever created – three minutes of sheer, muscle-cramping agony. It's right on the cusp of aerobic/anaerobic capacity, hovering between sustainable and non-sustainable effort, and demanding that you work the body to its limits. You can only exercise for long periods at a level where the heart can pump hard enough to get oxygen to the muscles and recycle lactic acid.

Push too hard and the heart can no longer meet the demand; the lactic acid builds up in the muscles and forces you to stop. It's a fine balance, and it's the reason why some athletes (Chris Boardman, the Olympic cyclist, for instance) monitor their heart rate throughout competition, to constantly check they aren't going at it too hard. With training the ability to tolerate lactic acid can be increased, but training is something I haven't been doing for a while, so my tolerance is low. I had barely started before my muscles were awash with lactic acid, screaming at me to stop. I thought I was going to die. I certainly thought I was going to have to give in to the agony and quit the performance. Out came the will of iron, branded into the psyche of all trained dancers, and I struggled through. But I must have looked as though I really had danced myself to death. In my efforts to keep going, I managed to land awkwardly and I now have a very swollen toe. I hope it's nothing serious. An injury is the last thing I need right now.

10th November 1997, London
Another great rehearsal at Barons Court with Cathy Marston. I tried out the 'cheap and cheerful' version of the costume we picked up two days ago, halter-neck top and bootleg pants, and it worked perfectly well. Jonathan Cope came up with yet more extraordinary choreography which in this instance has me dangling precariously by a hamstring over his right shoulder. Although I'm still weak from the salmonella, I feel surprisingly good after yesterday's torturous escapade at Roehampton, but I now have a severely swollen digit. It's a perfect pizza of a toe, a cornucopia of colours fit for a bishop's robe. The physiotherapists tell me that it probably isn't serious; avulsed ligaments rather than a break. Funny to think that even tiny toes have all the structural requirements of the rest of the body – ligaments, muscles, tendons and bones. Fortunately, when they're injured it's not such a big deal, once the initial pain wears off. I was able to rehearse without any difficulty. I'll have to be careful though; if I start to favour the injured toe to avoid the pain I might cause problems elsewhere. The hip bone really is connected to the thigh bone, and so it continues all the way down the body from the head to the toes. A shift of one or two degrees at ground level equates to quite a major adjustment higher up, altering the alignment and creating dangerous tensions as the body struggles to stay upright. All in all though, it was a good day, and I limped home to put my toe on ice.

I spent the evening reading through the lecture I had given at

London's Royal Society for the Arts a year ago in October. I'm due to give a repeat performance next week at Dean Clough, a rather special arts centre in Halifax, where the society has its northern branch. I have to make a few changes. Mostly, though, I am disturbed to see that issues I addressed tentatively a year ago – the blurring of distinctions between genuine art and mere self-expression, the plague of a government in thrall to market survey, the erosion of artistic presence in our educational system – are now swelling problems, as prominent and painfully obvious as my fourth toe. The main difference now is that back then, I blamed the tabloid press for decrying the arts as élitist. These days the respected broadsheets and the Labour government are joining in the chorus of denunciation. In his first major speech last May, for example, Chris Smith, Heritage Secretary (as he was known then) generously proclaimed that the arts are for everyone. Good start, but he went on to equate rock star Jarvis Cocker with opera singer Jessye Norman, unable to resist the allure of alliteration and missing entirely the point that you don't open the arts to everyone by labelling every kind of entertainment and hobby as 'art' and lumping them all together in a populist pick and mix. In what was perhaps a thinly disguised swipe at the Royal Opera House, Smith added: 'cultural activity is not some élitist exercise that takes place in reverential temples aimed at the predilections of the cognoscenti. The Lottery is, after all', he continued, 'the people's money. More of it should go to where the people are.'

18th November 1997, London–Halifax–London
I feel pretty exhausted after two high-speed days in the fast lane. I've been up to Halifax and back in forty-eight hours. Several months ago, I had a call from Sir Ernest Hall, who had read my lecture to the RSA and invited me to Halifax to deliver it at Dean Clough. Ernest is a template for life as it could be. He was born into a poor family and, as a young boy, discovered a natural ability for music and a love of the piano. After four years at the Royal Manchester College of Music he realised that he would never attain the high standards he set for himself, and so gave up music to enjoy a very successful career in business. Now, decades later, he has returned to the piano and has even embarked on a recording career. I met him in London last spring and we pencilled in a date for the autumn. I then heard nothing until about a month ago, when Ernest sent me a letter saying how much he was looking forward to seeing me again. Fortunately, the pencilled date was still clear but I had sandwiched it in

with an interview and the Dorling Kindersley sales conference where I was due to talk up *The Vitality Plan* to the DK sales reps. There was no alternative but to take a deep breath and set out on a couple of days of non-stop travel up north and back again, alighting just long enough to deliver a couple of lectures, two hundred miles apart.

After a breakfast interview for *The Vitality Plan* at a London hotel, I took the train up to Halifax. Ernest met me at Dean Clough. What an extraordinary place it is – Ernest calls it his 'practical utopia'. Dean Clough started life in about 1850 as Crossley Mills, an enormous Victorian carpet mill in the heart of Halifax whose looms finally ground to a halt in 1982. Ernest bought the place the next year with a vision of creating a centre where business and the arts could mutually co-exist, a perfect symbiosis with the former supporting the latter, and the latter enhancing the former. Together with his son, Jeremy, he has spent the last fifteen years transforming the mills into a rich cornucopia of commerce and creativity. Against all odds, he has done it, combining galleries, a theatre, and studio space for world-renowned artists with various large and small businesses. The commercial success allows Ernest to support a wide range of non-income-producing activities in the arts and education. What he does there governments and state-subsidised arts centres could well learn from.

At my instigation, and with half an hour to spare, Ernest whisked me off to a magical place nearby, Eureka!, the museum for children founded by Vivien Duffield. Both personally, and through the Clore Foundation, Vivien is an enormous benefactor of education and the arts. She is also, as Chairman of the Opera House Trust, largely responsible for raising the £100 million needed for the redevelopment of the House. It isn't *all* coming from the National Lottery. Ever since I first read about Eureka! I have longed to visit and see what it is all about. A museum for children seems to make such perfect sense, as I firmly believe that there is no point in dragging kids to museums and galleries for 'grown-ups' unless you prepare them properly for the experience. Even then you risk losing their interest pretty early on. Every child wants to touch things, pick them up and explore. Museums are generally full of signs and guards saying DO NOT TOUCH. At Eureka! there are no such restraints. The only thing I was asked not to touch was a fuse box that I mistakenly thought might be part of the exhibition. Although we had to dash to get round it – there is so much to see – I had the most wonderful time. I was like a – well, like a child again. There are displays on the human body,

Baby ballerina, aged seven, at the Janice Sutton School of Dance in Skegness, Lincolnshire.

The Royal Ballet School, White Lodge, now twelve and dancing away from home for the first time.

The Royal Ballet Upper School, Talgarth Road, London, at sixteen. Niccy Tranah and I do a photo spread for *Jackie* magazine.

Dancing at the Prix de Lausanne in 1980, performing *Giselle* for the first and last time in my career.

FACING PAGE:

Top: On stage at Covent Garden in 1990. Dame Ninette de Valoise corrects me in *Les Sylphides*.

Below: In my first principal full-length role – *Swan Lake* in 1990.

Making the leap from the *corps de ballet* into soloist roles in 1985. This photo appeared in *Harpers & Queen*.

Sleeping Beauty, first performed in 1995 and only ever danced by default. The good …

… and the bad. Gamzatti in *La Bayadere*, first performed in 1990 and since danced with at least fifteen different partners.

Making-up in the old dressing-
room at the Royal Opera House,
Covent Garden.

Dr Bull receives her honorary
degree at Derby University in
January 1998.

Launching the Silver Seraph, the last British Rolls-Royce, in March 1998.
From a cover photo shoot for *Country Life* magazine.

Rock chick with all-areas access on
the Bridges to Babylon tour,
October 1997.

With Torje on a glacier in Norway
in May 1998. Home at last.

communications, the home, machines, music – you name it. Endless
themes and topics. Everything, but everything is interactive. I so wish
that there had been something of this sort when I was young, to gently
introduce me to the wonders of the world around me and within me. I
very often find myself unable to really appreciate essential everyday
miracles – comets, sunsets, technology, human life – because these tools
to wonder weren't available then. It's like asking a seed to take root in
stone. The only way to create a fertile soil is through actively discovering
for yourself, and Eureka! is a wonderful starting point. I think Mrs
Duffield should build satellites of Eureka! everywhere. It occurred to me
as I wandered around that the person who facilitated all this was the
same woman taking flak at the moment for allegedly supporting élitism
and exclusivity at the Opera House.

Returning to Dean Clough with Ernest, I gave my lecture to a
surprisingly large audience and engaged in lively discussion afterwards.
People are usually very kind to a poor dancer forced to speak in public,
but I actually enjoy the give and take of questions which force me to
argue and prove my points. When I originally gave the lecture, to an
overflowing crowd at the RSA in 1996, Lord Gowrie was in the chair.
Like the consummate gentleman he is, he attempted to shield me from
some of the more difficult and vociferous questions which followed.
Although I don't remember doing this, apparently I waved his gallantry
aside and insisted on defending myself. After a busy day, I stayed in
Halifax overnight, awoke before dawn and took the first train to London
for the DK sales conference at the Strand Palace Hotel.

21st November 1997, London
It's that time of the year again. For most mortals, there are four seasons,
but for a preserved sector of society, a sector blessed with generosity of
character and cash, there are five: Spring, Summer, Autumn, Charity
and Winter. For some reason, the dull months between summer
holidays and Christmas celebrations are deemed to be the perfect time to
persuade people to open their hearts and wallets by enticing them to
fund-raising events. Not that I often get invited. I'm usually the thing
they are paying to see. In the past eight days, I've been involved in four
such bashes, three as participant and one as spectator.

The first was last Wednesday, a fund-raiser for The Place, the
foremost space for contemporary dance in London. I had a surprise call
about two months ago from Mark Baldwin, a choreographer who used to

dance with Rambert Dance Company. Contemporary choreographers don't usually call ballerinas at home, as the twain rarely meet. But he asked me to dance in a piece he intended to make for Cut and Thrust, a charity evening at the minimalist Saatchi Gallery in North London, where ten dancers would wear frocks by British designers and perform specially created snippets. The dresses would then be auctioned off (sweat included free of charge) and the money raised put towards the theatre's redevelopment. Mark was paired with Neil Cunningham, the designer who made waves recently by dressing Ffion Williams (soon to be Hague) in a lace dress which the press touted as 'see-through'. In fact, it was nothing of the sort, but the press are known to poke holes wherever they can.

Mark and I met at Neil's salon, in Sackville Street off Piccadilly, to choose an outfit, a procedure which, for me, is even more delicious than choosing chocolates. We went for the most tasty creation in coffee chiffon. From the front it looks like a charming and innocent evening gown, the sort of thing Audrey Hepburn might have worn, teamed with outrageously big hair. But hidden from view at the back is a veritable cascade of fabric, frothy and cappuccino-like, which severely restricts any serious movement. Mark was intending to make an energetic little number, but in the end he had to go with the gown and resort to minimalism. (This was no bad thing as far as I was concerned, as I am only now, finally, recovering my strength from the salmonella bug, and besides, concrete gallery floors are not the kindest of surfaces to dance on.) I wasn't the only ballet-dancer involved; Antonia Franchesci, ex-New York City Ballet, was also performing, and made up for my lack of exertion with an exhausting number choreographed by Wayne McGregor, dressed in a practical flapper-like dress by Julien MacDonald.

The evening went off without a hitch, although the gallery was so packed that there were complaints from the crowd that they couldn't see. At the end of it all, I had to give an impromptu speech, as the promised 'celebrity' failed to show up. I never did find out who it was. Without a script to follow, I improvised on the usual themes: money, governments, lovely art – my hundred greatest hymns. 'Oh God, not her again', they must have been thinking. But they listened and laughed when I complained that entering the world of contemporary dance for an evening, like Cinderella at a different ball, was not all that different from a night at the opera; in addition to the luscious gown, I was wearing a tiara.

The second event was at Her Majesty's Theatre in the Haymarket on Sunday evening, a gala in aid of another dance charity. It was a less adventurous affair in some ways, as it stuck to the traditional 'gala' format: famous-ish dancers performing solos and *pas de deux* from the repertoire of various companies around the world. But this one differed slightly, in that it was rather good. Galas are generally very hit and miss in terms of entertainment value. They start out with the best and most ambitious of intentions, and then dancer after dancer drops out until the audience is left paying inflated prices for something they could see any night of the year at any ballet performance. Although *Night of the Stars* had one or two casualties, it also managed to boast principal dancers from Stuttgart, the Paris Opéra, Munich, Birmingham Royal Ballet, Phoenix as well as a strong contingent from the Opera House. The interesting thing for me was how few strictly classical pieces there were on show. A few years ago, an evening like this one would have had at least three big tutu numbers – *Don Quixote*, *Swan Lake* and *Sleeping Beauty* for starters. This one was light on virtuosity and heavy on contemporary. Nowadays we all want to be modern. It's not so daunting and there are fewer icons to live up to.

I was dancing with Jonathan Cope the *pas de deux* I have been working on recently with Cathy Marston for Dance Bites. We thought it would be a good chance to give it a pre-première airing, and it also had the major advantage that we wouldn't need extra rehearsals. Charity galas usually take place on a Sunday, when a dancer's biological clock is screaming 'REST darling', so the more familiar (and less taxing) the number, the better.

There's also the worry of performing tricky footwork on an unfamiliar surface. You never quite know what the stage is going to be like when you get yourself into these things, and it's less chancy to turn up with a bit of lycra and a familiar DAT tape than to worry about *fouettés* on what could be the equivalent of the Black Run at St Moritz.

Event number three was one of pure spectating in which I got to dress up and play the guest. It was the concert and dinner at London's Royal Festival Hall on the South Bank to mark the fiftieth wedding anniversary of the Queen and Prince Philip. I was invited by Elliot Bernerd, Vice-Chairman of the Board of the South Bank, and Chairman of the Foundation which is raising a great deal of the money needed to match whatever Lottery award we get for the South Bank's redevelopment. (When *will* we find out?) It was a pleasant but uneventful affair attended by many of the crowned heads of Europe. As I was chauffeured there in my regular Cortina minicab, I passed a coach and glanced up to catch sight of Princess Anne. The entire Royal Family was going south of the river by bus.

The fourth and final charity extravaganza was last night, at the Savoy Hotel. Besides the obvious 'warmth' factor of giving a little back, dancing for charity can also be fun, especially when the performing bit is over and done and you get to dress up and join in the party afterwards. Apart from providing the frock for Cut and Thrust, Neil Cunningham generously allows me to raid his closet for the odd event when I need to look my best and tonight I wore his same cappuccino design but in blackest espresso.

I had been drafted in as a replacement for Leanne Benjamin who has injured her foot. In the event, it was a good thing that she didn't dance here; she was going to do a *pas de deux* from *Manon*, with Bruce Sansom, but the performing area was so polished and glossy that it was better suited to Torvill and Dean than Fonteyn and Nureyev. It was lucky that Ashley Page and I were doing 'something modern' – the *pas de deux* that we danced at July's Opera House closing gala. The piece was never intended to survive longer than the duration of an unofficial summer tour in 1991, but it is so good and so useful that it's come out time and time again, like a favourite outfit. Easy to wear (no uncomfortable bits) one size fits all (four very different dancers have performed it without adjustments) and appropriate whatever the occasion (Royal galas, open air theatres, hotel ballrooms). It has a rather sexy score by Orlando Gough (and yes, it's on DAT) which sat very nicely between the hors d'oeuvre and the main course at last night's dinner. The last thing the boisterous guests wanted to do was concentrate on difficult dance, and although the volume of the conversation went down slightly, it was by no means silent during our performance. At least I did my bit for Dr Barnardo's. I certainly couldn't have afforded to join in at the auction which followed, when bidding for glamorous trips and trinkets started at a grand and went upwards by noughts. But the drunks at the table behind me stunned us all when they started the bidding for the Sotheby's catalogue of the auction of the Princess of Wales' dresses at a staggering £20,000. Nobody bothered to compete and it was theirs.

A friend chauffeured me home afterwards, so at least I left the party in style. Back home I packed up my borrowed finery in the store room and retrieved my suitcase while I was there. The company leaves for

Madrid in five days' time and I'm determined not to leave the packing until the last minute.

30th November 1997, Madrid
Sunday evening: I'm in Spain with the company for seven performances of *The Sleeping Beauty*. We arrived here on Thursday, and this is really the first moment I've had to sit down in my room with my computer. The first day of a tour is always a bit hectic. We usually arrive in a city the day before the first night, so we have to rehearse on stage during the afternoon of the opening. If we're sticking to the same repertoire, things get much easier once the first day is over; all we have to do from then on is perform. This week, I'm only dancing the Prologue Fairies and the Bluebird in Act Three, not the lead role, so I can look forward to a relatively easy time. It could even be fun; a week in this wonderful, sun-drenched city, a lovely hotel and none of the stress of being top dog. I must confess that although I appreciate how lucky we are to travel to far-flung corners of the world for months at a time, I'm looking forward to the prospect of being back in my own bed by the end of the week. There are dancers in the company who love the gypsy lifestyle of touring, but I've never been intoxicated by the realities of dancing away.

Madrid looks and feels terribly European; every street warm and stony, and alleyways full of hidden delights. The architecture is elegant and historic, and whispers to me of Moorish intrigues. I'm having a hard time equating the concept of work with an environment that is screaming 'holidays'. I want to stop in every café I pass, drink *café con leche* and sample all the different pastries. Madrid is a city for sitting, seeing and shopping, not for donning ballet shoes and tutus and hopping around on *pointe*. Mercifully I don't have to do an awful lot of that, although opening night was a close call.

Sylvie Guillem, prinicipal guest artist, was scheduled to dance Aurora, but she has just returned from a mammoth concert tour of Japan built solely around her, thirty-nine shows in about as many days, and her left foot has had enough. She desperately wanted to dance yesterday evening but she wasn't at all certain that she could get through it. So having danced my 'fairyation' in the Prologue, I slipped into a spare Aurora costume, fresh out of mothballs, and hovered in the wings, Sylvie's official 'stand-by'. In the event she did a wonderful show, despite being in considerable pain, and my Aurora never saw the light of day. The costume went back into storage and I changed into the

Bluebird frock, as scheduled, to perform in the third act. To be honest, I was mightily relieved, as I'm not at all sure I'm up to the challenge of *Sleeping Beauty*'s three acts of technical feats. Although I feel fully recovered, the salmonella poisoning way back in September took its toll on my fitness and I wouldn't particularly like to test it out in public just yet. If Sylvie's foot *had* given way, I would have had to rely on pure adrenalin and good luck to get me through.

Madrid is a late-night city. Eating before 9 p.m. is uncommon, and things only really start to warm up after about 11 p.m. – closing time back in London. Saturday's performance began at 9.30 p.m. and finished at half-past midnight. At 1.30 a.m. I was with a small group of friends, eating cake and drinking (decaffeinated) coffee in a *calle* which, despite the lateness of the hour, was as busy and buzzy as Oxford Street on Christmas Eve. Exhaustion finally took over and we left, but none of the locals showed any signs of flagging.

Consequently I have been keeping rather odd hours. Today I slept until 2 p.m., and then felt guilty that I had wasted the wonderful winter sun. I managed an hour's walk before class, around the Palaccio Real and then meandering through the little alleyways of the city, hoping to lose myself in Madrid. The people here are refined and stylish, and *le tout* Madrid seemed to be out for a stroll. One *señor* I passed was humming snippets of opera to himself as he ambled along. The entire population was elegantly dressed in the muted browns, greens and yellows that well-to-do Europeans wear of a weekend. And then it struck me: I hadn't seen a single shell suit. Mind you, I was in a very regal part of town and seeing Madrid at its very best.

December 1997

Can it really be the last month of the year? It is definitely true that the older you get, the faster the years go by. Dancers are in the unusual position of retaining the same annual 'structure' that makes a child's life pass so slowly – seasons that run with the school year from September through to July, with lingering summer holidays to follow. When I was a young dancer, time for me seemed to move at a much slower pace, much more akin to childhood. Now, as I add in extra, non-dance activities, the pace of being actively human quickens. The future is racing towards me.

Another late night yesterday. I went to a flamenco club with Viviana Durante, and now we both want to give up ballet and learn to play the castanets in Spanish doll skirts. As a tourist it's always difficult to find the best of anything without insider advice, and I'm pretty sure that the club recommended to us by the hotel was not the greatest flamenco venue in Spain. Nevertheless, though the wine was dreadful, the dancers were wonderful, and as usual, the older they were, the better they danced. I was reminded of one of last year's 'Best of' summaries which announced that 1996 had been the year of the 'older dancer'; I narrowly beat Joaquin Cortes' uncle to be named as the *Independent on Sunday*'s Dancer of the Year.

Flamenco dancing is unlike ballet dancing, in that the dancers aren't required to bother about playing to the audience. Indeed, the more surly and contemptuous they are of everybody the better. We, the spectators, are left feeling privileged to have been allowed to witness what looks like a private ritual. And it is totally mesmeric; the insistent, rhythmic beating of the heels is positively hypnotic. I'm sure this same quality of rhythmic repetition, also present in Celtic dancing, had a lot to do with the success of Riverdance. Apparently we as humans respond to pulsating and insistent rhythm because it is similar to our heartbeat, but I can't help wondering if there is a more basic and even primitve appeal. Rhythmic, pulsating and insistent describes something more erotic than the heartbeat. I think all dancing is, to a greater or lesser degree, sexual;

it's a way of making love in public without upsetting anyone. In classical ballet the sexual undertones are well hidden beneath layers of refinement. In flamenco they simmer just below the surface. Until he became so over-exposed, every woman's fantasy was the dark, brooding Joaquin Cortes.

Today, as usual, most of Madrid's museums and galleries were closed to coincide with our day off. At least it didn't rain. Normally, you can guarantee that if we aren't working it will be (a) rainy and (b) closing day for most major attractions. But today has been glorious. Despite what everyone told me before we left home about rain, Spain and the plain, the sun has worked overtime, cranking up today's temperature to a steamy 22 degrees C.

I felt so guilty about sleeping through my free hours yesterday that I decided to make up for it today by visiting everything that was open. I started out at the Palaccio Real, no longer the permanent home of the Royal Family (apparently they have downgraded to a sort of Barratt Palace), but still in use for state occasions and, most recently, the 1991 Middle East Peace Conference. From there I strolled via the Plaza Mayor (every town should have a tacky Christmas market) to the Reina Sofia, Madrid's collection of modern art. Not having had much of an education in art history I sometimes find it difficult to get my head round a lot of it – movements, schools, styles, that sort of thing. I probably have as decent an unpractised eye as anyone who enjoys looking at paintings and sculpture, but once the points of reference become more obscure, objects become a metaphorical blur. For some reason, today I was extraordinarily clear-sighted. Even without much explanatory text in English to go on, everything I saw seemed to make perfect sense. In turn, I found myself delighted, disturbed, ecstatic, shocked and profoundly moved by the art on display. Spain has over the years produced some of the most vibrant and exciting art of modern times, and the Reina Sofia has four floors brimming with it, culminating in a rich and masterful selection of Picasso, Miro and Dali. I'm perfectly willing to confess to my own naïvety, but it all seemed to me far more sensational than the exhibition I saw at the Royal Academy's recent *Sensations*.

Why, by the way, do people who make their living out of tourists always behave so contemptuously towards them? It's not just a Spanish thing; I'm sure we've all encountered it in other places. Today, in six hours of being a tourist, I was only once treated with what I would call the minimum of courtesy, and that was by the man inside the Reina Sofia who was giving away condoms to mark World Aids Day. But if you're handing out contraceptives in a Catholic country, it's probably wise to take the added precaution of wearing a smile.

2nd December 1997, Madrid
Madrid continues to work its magic on me. I spent the morning in the Prado, wandering in amazement through room after room of Spanish genius. Perhaps there is something special about seeing art in its native country, or perhaps there is just something special about the Spanish artists. The range of work produced by Goya, for instance, from stuffy court portraits to the dark and sinister expressions of a sick and aged mind is truly astonishing, and I asked myself whether I could ever hope to claim so many outstanding performances in my own career.

Going to class at the theatre, I bumped into dancer Elizabeth McGorian. She was on her way to buy a ticket for tonight's performance by Antonio Canales' flamenco company and offered to get one for me, too. Elizabeth is probably the company's most adventurous tourer. Never one for ordering room service when there's a whole town to be consumed, she generally has more bizarre and exciting experiences in a day than most people have all year. Like me, she is loving Madrid, and firmly believes the god of touring is working overtime this week to deliver pleasure. I think he does so well for Elizabeth because she works so hard as his disciple. They make a date in every place we alight and he never, ever stands her up.

Canales' performance had been recommended to her as she was having a drink last night in a wonderful old bar, on yet another of her nocturnal jaunts. It was taking place in a theatre, unlike the club flamenco I saw earlier in the week, and Elizabeth had been persuaded that she must sit in the front row. In the event, I think we were lucky to get tickets at all, as the theatre was packed with locals, the Madrilenos. Not knowing what to expect we did our best to translate the Spanish programme notes into English, and managed to work out that there were two pieces, the first a version of Lorca's *The House of Bernarda Alba*, and the second a dance inspired by Picasso's great war painting, *Guernica*. But we were a little confused. As the company is about to revive its own version of *Bernarda Alba* (*Las Hermanas*), we both know it is a play about a family of sisters. But the entire cast seemed to have men's names. The curtain went up and we pretty soon realised why. They *were* all men. Although there are some woman in the company, Canales had obviously decided to make this piece on the men. It helped that most of the guys were extremely beautiful, and after a few minutes, their gender became irrelevant. Canales himself played the mother and was absolutely extraordinary. It was the most gripping piece of theatre I have seen in a very long time. The amazing commitment of flamenco dancers which was evident even in the tourist club the other night made what could have been a disaster (imagine conceiving a flamenco version of *The House of Bernarda Alba*?) into a stunning theatrical *tour de force*.

Canales is both lead dancer and choreographer of the company, and in a very different mould from Joaquin Cortes, now perhaps flamenco's more famous exponent outside Spain. Canales is a little heavier, slightly older, less overtly sexy (consequently much sexier) and rather modest. He isn't an oil painting, and neither does he try to be. You could pass him in the street and, unless you caught his eye, you'd walk right on by and not even notice. But once he starts to move, he dances straight from his heart, no holds barred, and watching him is a powerful and, for me, humbling artistic experience. Great flamenco is like great sex; it goes on for ever and hovers permanently and dangerously on the edge, working the audience into a lather of frenzied excitement and final explosion. When it comes to an end the entire audience is on its feet in a state of euphoria, and for the first time in my life I have the strange feeling that I should be bowing to the dancers rather than the other way round.

Afterwards, Elizabeth's god of touring guided us to the most perfect bar and on to a garishly painted restaurant with an indoor courtyard where we ate platefuls of paella and drank rough Spanish wine. Despite being unchaperoned females (and Elizabeth is a supermodel *manquée*) we're not bothered at all by unwanted approaches. But then we're still so wrapped up in the performance we've just seen and in company gossip we've just heard that it would have to be Canales himself to get our attention.

Johanna Adams (stage manager) joined us after she had finished work, and broke the mood when she told me that two company meetings have been called tomorrow to announce the findings of the Kaufman inquiry. Gerald Kaufman and his Select Committee regrouped after the long summer recess to continue their explorations into the workings of the Opera House. The final sitting was on November 14th, and the investigations are now complete. The report has already been released to the principal players at Covent Garden, but it's officially embargoed until noon tomorrow. There is a general sense of nervous anticipation.

3rd December 1997, Madrid

I finally got to bed late last night at around 3 a.m., and failed to reappear until well into the afternoon. It's amazing how quickly my internal clock has adapted to the hours kept here in Madrid. Consequently I missed the first company meeting, but I was around for the repeat performance, just before the show. By then, of course, I had heard a variety of convoluted versions of Kaufman's report from dancers who had made it to class this morning.

The Chinese whispers were frightening enough, although I didn't actually believe that the word 'philistine' could *really* have been used in the document. I was sure this must have been an embellishment on the part of the messenger, not the message itself. When I finally saw a written summary of the major points put together and circulated by the Opera House, I was staggered. It was pretty obvious from the proceedings that the report would contain a lot of Kaufman's own brand of pugnacious rhetoric, but I couldn't believe that a government document could read quite so much like a cross between an end-of-term report and a curmudgeonly Victor Meldrew monologue. The testiness of its tone was quite distasteful. Never mind the recommendations; some of them may be just, others most certainly are not, but the tone of it, the lack of faith in anyone's best intentions, despite the outcome, rent another hole in the tattered remnants of my hope that this Labour government might do something positive for the arts.

The gist of Kaufman's report is that the Opera House Board and Chief Executive Mary Allen are to be held responsible for the situation in which Covent Garden now finds itself, a conclusion I find very hard to accept bearing in mind that Mary has been in her job for only about three months. Everyone knows the arts world works several years in advance in its planning and budgets, and whatever is happening now probably has a lot to do with seeds planted long ago and by previous administrations. It seems to most of us that Kaufman wants to get Mary for decisions she took during her time as Secretary-General at the Arts Council. But if that is the case then he should launch a fresh and separate investigation on that matter alone. The inquiry's determination to find a villain in the drama is all a far cry from the current Truth Commission hearings in South Africa, where owning up to your mistakes ensures forgiveness and redemption.

The upshot is that Kaufman's committee has overstepped what I would have imagined to be his remit. Not only has he made recommendations, he has also meted out punishment in advance should those recommendations not be followed. I find it all very chilling. What happened to the cherished 'arm's length' principle of arts funding? I think we all knew there would be changes in the way the arts are funded under Blair's administration. But surely there needs to be some debate about what the changes should be before Gerald Kaufman and his colleagues go ahead and blow away the Arts Council. Since 1945 the scenario has been that the government allocates funds to an independent body who are best positioned to make decisions about how to apply that money. Apparently the directive now is 'independence with co-operation', a phrase passed on to me recently in private. New slogans to subtly alter policy, or to cover up the fact that there is no policy at all?

Nicholas Snowman, Chief Executive at the South Bank, very kindly faxed me some of the press comment on Kaufman, and again I saw how public opinion is swayed by the spin that different commentators put on events. The fairest comment – or rather the one most in tune with my own thoughts – came from Norman Lebrecht in the *Daily Telegraph*. He describes Kaufman as 'the kind of chap who pulls on dancing shoes only to attend a funeral' and accuses him of offering no prescription for the future beyond 'sack 'em all and sod the lot'. He, alone amongst commentators, describes Kaufman's 'do as you're told or there'll be no pocket money' stance as 'an unconstitutional interference in the affairs of an independent company'. In a sharply observed yet generous article, Lebrecht argues that this line of action would be the beginning of the end for the Opera House.

Amongst the other clippings was a diary column from the *Spectator* by the great Kaufman himself, in which he explains why he had persuaded his colleagues to pursue the inquiry. The tone is jovial, verging on the smug, and it seems to me strikingly tasteless at a time when several hundred Opera House employees are wondering just how much their jobs are on the line. What upset him were the Opera House patrons 'air-kissing' and pre-ordering smoked salmon sandwiches for the intervals, something I'm sure Kaufman has never done. Setting up as a man of the people, he obviously feels we should greet each other with a 'high five' and munch chicken nuggets between acts. (We do both these things, in different circumstances, but isn't democracy about personal freedom?) With supreme hubris, he even congratulates himself that he can take the credit for the fact that the air-kissing will evaporate after the redevelopment.

Kaufman claims to be a long-standing supporter of the Opera House. But now that he can afford the 'better' seats downstairs, he misses his mates, the true opera and ballet lovers upstairs in the amphitheatre and upper slips. He despises sitting amongst what he would consider to be the *arrivistes*, people who aren't the least aware that Mozart composed *The Marriage of Figaro* until they open their red-and-gold crested programmes. In the widely held and erroneous belief that the Opera House somehow chooses its patrons and specifically excludes 'the people', he arbitrarily decides it's time to sort the place out. Rather than devoting his energies to lobbying for an increase in the provision in schools so that more people might be aware and knowledgeable about the arts, he attacks the art itself and the people who make it happen. Gerald Kaufman's report I can handle; his attitude, clearly apparent in this *Spectator* article, makes me livid, and an 'angry of Little Venice' letter starts to take shape in my head:

> Well, Mr Kaufman, I've got news for you. Right up until last July's closing gala, the opera and ballet lovers were there in full force, and you might have done better to simply go upstairs and join them instead of launching your own private vendetta against the place. You see, their seats are being subsidised by the smoked salmon eating, air-kissing patrons downstairs, a job that your government (and, to be fair, the last one) fails miserably to carry out. With the antagonistic tones of your report, you have risked that delicate balance, not one I particularly like, but the only option in the absence of an arts subsidy which fails even to approach the levels of any other civilised nation. The press fiesta which greeted your report will have deterred thousands of people who might otherwise have rather enjoyed a night at the opera or an afternoon at the ballet from ever considering it. The new wave of populism rolls onwards, and the government surfs along on the crest of it.

There was a point, back in 1781, when the Opera House closed Parliament by presenting the two Vestrises, father and son, in the same performance. Honourable Members were so keen to see this artistic phenomenon for themselves that sittings were suspended while they trooped up Whitehall to Covent Garden. Now, in a reversal of circumstances, this performance in Westminster is threatening to close the Opera House instead.

6th December 1997, Madrid–Palm Beach, Florida
Woke up to a winter wonderland. Snow. In Madrid? A complete change from the sunshine of the last four days, and much closer to the sort of winter temperatures we were expecting here. It's freezing. I made my way into the theatre like Good King Wenceslas, the snow driving a horizontal path straight into my eyes, and my long black coat pulled up to shield my face.

We finished a successful run of *Sleeping Beauty* with a show that almost failed to happen. As stage management called the half, the thirty-minute warning before curtain up, the backstage computers which control the on-stage cues crashed, threatening to scupper the performance. The backdrops and wings could be flown in manually, but there was no way of getting them back out again. I always idly wondered how much smaller a room might get over the years if you just layer new wallpaper on top of old. Tonight we could have found out. By the final act, with scenery from three previous acts already crowding the stage, we could have been dancing on a six-inch strip in front of the footlights.

In the end, a combination of ingenuity, hard graft and positive intentions ensured that the show went on. It was a bit of a sad occasion as we were saying goodbye to Tony Bourne, a soloist in the company whom many of us have known for about twenty years. With the help of the Dancer's Resettlement Fund, a lifeline for dancers who invariably leave the company unqualified to do anything except dance, he is formalising what has been a long-standing hobby and will set up trade as a builder. For the last decade he has been the first line of enquiry for anyone with a new kitchen to fit, so he'll never be short of clients in the years to come. We had a small party for him, organised by two Spanish girls who spent a brief but memorable couple of seasons with the company. Despite having slept through the best part of today, I only lasted until about 2 a.m. when I crawled back to the hotel. But then I did have quite a day ahead.

I had been toying with the idea of doing something flamboyant this weekend, but I only made the final decision at about 4.30 p.m. when the travel agents emerged from their afternoon siesta. Determined to take advantage of the gift of one of those rare three-day weekends, I decided to fly to see Torje – in Miami. I know, a bit of a splurge, but you have to take these opportunities when they're on offer. If you spend your life waiting for the *perfect* circumstances, you'll wait for ever, and besides, I haven't seen Torje since October. So at 12.30 p.m. on Friday I was sitting on a bargain flight headed to Miami International, with an unusable return ticket in my pocket. This particular cut-price airline only operates on Tuesdays and Fridays and I have to be back at work, in London, on Monday morning. I wanted to surprise Torje, but as I needed him to find me a seat on a plane home, I decided to call before I boarded the flight. And a good thing I did. Although he is staying out in Palm Beach, the Rolling Stones had a concert on Friday evening in Miami itself, the single *Bridges to Babylon* show in the home of the Dolphins football team. Had I jumped into a cab intending to arrive in Palm Beach and yell 'surprise', I would have had to spend the entire evening in the lobby, waiting for Torje's return.

The god of touring obviously flew with me and I had the luxury of an empty seat to one side. I was able to adopt the foetal position and get a few hours' sleep. At about 4 p.m. local time, I asked the hostess why we hadn't landed; the travel agent had told me we would arrive at 3 p.m. 'Oh no, that's in the summer. In the winter we have to fly against the jet stream, and it takes at least two hours longer.' What? I had planned to have an hour or so in the airport to affect the transformation from ballet dancer to rock chick, but now I had to do the trick on the plane. Torje was expecting me at the gig at about 5 p.m., so I was seriously behind schedule. When we eventually landed, at 5.20 p.m., I raced through the airport and hopped into a yellow cab. As I heard myself asking the driver to 'take me to the Orange Bowl, backstage area, please', it dawned on me that there could be problems ahead. I had no ticket, no identifying 'laminate' (vital neckwear at a rock concert) and not a clue about the lay-out of the stadium. It was going to take all of my charm, ingenuity, and maybe even my English accent to get through the impenetrable security cordon that surrounds a Stones concert. There would be no point in asking for Torje, as the local heavies wouldn't have the slightest clue who he was. And asking for the Stones, either collectively or individually, would have had me ejected before you could say Jumping Jack Flash. The cab driver didn't know where backstage might be in a football stadium, so he dropped me at what he thought was the right end. Miracle of miracles, he was spot on. Dressed in my Madrid winter coat (it was still snowing when I left) and dragging my wheelie bag behind me, I walked off into the humid Miami night, wondering how in the world I would get in. I suddenly remembered Miami's recent problems where crimes against tourists are concerned, and I prayed that I wouldn't be thrown out when I tried to penetrate the inner sanctum without the sacred laminate.

Fortunately, I know the magic word – or rather two words. J__ C__. Head of security for the Stones (and most other top rock bands) for as long as anyone can remember, JC is, without doubt, a legend in his own lifetime. The mere mention of his name and the barriers parted miraculously like the waters of the River Nile. Within minutes of getting out of the cab, I had located JC and found Torje, whose embrace included an 'All Areas Access' laminate which he placed lovingly around my neck. I was safe and now ready to rock 'n' roll. Once on the right side of the divide, the *Bridges to Babylon* lounge is heaving, packed with familiar faces and familiar types; the people who get the show on, recognisable by their 'All Areas Access' and their air of efficiency, and the people who have somehow managed to beg, steal or borrow a guest pass, a 'local'. Torje slips in and out of my grasp like a freshly caught fish; just when I think I have him to myself for a few minutes, the walkie-talkie crackles into life and he's off on call yet again to attend to the needs of the performers. At about 9.15 p.m., JC's voice booms across the room: 'That's it, folks, need to clear the lounge now, thank you, show's about to start.' Actually, the show has been going on for some time, but no one with a backstage laminate is remotely interested in the opening band. They're only here for the Stones. Now, though, JC forces them out into the crowd, and the musicians start to gather in the lounge. At this point I usually disappear myself, and tonight Torje escorts me through the barriers to my place in the lighting tower just as Keith Richards rips into the opening chords of 'Satisfaction'. Dum-dum, dum-dum-dum. A small sound starts somewhere in the crowd and rises like a whirlpool in reverse as 60,000 people cheer. In less than twelve hours I have crossed the Atlantic and the divide from my own rarified theatrical world to one which is popular to the core. I feel like I've passed into another, alternative reality.

After the show, we do a 'runner', escorted by Miami's cops on motorbikes, and get back to the hotel in the small hours. I finally have Torje to myself and the gap of the last six weeks begins to close.

Next morning, while Torje is working, I rummage through my bag and pull out a sheaf of faxes which arrived just before I left Madrid. The news, as I half expected, is that Lord Chadlington and the Board have all resigned, as Kaufman requested. But Mary Allen, Chief Executive, with the firm support of both the Opera House staff and the Culture Secretary, is weathering the storm and standing firm. Some of the former Board are staying on temporarily in a 'caretaker' capacity until a

new one is assembled. I can't help but think that the way boards have
been constituted in the past must now undergo a serious rethink. If non-
executive and philanthropic boards are to remain unpaid their
membership will inevitably go to people who can afford to take it up.
Most people don't have the time or money to devote their working hours
to anyone other than their employers. I only manage to sit on the Board
at the South Bank because I have sympathetic bosses (Anthonys Dowell
and Russell-Roberts) who recognise the importance of having younger,
artistic representation at board level. I also work a completely bizarre
schedule which usually permits me to be free to attend afternoon
meetings. But there's an awful lot of work and obligations involved,
forests of papers to be read and serious decisions to be taken at every
turn. It may be that it isn't fair to ask people to bear this weight of
responsibility without appropriate remuneration.

A word has to be said in favour of poor, maligned boards. Apart from
the fact that they do it all gratis, we shouldn't forget that a great many
board members also give a huge amount of their own money to
institutions like the Opera House. It's all very well to adopt the 'sod 'em
all and sack the lot' attitude, but individual board members over the
years have contributed literally *millions* of pounds to the arts; in July of
this year, Vivien Duffield and Sir John Sainsbury rescued the House
from insolvency with personal loans totalling two million pounds. It is
rumoured that Mrs Duffield has pledged a further twenty million to the
redevelopment of Covent Garden. That money not only pays for
smoked salmon and champagne, it also subsidises companies which can
be seen at any performance for less than the price of a ticket to a football
match and, on occasion, for less than a tenner. It's cultural Robin
Hoodism; we borrow from the rich to subsidise the poor, and if that
involves one or two swanky galas and sponsors' parties, so be it. Dancers
dance just as well whether the audience has paid £200 or £2 a seat.

10th December 1997, London
Back in the real world and an empty home without Torje. Given the
turmoil created by Kaufman, it is all surprisingly calm and for the last
few days Covent Garden appears to have stayed out of the papers.
There's more drama in Ambridge right now on Radio 4, where Eddy
Grundy, a wheeling-dealing regular in *The Archers*, has been falsely
accused of committing GBH. I, like the rest of the nation, await his fate.
We all know it was a set-up. I feel as if we at the Opera House are

awaiting judgement, too, but from a court higher than Kaufman's: the court of public opinion. I think people are more likely to have sympathy for Eddy Grundy than for us at the Opera House.

At work, dancing on through the in-house drama, we have started to rehearse for the Christmas season, which will take place this year at London's Royal Festival Hall. I will be dancing one of the leads in *Les Patineurs*, Ashton's ballet about ice-skating. I found out on Monday that Nicky Roberts will be out of action. She's pregnant with her second child. So I'll be picking up extra shows over Christmas. But I'm not complaining; it helps to assuage the guilt I feel that everyone else had to do my work at the Labatt's Apollo, while I was down with the dreaded salmonella. Besides, *Patineurs* is hardly the toughest ballet in the world. It opens the programme, followed by *The Tales of Beatrix Potter*, a jolly piece which disguises its cast beneath layers of fur. So I'll be home by 8 p.m. while the rest of the company is still bunny-hopping.

A note pinned to the board today requested that I go and see Jeanetta Laurence, Anthony Dowell's artistic administrator. Jeanetta was a dancer herself, and she has retained the look of a ballerina, slightly built and slightly gamine. As her desk is invariably a mountain of paperwork, you don't often see much more than her head peering over the top of it. When I was trying to squeeze through the bottleneck of the soloist ranks on to the spacious plateau of principal status, the yellow slip of paper with its handwritten 'Please see me/Anthony after class' would flick a switch in my stomach, setting it to 'slow tumble', as I debated whether the news would be good or bad. Nowadays it is more likely to be information, requests or discussion, although I am mindful that there is one more 'yellow peril' still to come. A dancer's life doesn't go on for ever.

Today Jeanetta wanted to update me on the 'P3000' project. About a month ago, she had pulled me into Anthony's inner office, deeply conspiratorial, and after swearing me to secrecy, asked if I would be interested in launching the first new Rolls-Royce in eighteen years. Would I? You bet I would. Do they give me a car? Jeanetta said no, and as it was all still top secret and very provisional, mum was the word. It was a brief conversation, and I tried hard to forget about it. The agency dealing with the launch wanted a dancer, but they were looking at other options as well. It all sounded like wonderful fun, and I hoped I'd be the option they'd eventually go for.

Now it seems that the project will happen. The idea is that I go up to a castle in the wilds of Scotland and dance, on five consecutive evenings, a specially created solo on a stage shared with the new car. The audience would consist of various invited automotive and lifestyle journalists, and there would be dinners and general festivities to follow. Very unlike the sort of thing I get asked to do; I won't have to open my mouth for a start. Tomorrow I am going to meet the agency who have dreamed up this whole project, so I will find out how close to reality it actually is.

Later on I had a meeting at the Opera House to discuss the staff catering arrangements for the new theatre. Louise Shand-Brown, the company manager, received a fax in Madrid last week asking her to put together a small group to represent the interests of the dancers, with a whispered added note that 'apparently Deborah Bull has strong views on the subject'. Too right. I'm not sure all the other dancers would be too pleased to know I was putting them forward, though. To balance things out, Lucy Haith, one of the company physiotherapists, and Louise came along too, and it turned out that we were all after the same thing: fresh, simple, good food available throughout the day. Not a lot to ask.

I just hope Chris Smith lets us know before too long exactly how many companies he would like to shoehorn into the Opera House. We'll need to know how many we're cooking for.

12th December 1997, London
A full day at the office. I had to be up early to go and meet the agency who are dealing with the top secret P3000 launch. It all sounds highly glamorous; Rolls-Royce haven't produced a new car since the Silver Spirit in 1980 and the motoring world is understandably all in a lather about this one. The press launch in January is intended to combine 'the traditions and heritage of Rolls-Royce with the bold innovation of the new design'. The physical embodiment of these lofty sentiments is to be little old me – the tradition and heritage of a Royal Ballet ballerina dancing original choreography by Ashley Page, to a newly commissioned score by Orlando Gough. I will share a tiny stage with the *real* star of the show – the Silver Seraph, a name that is highly classified until the official launch on January 6th.

And it really is going to happen. I attempt an air of detached cynicism (a much stronger basis for negotiations), but inside I'm all bubbly. I shall try to keep a space available for the disappointment of it all falling through, particularly in the light of the recent announcement that Vickers, who own Rolls-Royce, are putting the company up for sale. I learnt a long time ago never to count my Rolls-Royces before they're launched.

Spent the evening at a private viewing at the South Bank's Hayward Gallery – *Objects of Desire*, the exhibition that I tried (and failed) to see in New York. Some of my fellow South Bank Board members were there too, and the talk was understandably about yesterday's Arts Council decision – or lack of it. The South Bank Lottery application has been batted back and forth like a Wimbledon volley. And to mix my metaphors, every time it has come back from them to us, the goal posts have moved. Our final, revised application was an heroic effort on the part of Board members (unpaid, and working all hours God sent) to meet yet another set of criteria. Yesterday, the Arts Council met to consider their final judgement. The conclave assembled for the last time, and eventually the plume of white smoke was spotted over the Council's headquarters in Great Peter Street. They had come to a unanimous decision. They are totally in favour of the concept of redeveloping the site and sheltering it under Richard Rogers' 'glass wave', but unable to award the full amount without approval from the Department for Culture, Media and Sport. Amongst us, reactions are mixed: those who have really put in the hours on re-working the proposal feel disappointed and frustrated that having met all the conditions, the South Bank has been told yet again that the money isn't guaranteed. As a relative newcomer to the South Bank, and an old timer where the uneasy marriage of Lottery money and public opinion is concerned, I think the Arts Council have been extremely bold. It would have been much easier to pander to the current public mood and turn the application down. But they have stuck their necks out and said they believe in it. Now we need the same sort of bravery from Mr Smith and his colleagues in government.

I met Tony Blair for the first time last week when we were both having dinner in the same London restaurant. It was a movers and shakers evening at which the Prime Minister and his wife sat at one table, and dotted around the room were writers, journalists, actors, editors, arts administrators, news readers, ballet dancers and composers. Blair is much taller than he appears. I wonder why he looks so short on television? Perhaps he surrounds himself with seven footers. In the brief minutes I spent with him, I found myself peering closely at his skin to check if he really does wear make-up. In an unobtrusive walkabout, the Prime Minister went to greet the composer Harrison Birtwistle, and was clearly overheard to say 'what you do is more important than what I do'. If you really believe that, Mr Blair, say it again, in public – I dare you.

15th December 1997, London
The Christmas silly season is on. Off to ITV to record a snippet on the 'twelve Lords a-leaping' of the famous seasonal song. My task was to tell Peter Hayes (political correspondent for Central TV) about the difficulties that would be involved in teaching twelve members of the Upper House to 'leap'. I'm not sure if he actually intends to try this. I think he has one volunteer, Brian Rix, he of the 'Whitehall farces'. Although he is an elderly Lord, and a surprisingly sprightly one at that, I'm not certain he counts. He's a man of the theatre and once a performer, always a performer. Dancing is like riding a bicycle; something you never forget. I suggested that the simplest way to make them all leap was to publish a white paper on the abolition of the Upper House. That would start them jumping.

16th December 1997, London
My second South Bank Board meeting, and predictably the main item on the agenda was the Arts Council decision of last week. The press had apparently carried articles over the weekend claiming that the entire Board had threatened to resign if the award was not forthcoming. News to me: I, for one, hadn't threatened, and as far as I am aware, neither had anyone else. But distortion in the media is hardly news these days. The unanimous feeling was that resignation was the last thing we should do. I personally feel that the Board (and I don't include myself, as I am too new to it) have throughout this whole scenario behaved professionally. Resignation would be a supremely childish (and futile) gesture at this point.

As at last week's Hayward event, individual moods varied, but overall there is more optimism than despair. It seems that we have every ingredient in the pot for a successful result – the only thing lacking is the vociferous public support to whip it all together. From what we can gather, the arts community is entirely behind the project. And like it or not, artists constitute the people, too.

19th December 1997, London
Had lunch with Siobhan (Sue) Davies, the choreographer, and Michael Morris of Artangel, an organisation which facilitates one-off artistic

collaborations. We are now on to the planning stages of our project, although we still aren't sure where and when it will take place. Co-ordinating the two of us is a pretty difficult process, but Michael works hard to keep us in touch and juggles adeptly to make things happen. I am so excited about working with Sue. I have always been a fan of hers, right back to my days as a ballet student, when I would rush off to see contemporary dance at every opportunity. As a dancer Sue was wonderful, and as a choreographer she is probably one of the most respected and distinguished in this country.

I have an idea that the working process will be rather different from what I am used to. Sue doesn't work in the hallowed tradition of 'choreographer knows best'. Instead she draws on the skill and input of her individual dancers to help shape the piece she's making. I'm sure she's nervous about going into the studio with someone who is, at least as far as her work is concerned, a novice, and I'm sure as hell nervous about exposing myself to her. But I'm more than willing to risk making a fool of myself in order to collaborate with Sue. Inevitably the conversation over lunch turned to the current situation at the Opera House. I realise it has provoked an outpouring of resentment from independent dancers about the inequity of so much money funding one institution while others find it hard to secure cash for single projects. But Sue wasn't so harsh about it. Classical ballet is one of the main reasons why other forms of dance (at least in the Western world) exist. Reaction against ballet's rigidity and all its constraints started a line in contemporary dance which can be clearly traced from Isadora Duncan, through Ruth St Denis and Ted Shawn, Doris Humphrey, Martha Graham, Merce Cunningham and Robert Cohan to Siobhan Davies. Sue, with her gentle wisdom and her unselfish nature, understands the importance of ballet and its relevance to everything else that goes on.

23rd December 1997, London
The grand opening night of The Royal Ballet's Christmas season at the Royal Festival Hall on the South Bank. I was one half of the pair of blue girls in Ashton's *Les Patineurs*, replacing Nicky Roberts (pregnant), who should have been replacing Leanne Benjamin (injured). It was my first outing on this stage. We should have been here last night for a run-through, but as always happens things fell behind schedule and half the rehearsal had to be cut. My half. But at least we knew in good time so it wasn't a case of hanging around for nothing.

It's no wonder things start to go awry when we try to 'get in' to a new venue. I can only marvel at the ingenuity it must take for the Opera House stage crew to transfer entire ballet sets across London and recreate them in a space designed for concerts. It must be a bit like moving the contents of a five-storey house into a top-floor flat. In theory it might be possible, but it isn't until you try cramming it all in that you find out just how tricky it is. I'm never surprised when we run late on 'get in' days, only amazed that we 'get in' at all.

The Festival Hall is a rather nice place to perform – well, I would have to say that, wouldn't I, being a member of its Board. But it is well laid out and the dressing-rooms are very close to the stage, if a little cabana like. Traditionally, English National Ballet have performed here over Christmas. But they have managed, this season, to get hold of the Coliseum, the theatre in St Martin's Lane which they hope to secure as their London home. Apparently, English National Ballet didn't really like performing here at the Festival Hall, as it presented two practical problems. First, there is no 'fly tower' so stage sets have to be reconstructed in order that they can glide on tracks, like the smoothest of 'swish' curtains, rather than 'fly in' from above. Second, the stage is designed for concerts, so it is tightly ring-fenced in by choir stalls, tiered ranks of wooden steps on both sides. Until this year, it was impossible to exit the stage without running up a flight of stairs. At the insistence of The Royal Ballet management, some of the choir stalls have been removed and you can now get into the wings unimpeded and without using crampons. Poor English National Ballet had endured the uphill hike for years and I'm sure they're enjoying the well-deserved comfort of the Coliseum.

The mocked-up stage feels surprisingly solid and permanent, and there is something about being away from the hallowed gilded proscenium of the Opera House which takes the edge off pre-performance nerves. I have always said I'm a much better dancer in school gyms and hospital visiting rooms than I am at the Opera House, and sure enough, I danced pretty well tonight. It being the night before the night before Christmas (Norwegians celebrate the 24th not the 25th) I didn't hang around to watch *Beatrix Potter* but rushed back home to see if Torje had decorated the tree. He flew back yesterday from the US for a short Christmas break, and he is already hard at work dealing with all the technical hitches around the flat that trip me up in his absence.

26th December 1997, London

Back to class, and a feeling of virtue that I'm at work while the rest of
the country is still at play. I don't really have a busy day; class, a fitting,
and a run-through with Ashley Page of the 'Dance of the Silver Seraph'
for next week's Rolls-Royce gig. Most of the dancers have two
performances. Christmas is the busiest time of the year for the ballet as
it is for the Church; its merriment is slightly muted for the vicar who has
to deliver midnight mass and an 8 a.m. communion service, and the
dancers who have to get up the next morning and spin their way through
Les Patineurs. I know I would have had fewer glasses of wine with my
Christmas lunch if I was due to perform today. I wonder why people
want to leave their warm homes and all those new toys and come to see
the ballet on Boxing Day. Perhaps there's an element of vicarious
exercise in watching us work up a sweat, but I guess it just wouldn't be
Christmas without a trip to the pantomime. The Royal Ballet's
programme this year certainly reflects the pantomime spirit. *Beatrix
Potter* is fast becoming one of our Christmas staples; it sells out as soon
as booking opens, and the audiences, adults and children alike, love it.
Not so the critics, and the dancers aren't very keen either. Just imagine
dancing in a costume which weighs over a stone and a mask which
reduces your field of vision to a pin-prick and you'll realise why.

After class, I tried out my Rolls-Royce costume, an ingenious creation in
silver satin, designed by Tanya Spooner, which manages to evoke the lady
on the bonnet and yet allow me enough freedom to dance Ashley's choreography. A clever construction. We have all been working prestissimo
on the project, as Christmas has come right in the middle of it all, denying
us two crucial working days. I leave for Scotland on January 4th, and the
New Year fiesta will cut another chunk from the time we have left.

Spent the evening watching the broadcast on BBC 1 of the *Steptext*
performance that we recorded back in the summer. The supreme effort
which went into dancing *Steptext* didn't come across at all. It looked
about as taxing as a trip around Tesco. As I very rarely see myself on
film, the image I have of myself is based largely on my reflection in the
rehearsal studio mirrors. Despite the fact that everyone and their aunt
owns a home video camera, it's only just becoming common practice for
us in the ballet to use video in the rehearsal room. Some companies
record their rehearsals all the time, but as we use live musicians in the
studio as well as on-stage we run the risk of conflict with the unions.
Now, with the advent of handheld miniature video cameras, it's all less

formal and even choreographers working with The Royal Ballet frequently video their work during the course of rehearsals. I am looking forward to the time when we use video as a matter of course for the entire repertoire. Sometimes the only way to really accept your own mistakes is to see them for yourself on the screen.

I generally don't watch the archive recordings that are made of the dress rehearsals until the work comes up again for revival, sometimes years later. I only once made the mistake of going into the video room before a first night. It was the opening of *The Planets*, and David Bintley had choreographed a beautiful *pas de deux* for Jonathan Cope and me. It wasn't the sort of thing I am normally cast in – languid and lyrical rather than spunky, swift and bloody hard – and I enjoyed feeling like a different dancer. There were so many favourable comments (including 'is that the French girl?' from Princess Margaret) that I decided to go and see if I *looked* any different from normal. Hmm. That was the last time I made that particular mistake.

29th December 1997, London
Monica Mason, The Royal Ballet's Assistant Director, called me at home this evening. Whenever I get a call from management I mentally fast-forward, in the space between 'hello' and 'it's Monica', the entire repertoire and casting possibilities to see just what I am about to be asked to do. Tonight I drew a blank, as Monica is not directly involved with *Patineurs*, the only ballet I am dancing this week.

She had something far worse to tell me than anything I could have anticipated. Paul Andrews, the designer for Cathy Marston's piece, died in hospital yesterday evening. Apparently he suffered a massive asthma attack on Christmas Eve and has been on a life-support machine ever since. He was twenty-nine.

Paul was the first designer I ever started to become close to. He was the first designer who had ever asked my opinion about fabric swatches and colours. He was the first designer I've ever been shopping or had coffee with; last month, when I managed to costume myself for the gala preview of Cathy's *pas de deux* for less than £50, he sheepishly spent almost twice that on a pair of shoes, admitting that he had something of the Imelda in him. In short, he was the first designer I had ever had real, personal contact with and I remember feeling so excited about that. Aside from this, he was one of life's truly good people. It's tragic that his life has been cut so short.

January 1988

1st January 1998, London

New Year's Day and I am back in the theatre waiting for another journalist. *The Vitality Plan* comes out later this month, and I seem to be doing interviews and photographs at the rate of one or two a day at the moment. There is still such wonderment and surprise at the idea of a talking, writing dancer that every time one newspaper article appears it spawns another two or three in its wake.

It's good to be back in the theatre after such a bad start to the season. This is the first time I have danced in this country in about six months, and I'm having a lot of fun telling people that I'm the first Board member ever to tread the boards here at the Royal Festival Hall. To be perfectly honest, I'm not sure if this is entirely true, but I'd be willing to bet I'm the first Board member to *dance* here, and probably, for that matter, in any London theatre. One Board-a-leaping.

The theatre is deathly quiet backstage but the foyer is as lively as ever. Entering through the front of house, I was amazed at the number of people who had ventured out after last night's revelries. There was a 'foyer event' underway: a free concert with a huge audience who were enjoying the music while they ate lunch or had a drink. This is one of the things I am most looking forward to when the new House finally opens – the ability to welcome the public at all hours. It's all very well for people to complain that the theatre is locked to the general public during the day, but we are severely limited by the fact that the Opera House was built over a century ago in the middle of a large fruit and vegetable market. It wasn't designed to be operational before 7.30 p.m., and we have nothing to offer in terms of all day entertainment. The Festival Hall is a relatively modern venue, completed in 1951 as the centrepiece for the Festival of Britain, and designed with a very different and populist philosophy. It was always intended to do more than admit a small selection of people from curtain up onwards. But give the new Opera House a chance. I think it can work.

4th January 1998, Ackergill, Scotland

Today is the start of the P3000 week and Ashley Page and I met up at

Heathrow Airport early this morning to fly up to Ackergill, Scotland. There is a local airport in nearby Wick. But with no direct flights from London the journey involved a change of planes (and a long delay) in Edinburgh. I'm not a hugely enthusiastic flyer, and the announcement that the plane I am about to travel on needs a spare part never inspires me with much confidence.

Once the part arrived we flew the last leg of the journey on an eighteen-seater prop-driven plane which seemed to me to be pretty much on its last legs too. We took off in a hailstorm, and the plane bounced around as it climbed through the clouds. I finally understood why plane jargon is all based on the nautical – in a propeller plane, the experience of flying is much more akin to life on the ocean wave than the thrusting jet-propelled sensation that we're used to nowadays. We bobbed all the way to Wick. When we finally touched down, our band of merry men – Becky McBride from the R-R's PR agency, four musicians, Ashley and me – sat obediently and waited for the OK to disembark. After a while we realised that the majority of the passengers (several Mrs Doubtfires amongst them) were patiently waiting for us to get off. They were all going on to Shetland and Wick was little more than a bus stop.

But what a stop. I'm not sure I will ever leave here. Ackergill Tower is without question my ultimate holiday destination. Not that it's easy to vacation here: apart from the transport logistics, it isn't exactly the sort of place you can just turn up for a few days. They do host occasional 'open' weekends, but they cater in the main for conferences and events and, well, P3000 launches. The tower sits in splendid solitude at the edge of the sea, a relic from the days when we had to guard against the marauding Norwegians (apologies to Torje). It dates back to the 1400s, although the Victorians left their customary mark in the form of extra wings and various add-ons to the original. One of these add-ons is a converted stable block, referred to as the Opera House, and I have to confess that I had my doubts, viewing it from the outside. It looks like a lock keeper's cottage. Inside there is an anteroom, and then, through a green baize door, it opens out into a tiny theatre with a stage five metres by four. On one side there is a large window, allowing scenery (and motor cars) to be manoeuvred into position on the stage. In three neat rows sit eighteen high-backed chairs, upholstered in tartan and lined up expectantly. It's all totally delightful, and I'm looking forward to the arrival of the car in the morning and the process of getting the show on the road.

As we can't start work until the vehicle is in position, we abandoned the rest of the evening to a musician's snooker match and a wonderful dinner. It seems that nothing here is too much trouble. Ackergill elevates the idea of service to a totally new level of luxury.

5th January 1998, Ackergill
Woke up to brilliant sunshine and fabulous views along the beach. I took the bull by the horns and dragged myself out for an early morning run, my somewhat unconventional way of supplementing training and increasing fitness. Although I'll be working fairly hard this week, I need to start thinking about *in the middle, somewhat elevated*, another piece by Bill Forsythe (choreographer of *Steptext)* which I'll be performing on the Dance Bites tour in late February. We last danced *middle* in 1993, but this time I'm cast in a different role, and it's hard to know, as yet, just how fit I'll need to be. If Bill's other works are anything to go by then I'll have to be in pretty good shape. Hence the morning training. At long last after the salmonella poisoning last September I feel well enough to push myself hard.

At about lunchtime I heard a rumbling outside my window. Three high-sided vehicles were progressing slowly towards the little 'Opera House'. The Seraph was about to arrive. I rushed over, not wanting to miss any of the action and keen to have one of the first pictures of the car. We all had the same idea but Becky McBride put an immediate stop to it, fearing for her job if we all turned up at Boots with a film full of highly sensitive pictures for development; the launch itself is embargoed until the end of February. I find it hard to believe that the world's press will adhere to the restriction, but R-R have no option but to launch it now if they want magazine coverage at the same time. The newpapers can turn stories around quickly but magazines have a very long lead time.

After an hour or so of fun and games while a remarkably confident mechanic endeavoured to reverse £150,000-worth of motor car through the window and on to the stage, we finally got to work. With a car parked on it, the stage went from small to minuscule. But we dancers are trained to cope with adverse conditions, and after the obligatory whinge, I set about making the choreography fit the dimensions. We had created the dance in a fairly large studio, but Ashley had sensibly marked out the boundaries and the steps were made with a limited space in mind. And the instinct for survival is pretty strong. When you know you have a brick wall on one side, a glass window on the other, a drop

at the front and a very expensive piece of metal at the back, you watch
your steps.

At about 7 p.m. we allowed an advance party of R-R executives to
come in and watch a dress rehearsal. Richard Charlesworth, Head of
Public Affairs for Rolls-Royce, commissioned the piece and the
reponsibility for its success or failure rests on his shoulders. In some
ways it was more nerve-racking than a real performance – dress
rehearsals are often like that. But he seemed pleased, and I must say,
leaving the dancing aside, having four musicians playing live in such an
enclosed space is thrilling in itself. Orlando Gough has scored the piece
for piano, violin, cello and trumpet, an unusual combination, but very
powerful. All in all, combined with the splendour of the surroundings, I
don't think tomorrow evening can fail.

6th January 1998, Ackergill

The day of the first night. In the afternoon we gave another advance
showing for the Chief Executive, Graham Morris, and then, after a late
lunch, it was time to do it for real. From the safety of my room, I heard
the pipers announce the arrival of the first group of journalists and then
I crept over to the Opera House. My involvement was supposed to be a
surprise but Clive Aslett, editor of *Country Life*, was here and I knew
that if he saw me the secret would be out. I was pretty certain I could
have stripped naked and danced the can-can before any of the motoring
correspondents would have recognised me. I was an added attraction to
be upstaged by a car. I got ready in an upstairs room with a rickety
wooden floor, the tapping of my pointe shoes upsetting the R-R team
below who were being either briefed or debriefed. I never did work out
which was which. At 7.45 p.m. it was time for curtain up on the world
première of the now-titled *Silver Lines of Grace* – except there is no
curtain. So I entered via the kitchen and crouched down, centre stage, in
darkness. The piano sounded its opening notes as the lights came up and
there I was, motionless, wings wrapped about me and silhouetted like
Boadicea. Then we were off, up and down the diagonal and round the
stage in as many variants as Ashley could think of in his efforts to make
the most of 20 square metres of stage. All premières, even here in the
remoteness of Scotland, have their own sense of excitement – a bit like
the nervous anticipation of watching someone open a present you have
very carefully chosen and feel sure they will love. At the end of the
performance, the backdrop falls to the floor and the Seraph is revealed in

all her silver splendour. There were bravos from the packed house of twenty, all splendidly kitted out in full Highland regalia. But I'm not sure if the noise was for my performance or (more likely) for the vehicle parked behind me. After I had finished I did what the Stones call a 'runner' – into a dressing-gown, into a waiting vehicle and back to the Tower. The only difference was that I had a glass of Krug forced into my hand. Hey! I could get used to this. Seven minutes of dancing and the rest of the day in luxury. That's what I call a proper job.

9th January 1998, Ackergill
My final full day here at Ackergill. It has been the most wonderful and stress-free week and I know that I will suffer withdrawal symptoms when I get home. Not that it hasn't been hard work. My role includes heavy socialising and nightly haggis as well as dancing. However jolly that may sound it can actually be quite demanding. At least I don't have to get up at 6 a.m. The R–R team are dragged from their beds an hour before the guests to be briefed (or debriefed) despite the fact that they have to be the last to retire. Today everyone is confessing (in private) to a slight fatigue (me included) but in true professional style we all remain full of charm.

At about 4 p.m. the final group of journalists arrive. Tonight it is 'the rest of Europe'. Yesterday we had the Germans, prior to that the Japanese and on Tuesday the Americans. For the past two evenings the weather has been kind, and we've had a post-prandial bonfire on the beach. Wrapped up in Barbours and wellingtons against the January night, a bemused collection of journalists has processed down to the sand-dunes where a Land-Rover waited, loaded with hot coffee and an array of liqueurs. On a nearby rock sat Donny, leprechaun-like, softly coaxing tunes out of his squeeze-box. The Chief Executive and I led the party in 'Strip the Willow', a traditional Scottish folk dance, and then we laughed to the point of tears as we tried to marshal ten non-English-speaking journalists through its intricacies. As the fire roared and the ocean seethed behind us, it occured to me that they must have thought they'd landed on another planet. Worse, though, my heart ached at the thought that this particular moment of pure, unadultered happiness could never, ever be repeated.

11th January 1998, London
My week in Ackergill went from better to better, right up to the moment of departure; flowers after the last performance and a Rolls-Royce to take

me to the airport. The fall back to normal got harder and harder from that point on.

The airline which flew me home did its best to make the return as difficult as possible, both losing and destroying my suitcase, and then having it delivered at midnight in the most surly and unpleasant fashion possible. As usual my answerphone had burst its banks with a series of increasingly frustrated callers, first asking and then demanding that I call back. Am I such an unfriendly, inefficient person that people assume I am simply ignoring their calls? Do they never stop to consider the possibility that I'm not returning their messages because *I haven't heard them and I'm not at home*?

I've had a week without television and radio, and I'm very behind on what's going on both on the world stage, and in Ambridge. (I'm a Radio 4 addict, with *The Archers* the highpoint of my listening schedule.) So it's news to me to read that Covent Garden is rumoured to have a new Chair, Sir Colin Southgate, Chairman of EMI. He's the man reputedly responsible for signing the Spice Girls. Evidently he's a man who sees potential in unexpected quarters. It would certainly seem so, if he's thinking of taking on the hottest seat in the arts world at this particular time. If *he* can't popularise the company, I don't know who can. After all, we're most of us by turns scary, sexy, posh, juvenile (occasionally), sporty *and* totally talented.

The same article reminds us all in a tiny paragraph, low on words but big on import, that Gerald Kaufman's Select Committe will be reopening its investigations into the House later this month. I have also seen and heard suggestions that discussions are under way about the possibility of privatising the opera while leaving the ballet subject to public funding. It seems that even Lord Chadlington's and the entire Board's resignation weren't blood money enough to rescind our sentence. The case continues.

All this left me wondering yet again just why people are willing to get involved with such copious amounts of unpaid work. Southgate's time and energies must already be heavily committed elsewhere. After all, you don't make £800,000 a year by doing nothing. But he (and, allegedly, Gerry Robinson, who is tipped to take over from Lord Gowrie at the Arts Council) has been 'looking for a prestigious public office for six months'. Why? After the very public fate of several 'good men and true' over that same period of time? Did they suddenly wake up one morning to think, 'life's too good. I should suffer a bit. I know – I'll go and get myself an unpaid, non-executive job in the arts. That should do the trick.'

This might be a good moment to ask just why *I* agreed to become involved in unpaid public service, both at the Arts Council and on the Board at the South Bank. I did have to think a bit before coming up with the answer but I concluded that the situation is different for me. I have, for the last seventeen years, been directly affected by the decisions of people in 'prestigious public office'. My life has been shaped by those decisions. The arts are what I do. I'm a main ingredient of the recipe, neither the head chef nor the *maître d'*. As such, I feel I have quite a lot of first-hand knowledge about what it feels like when the heat is turned on. I've come close to getting burnt. Now that I'm a bit older (although I deny I'm fully cooked), I'd like to make that knowledge available. It might help people get a clearer picture of what goes on behind the scenes.

14th January 1998, London
I started my week with Sue Davies, on our collaboration for Artangel. I have wanted to work with her for so long that I find it hard to believe we have finally got it together. We worked in a church close to the Holloway Road, up in North London. No shower, no canteen, and very little heat. I am ashamed to report that for many, many dancers, these conditions are the norm. St Luke's is a working church, but as most churches are fairly quiet during the week, this one has sensibly decided to try and boost its income by hiring out the space. I did my warm-up barre holding on to a table which was draped in cloths and looked suspiciously like an altar. It couldn't have been. It wasn't in the nave, for a start, but I did wonder if I was doing something slightly sacrilegious. I took comfort in the lines of the Christmas carol: If I were a shepherd, I would bring a lamb, and so on. Well, I'm a dancer.

Sue arrived laden with books to provide a starting point; pictures, patterns, designs, anything to spark the imagination. She asked me to choose a motif, and then left me alone to set about making it into a sequence of movement. As a dancer I've never been asked to work this way before. Most rehearsals I've ever been in begin with 'you start in the corner and do this'; with Sue, it's more a case of entering into a choreographic dialogue. Together with the dancer, she builds up a vocabulary of movement, and then, over a long period of time, forms those sequences into a structured piece. Today, in hours of concentrated work, we came up with four little motifs. It might not sound like a lot but, basically, I'm learning to speak a new language here and Sue is enunciating slowly and patiently so that I will understand.

But it was very exciting for me to explore movement in another way. There is a difference, difficult to define but nevertheless marked, between the work I have done with contemporary choreographers and what I do in the classical repertoire. In contemporary dance there's a strong emphasis on movement; not positions, or line, not pictures that can be held for a moment and captured visually, but *movement*. The way you get from one position to another, making sure that the impetus comes from the right place, neither forcing nor faking. In a sense, the least important thing is how polished it looks, whereas in classical ballet hiding the effort and presenting a finished product is absolutely fundamental. For a choreographer like Sue process is every bit as relevant as product.

There's something different, too, about rehearsing in a style of dance which doesn't come so naturally to me. I noticed this for the first time when I worked with Bill Forsythe, on *in the middle, somewhat elevated*. Because I am having to analyse carefully everything I am told and link it very clearly to the physical sensation, the movement and the information knit together until one no longer exists without the other. Every step I dance triggers a checklist of the ideas which lie behind it. This gives me something to cling to, on-stage, when nerves threaten to take over, a sort of dancer's rosary. The problem with classical ballet, the sort of dancing I do for a living, is that it is second nature to me; I must have *learnt* it at some time, in the way that once upon a time I must have learnt to speak. But I don't remember the process at all. Nervous impulse can become physical movement without me knowingly engaging my brain. Because corrections are served up in a shorthand that we all speak fluently, they can become vague and general, like the Lord's Prayer – something we can all recite flawlessly until we *think* about it. Without thought attached, corrections fail to function as landmarks in the same sort of way. It all becomes a mêlée of 'I know I need to turn out/lift my working knee/point my foot' etc, but none of this can be grasped when things start to go awry and the movement goes off track. Sue's choreography, on the other hand, is going on to my internal hard drive with instructions attached.

I got up early this morning to go and appear (can you appear on the radio?) on Radio 4's *Midweek*. The news broadcasts were full of speculation that the Opera House would today announce its new Chairman. By 6 p.m., the Radio 4 bulletin had dropped that story, but instead confirmed the widely anticipated news that Gerry Robinson of Granada TV had secured Lord Gowrie's job at the Arts Council. Robinson is a big Labour supporter, and appeared, or at least spoke for the party, in the run-up to the election in May. The newscaster described him as 'full of Irish charm'. He will need all his blue-eyed charm and diplomacy if he is to remain friends with the government on a continuing basis. After he's spent a few weeks at the Arts Council he will see just how dire the (under) funding situation is. I know we cry wolf quite a lot, but that's because for many people in the arts world, the wolves really are outside the door, licking their lips in anticipation of a low-fat meal. I can understand that anyone looking in from the outside may be tempted to think we are just very bad at balancing books, and that applying a little business acumen will soon whip us into shape. But there's no business like show business, and I have a suspicion that our new arts supremo will soon be forced to report back that this is like no business he knows.

20th January 1998, London
The players are gradually beginning to take their places for the next act of the unfolding drama that is the Opera House. Who's going to get Hamlet's poisoned chalice? Gerry Robinson is presumably attempting to unravel the complexities of the Arts Council, and Colin Southgate is now officially on board at the Garden. I was interested to hear his initial sound bites. Under pressure from an insistent press corps, he disappointingly came out with the old chestnut (old but chilling) of 'bums on seats'. But he came up with another which was more original and probably very true. Apparently we need 'a little bit of love and leadership, and a cuddle'. A ray of hope.

Tomorrow is THE day – the launch party for *The Vitality Plan*. I'm about to become a published author for the first time. Never mind that the book has been on sale for the best part of a month at various shops across the country. It will still be officially launched with a celebratory drink at The Circle, a new restaurant by Tower Bridge, tomorrow evening. It has received a fair amount of publicity, including the inevitable article focusing more on Torje's famous clients than on the book itself. But never mind; mostly the coverage has been about the book and its contents, and the one column I was scared about gave it a very favourable review. Ever since Dorling Kindersley commissioned the book, I have dreaded opening the *Sunday Times* and seeing *The Vitality Plan* featured in 'Diet Watch', for the simple reason that I read the column regularly and invariably agree with the opinions of its author, Amanda Ursell. She talks good sense in a field more noted for its nonsense, and I would have had a hard time arguing the case if she had hated it. I flicked nervously through last Sunday's edition and, with great relief, came across one of the best reviews of my career.

Another Board meeting this afternoon at the South Bank – my third in about four months. I am gradually becoming familiar with my colleagues there (and they with me). Robert Saxton, the composer, is a fellow Board Room virgin, and together we are, meeting by meeting, becoming bolder and more relaxed in the presence of such artistic giants as Harrison Birtwistle and David Sylvester. At the top of the agenda, once again, was the hot potato of the Lottery bid. Approved 'in principle' by the Arts Council in December, we are now waiting to see whether Chris Smith's department will allow the Arts Council to 'draw down' money in advance, enabling them to pay up. Unfortunately, the longer we wait, the more the cost rises. Each month of delay adds a staggering £3/4 million to the price tag.

23rd January 1998, London
It's Friday evening, and I'm back at home after three days of non–stop excitement and two personal firsts. I've had a book published, and I've been doctored.

Wednesday, the day of the launch party for *The VP*, seemed to go on for ever. I started at nine in the morning at a studio off Lisson Grove, with sixteen local radio interviews, all via telephone, which stretched over six hours. That's a long time to maintain cheery author enthusiasm, and I learnt very quicky that the success of an interview depends more than anything on the personality of the disembodied voice doing the interviewing. They had all been issued with a press release which included sample questions intended to stimulate ideas, rather than to be read straight off the page. But it's amazing how many interviewers simply recited, as if from a script, word for word, the text they had in front of them. 'So . . . Deborah . . . what . . . is . . . the . . . basic . . . philosphy . . . behind . . . *The* . . . *Vitality* . . . *Plan*?' Would someone please wake me up at the end of the sentence? When so little vitality is coming down the line, it's rather hard to work up any of one's own. But occasionally the give and take was great fun; the presenter on Scottish radio opened with, 'Deborah Bull is a principal dancer with The Royal Ballet, she has just published *The Vitality Plan*, and she's a babe.'

From Lisson Grove I went (via my fabulous hairdresser, Laurent) to The Circle, a restaurant near Tower Bridge, for the book's launch party. I'm not sure what purpose these events are designed to serve, but whatever it is, I had a wonderful evening. I was genuinely surprised at the number of people who had showed up to celebrate with me, and I was particularly pleased to see Mary Allen, who aside from suffering the ongoing saga of the Kaufman inquiry (Kaufman: the sequel – just when you thought it was safe to go back into the Garden . . .) is also nursing an injured knee. Maybe Kaufman struck a low blow. Christopher Davis of Dorling Kindersley, who bravely commissioned a book on diet from a ballet dancer, said a few kind words, which was good practice for the eulogy I would have to endure the next day.

On Thursday afternoon, after guesting with Debbie Thrower on Radio 2, I travelled up to Derby to receive an honorary doctorate from its university. It's only the second time I've been inside a college. Really. The first was Oxford, to address the Union, and today I was receiving the University of Derby's highest honour. Nothing like working your way up from the bottom and missing out on the important bit in the middle, the college years. The years when I might, under normal circumstances, have been at university (ages 18–21) were wrapped up with being a ballet dancer, and all the ambitions that entails. I wouldn't change a thing about my life and the direction it's taken, but I do regret this one, missed, opportunity; the time to study and enjoy books and ideas in a structured environment.

I took the train from St Pancras at 4 p.m., and armed with a supply of newpapers, caught up on last week's events. There were a couple of scary stories in *The Times*. In the news pages, for instance, I read that when Lord Chadlington left the Opera House, £2 million of donations left with him. And amongst the letters to the editor I found angry and disappointed correspondence about the Education Secretary, David Blunkett's proposal to restructure the primary school's curriculum and push the arts even further out on to the peripheries. Oh dear. I feel hugely disappointed that with expert opinion pointing unarguably to the importance of the arts in education, Blunkett should blithely take yet another step in the wrong direction. After only nine months in power, this government is really falling out fast with the arts community. There were such high hopes back in May.

The train arrived in Derby at that dusky point when afternoon turns into evening. Nostalgia time. It's the city where my parents were born, brought up, met and married. But since the family moved down south before I was two, I don't feel very much like a local girl. Come to think of it, I don't feel particularly at home anywhere. Nevertheless, I was unprepared for the rush of emotion which met me as I got off the train and walked the short distance from the station to the Midland Hotel, where I was booked in for the night. All of a sudden I was struck by the notion that this is the city where my parents lived their dreaming years – the stage in your life when everything seems possible and heady plans are laid down for the future. Years on, some of those dreams are realised, yet inevitably, many of them turned to dust. But I guess every new child brings with it a fresh set of dreams and aspirations, a new scheme for the future. It felt very strange that being back in Derby to accept public recognition for some of the things I do might just be one of those hopes fulfilled. I wrapped up warm and took myself for a walk with the ghosts along streets with half-remembered names, then back to the hotel for an early night. I felt tearful and even unaccountably guilty about the sacrifices that have been made on my behalf.

After a restless night I woke up at 6.30 a.m., way in advance of the alarm call. I often find that when there is something important to do, I don't want to sleep, however tired I am. I go all Thatcherite and view sleep as an irrelevancy, wanting to get on and face what lies ahead. Doctor me and be done with it.

After a nervous breakfast, I was driven over to the Mayor's Parlour to dress up. I had already been warned that the honours procedure is every bit as complicated as a performance, and this morning I discovered that the costumes are every bit as good, too. I needed help to get into my gown, and I have to confess to feeling slightly disappointed that I wouldn't be wearing a mortarboard after all. Instead I was issued with a large black velvet floppy cap, complete with deep red tassles. I began to look the part. I hoped no one would ask me for my credentials.

My fellow honorand was Lucy Gannon, the writer responsible for numerous television drama series. She really is a local girl, born and bred here, and although her work forced her to move to London a couple of years ago, she won over the crowd instantly by announcing that she hates the capital so much she is already planning her return north. Together, Lucy and I pulled each other through what could have been a frightening ordeal. Our hosts were kind and hospitable, but this was another occasion when I felt like a total outsider. Not my world. When I was originally offered the doctorate, I telephoned Jonathan Powers, Honorary Vice-Chancellor, and asked him to take me through the entire awards hierarchy. I didn't have a clue what came after A-levels. Thanks to Jonathan's patient and lengthy dissertation on the subject, I now have a vague idea, but I wouldn't want to take questions on it.

Processing into Derby's Civic Centre, I felt like a fraud before the hundreds of students who had all put in years of hard work for their hand-shake and certificate. Lucy and I had arrived from London and done sod all, but we were each treated to a five-minute panegyric, the opportunity to address the assembly (I'd like to thank my agent, my mother . . .) and awarded a title – Doctor of the University. Dr Bull? Who, me? I don't deliver babies.

I must admit that I've had a bit of a problem with accepting this award, stemming mostly from the 'I am not worthy' syndrome that racks me from time to time. So much of my life and training is spent in being corrected, and so many of my efforts condemned with a no, no, no, rather than rewarded with a yes, yes, yes. I thought about this long and hard and squared it by seeing myself as a token; through an education in the arts, I inhabit a world where visions are broad, and options, theoretically, unlimited. So many people are not as lucky as me. I decided that I could accept the doctorate if I collected it on behalf of all the people who, in a better world, would achieve or should receive awards of their own. All in all, it was a strangely humbling experience. I travelled back to London on the train with my mother, who had arrived early this morning and with fierce maternal pride had enjoyed the day as much as I had.

30th January 1998, London –Portland, Oregon
This has been a week of early risings. As a rule, I try to limit the number of times I see the dawn to once or twice a year. One of the few perks of being a dancer is that class doesn't usually start until 10.30 a.m., twelve hours after curtain down, so my alarm is permanently set to go off at half-past eight. What a godsend for me, as I don't really do mornings.

But all week long I have been forced to break my rule and get up at silly o'clock. The company is officially on its 'mid-season break', a welcome chance to recover from the Christmas season before the Dance Bites tour starts up. Despite the fact that the holiday coincided *exactly* with Torje's two-week stopover in Hawaii, I have been stuck here in

London, continuing the publicity rounds connected with the launch of *The VP*. At the beginning of the week I made my début on the chat show sofa, dressed, I am embarrassed to admit, *à la* Jane Fonda – not exactly what I recommend in the book, but admittedly more fetching than the clashing Gore-Tex and cycling trousers I was wearing yesterday as I ran around Regent's Park. Yet although I was doing my very best to look like an all-singing, all-dancing fitness expert, even in my skimpy coral two-piece, I had to face a barrage of questions on the controversy surrounding the Opera House. Get me at my most vulnerable, I would. It was slightly comic that these two aspects of my life, so disparate in my own mind, should interlace here on satellite TV. But it was the final throes of weeks of *VP* publicity before I jetted off for a brief holiday in the US, and I suspect Britain will be as glad as I am to see the back of my leotard.

Just time for one more picture though, in Crewe, at the Rolls-Royce factory. I was shooting a cover for *Country Life* magazine, scheduled to appear in March, and I was posing in a Neil Cunningham gown as the Spirit of Ecstasy before a Silver Seraph. Since the intense week in Ackergill back in early January, the people at Rolls-Royce have become my new best friends. Our relationship has gone way beyond the mere commercial and is full of mutual respect. Long may our friendship continue, as strange to say, I do feel quite at home in the back seat of a Rolls-Royce . . .

My final lark ascension finds me *en route* to Portland, Oregon, effecting once again my miraculous transformation from ballet dancer and (now) published author to Rolling Stones groupie. When you have a boyfriend who tours with a rock band and a job which doesn't let you plan further ahead than a week at a time, you take your opportunities to meet up when you find them. So, Hawaii didn't work out: no matter, I'll go to Portland. As it turns out, it's a great place; a western American city with the feel of a frontier town. Now I know why America is so in love with its North West. Of course, Portland is an infamous place right now for having been home to one of Monica Lewinsky's early affairs, prior to her alleged main event with President Bill Clinton. Feeling certain that this minor *scandale* will leave the city unblemished, Torje and I add Portland to our list of possible retirement sites, along with Denver, Vancouver and Norway. We like the mountains.

It's hard to get a take on just what American public feeling is regarding the latest sexual upheaval in the White House. I should think an entire forest is felled daily to print the myriad American newspapers, with their weird and wonderful titles; the *New Orleans Times Picayune*, the *Atlanta Constitution* and the *Sacramento Bee*. But because there isn't a truly national newspaper, many publications tend to give precedence to local issues. Here in Portland, for instance, the big stories are the death of Colleen Waibel, the first ever Portland police officer to be killed on duty, and last night's Stones concert at the Rose Garden Arena. The band hasn't played Portland since the sixties, and the *Oregonian* yesterday reprinted two reviews from the show thirty years ago. Their critic at the time wrote that the Stones would get half of a guaranteed $30,000 from seat sales and 60 per cent of anything over $30,000. 'They should get about $18,000 from this performance,' she reported. *Plus c'est la même chose, plus ça change*.

I'm using part of this flying visit to work my way through Richard Hoggart's *The Uses of Literacy*. I first came across Hoggart a couple of years ago, when I heard him featured on another of my Radio 4 favourites, *Desert Island Discs*. He had just published *The Way We Live Now*, which I bought the same day and devoured with fascination. It increased my interest in reading the important book which launched him, back in 1957. I searched for it in endless bookshops, and eventually a customer at a store in Primrose Hill, overhearing my request, followed me next door into Cullens, and offered to send me his original, pristine copy, cover price 4s. It's shocking to see how pertinent it remains today, with its lucid and persuasive analysis of popular culture. Hoggart is bold enough to say that some things really are better than others, and that within culture there are distinctions. Novels *are* better than magazines. In today's stifling atmosphere of political correctness, you have to be one of a small and select band of cantankerous old men to get away with this kind of talk.

A prime example of all this was on last Sunday's BBC 2 discussion about the state of the arts in this country. Culture Secretary Chris Smith and a panel of arts folk discussed and took questions from the audience about hot topics like the Millennium Dome versus the closing of the Greenwich Theatre. The talking went on and on, intelligent but often unfocused, though it seemed that Sir Peter Hall (possibly not can-tankerous, but certainly iconoclastic) was the only person prepared to speak with real passion and intelligence, saying things which may be unpopular, but which I, for one, believe to be true. The arts may not be vote-winners, but we let them decline at our peril, and it is a government's responsibility to ensure that the conditions exist in which they can thrive. Whatever the general public perceives to be their image, the arts have precious little to do with glamorous first nights and gala performances. They challenge our intellect, deepen our emotions, and broaden our world-view. They humanise us, turning us from cretins into a civilised society. To quote the writer Howard Jacobson, 'when did you last see a thug waving a copy of *Middlemarch*?'

February 1998

1st February 1998, en route *from Portland to San Diego*
Has anyone else noticed the similarities between the roles of Kenneth Starr, the US Independent Counsel, and Gerald Kaufman, UK Chairman of the Select Committee on Culture, Media and Sport? The Independent Counsel Act allows Starr to justify his existence by pinning a crime, by whatever means, on his target, and *Time* magazine this week suggests that Starr won't rest until he succeeds. His investigation, *Time* says, is 'likely to launch from one allegation to the next, with its ending always just out of reach'.

And so with Mr Kaufman. I do have a sneaking suspicion that Kaufman is trying to find crimes, whether they exist or not, and Mary Allen is his target. He doggedly pursues her, convinced she's committed a transgression, but unable to come up with the smoking gun. He reports, she resists, so back he comes again with a new investigation and a vigorous attack. He seems determined to bring her down. As with Starr in his pursuit of the President of the US, there are endless accusations of malfeasance which both men hope will blossom into crime by their exposure to the light of day. Both, too, are masterful in their manipulating of the media. These independent counsels, or select committees, as they're known on this side of the Atlantic, are not governed by the same rules of procedure as a criminal court would be. If they were, their lines of questioning, and without a doubt the *tone* in which they do the asking, would have been ruled inadmissible. And as for Kaufman's final ruling on the whole saga – well, I would be interested to hear whether twelve good men and true would reach the same conclusion on the hectoring evidence presented by Kaufman. Twisting the evidence so that it 'fits the crime' – 'I know they did *something* wrong, so I might as well get them for *this*' – is surely a crime in itself. Or did I miss something?

4th February 1998, in flight between San Diego and London
I'm in the air again, on the way home to my real life and more rehearsals for Dance Bites, which hits the road on the 23rd of this month. The long

Christmas and New Year holidays which the upper echelons of power enjoy brought a lengthy pause in the political machinations in the world of the arts. When I left London, it was all new beginnings as a change of cast was announced in crucial lead roles in the drama that is the Opera House. Sir Colin Southgate took centre stage as the new Chairman of the Board, and Granada Chairman Gerry Robinson entered from the left to take over at the Arts Council. God only knows who's waiting in the wings. Kaufman is probably hovering up in the flies, ready to drop yet another bombshell.

I did wonder why everyone who called me in the days before I left for the US were saying things like, 'I hear the Opera House is closing down for the next couple of years'. It seems that while I was celebrating the launch of my book last Wednesday, the *Evening Standard* was running an article (on page 17, mind, not even worthy of the front page) entitled 'New Chief May Axe Royal Opera Season'. The truth lurking behind the story seems to be that Phantom of the Opera Gerald Kaufman has suggested Colin Southgate consider 'curtailing or cancelling the present season' rather than let it continue 'on its present disastrous way'. So we can assume that Kaufman didn't come to the Royal Festival Hall, then, where the company had a hugely successful Christmas season, balancing the books and attracting consistently full houses.

Roll up, roll up. The circus is back in town, and Kaufman has roared back into the ring with his offensive assertion that 'no one appears to have lifted a finger to get a grip on the closure season' or reduce the Opera House deficit. When I was little, I was told to count to ten before I spoke. I have nothing against Kaufman's enquiries (though I do find them a little scary) and if there are things to be uncovered, let him be the one to do it. But please, Mr Kaufman, remember that when you make those sorts of remarks, you belittle the work we do. Everyone, from the youngest member of the *corps* to the Chief Executive of the House has put in endless amounts of effort to try and right what you described as several years of wrong. The Opera House is not its Board, or the changing guard of Chief Executives who have run it of late. It's made up principally of people who sing, dance and play there. People who design, build and usher. Management are but one part of a total effort to make an inert building come alive and stay afloat. You've made your suggestions in your report, and continually in the press. Now stand back a while and give us time to make them all work.

Christmas and the New Year had lulled us all into an uneasy calm, but the reconvening of the Select Committee last month has jolted us back to reality. My gut feeling is that the circus isn't leaving town yet. For God's sake, send in the clowns.

8th February 1998, London
Things have been worse than hectic since I came back from the States. I left San Diego on Wednesday morning, and arrived about 12 hours later at Heathrow Airport. By then it was 7 a.m. on Thursday, and after dropping off my bags at home I went straight in to work at Barons Court. Inevitably, when I could have used an early finish, I had a full day at the office; class, then rehearsals from midday until 6.30 p.m. I spent a chunk of that time working with Chris Saunders, one of the company's strongest partners, teaching him the *pas de deux* which Cathy Marston choreographed for Jonathan Cope and me to perform on the Dance Bites tour. Jonathan had been complaining of feeling unwell for months, and he finally succumbed to a severe throat infection just before we went to Madrid, in December, leaving me stranded without a partner. He's been out of commission since. By the end of today's call I think Chris could have happily strangled Jonny, ill or not. It's a tough and strange duet we've created. At no point during rehearsals would Jonny take the easiest or most familiar path. If he'd seen it before, he wasn't having it. So every lift, every grip is weird. The effect is wonderful – when Anthony Dowell saw it for the first time he commented that he thought his days of being shocked were over. 'Until today, I really thought I'd seen it all.' But all that innovation makes it extremely taxing, especially for someone of different proportions from Jonny. So much of partnering depends on the physical relationship between the two dancers, and when this changes, movements which were second nature suddenly refuse to work. And of course when steps are created on you, they are inevitably the sort of steps you favour. When the second cast tries to step into your shoes it feels completely alien, and in this instance, it hurt. Chris worked at it until his body couldn't take any more, and I doubt he'll be walking in the morning.

On Friday, though, I was in for a real surprise. I walked through the big studio at Barons Court on my way to class, and there was Jonny. Sick Jonny. We had given up on him; not necessarily permanently, but certainly for a good while yet. But there he was, looking so well that it made me realise just how bad he looked the last time I saw him. I told him his name was mud in the rehearsal with Chris yesterday, and he was confused. 'But why were you teaching it to Chris?' he asked. 'I'm going to do it.' It's a miracle, but one that I will reserve judgement on for a few days. Jonny is incredibly determined once he sets his mind to something – the work he managed while he was seriously ill is testament to that – but this is day one and it could have been the voice of optimism speaking.

I soldiered on through Friday, but by Saturday evening I was beginning to feel the effects of the week's toil and travel – long days at work combined with a sprinkling of jet lag. Past the point of fatigue, I spent a couple of hours tossing and turning before I finally dropped to sleep.

10th February 1998, Blackpool–Sheffield–London
My life swings from one extreme to the other. Sunday evening I was in Blackpool, with Amanda Jones of the Ballet Press Office. It's a far cry from Portland and San Diego. The rock doesn't quite match the rock 'n' roll I left behind, and I'm missing Torje. I'm here on company business, drumming up publicity for our forthcoming visit on the Dance Bites tour. Ticket sales so far are a bit on the slow side, and I am supposed to whip up some local interest. I only hope they aren't all fed up hearing about me after *The Vitality Plan* and I appeared in at least four national newspapers over the last few weeks. Perhaps we could try bribery – buy a ticket to see Deborah Bull dance, or buy two and you get a special reduction. In weight.

The past two days have been an interesting exercise in just how many interviews you can fit into forty-eight hours. For the record, I think it is seventeen, and that includes one book signing, one television, four radio, two photographs, six face-to-face, and three by telephone. I guess it's good practice for the upcoming US book tour, which I gather is a unique and totally exhausting experience. The past two days have been hard enough.

The Blackpool Grand, where yesterday morning's interviews took place, is a beautiful little theatre with a wonderfully hard-working team. In the summer they play host to the inevitable 'summer spectacular' and over Christmas, the perfectly predictable pantomime. For the rest of the year they try to redress the balance by presenting interesting and serious theatre and dance. A difficult trick to bring off, particularly in the light of an Arts Council report I read this afternoon about the links between venues, audiences and their expectations. It's asking a lot that the local population will accept and feel comfortable with two such contrasted theatrical experiences in one calendar year. Consequently, ticket sales have been a little slow so far. But the Blackpool Grand must be doing something right as they feel confident to have added (with Lottery funding) a fabulous studio theatre behind the auditorium.

After lunch, I went to Dillons bookstore for what my writer friend Sarah Stacey calls 'ritual humiliation' – the first book signing. A horribly exposing experience. You sit there, a stationary target, and wait for people to come in and purchase books which you then sign. Luckily for my fragile ego, I did have some 'walk-ups', and I signed the rest of the stock before I left.

After two radio interviews, one in Blackpool, and one in Blackburn, Amanda and I called it a day and headed to Sheffield, our next stop. This involved changing trains three times, and we finally arrived at 8 p.m. What we do for art.

Tuesday started even earlier, with a long taxi ride to Tupton, a Derbyshire village where I lived between the ages of five and seven. I was filming a nostalgia trip for Central TV, as a plug for both the Dance Bites tour and *The Vitality Plan*. I didn't sleep very well, and I suspect this was because I was nervous about going back to my roots. I remember Tupton fairly well, but only as a single, photographic image. In my mind, it's like one of those colourful boards kids have for their toy cars to drive around, marked out with the local school, fire station, bus stop, garage and other obvious sites. On my 'board', there is a church, a zebra crossing, a school and a sweetshop, all situated around one T-junction, but I can't summon up any of the emotions associated with these various landmarks.

We rolled up outside Tupton church at about 8.45 a.m., just as several five-year-olds were crossing the road, with the lollipop lady, from the church gate to the school. It's exactly the route I took every day on my way to the same school, dancing, rather than walking, and even though I remember so little of my childhood, it's a journey which is etched in my memory. It was all exactly as I remember it, although, of course, it seemed to have shrunk. The sweetshop was still there, very tiny, but closed now, and through the window I could see all manner of oddities – a Bakelite radio, two computers, racks of chewing gum and several unconnected parts of a bicycle. The bicycle wasn't the only thing with its parts unconnected. My life then seems to have no discernible link whatsoever with my life now.

Afterwards, we rushed back to Sheffield to start today's round of interviews at 11 a.m. Mostly newspapers, but one radio. The last was in some ways the hardest; not exactly the most prestigious, but it seemed to me to be the most important. It was with a journalist from the local university newspaper, a young law student with sharp features and an equally sharp mind. He was probably the smartest writer I talked to all day, and he wasn't interested in pointe shoes. 'I only have one question,' he said: 'How are you going to convince people that they really must come and see you?' 'This'll be a short interview,' I told him. 'That one's easy – you're going to convince them for me.' I'm used to a tough ride from the national papers, whose reporters seem, on occasion, to have the Opera House Board room wired, but you used to be able to count on the regional press to welcome an institution like The Royal Ballet with unquestioning delight. Not any more. There was no fobbing off this young man with vague platitudes about how everything is beautiful at the ballet. I got the impression he wasn't taking any shit, and neither did I want to give him any. No puff piece from this guy. He promised to come and see the show in a couple of weeks' time, and it'll be interesting to see what he makes of it.

At the end of a long afternoon, we took the train back to London, and I am now ready to collapse. Tomorrow it's back into the jaws of the company routine, with six hours of rehearsals, and still one more Dance Bites interview to do.

14th February 1998, London
I rush down to the front door to check the post. No deluge of valentine cards, unless they have all gone to the Opera House. There was just one waiting for me at Barons Court (I'm not even sure it was a valentine) with a cryptic message: 'Is she kind as she is fair? For beauty lives with kindness.' It surely can't be from anyone at work, as they would realise that in truth I'm much kinder than I am fair. Generally, in rehearsal, I'm not fair at all. I turn up looking like an old dog. It had me flummoxed for quite a while, my brain spinning to recall where I've seen the handwriting before. And then I remembered.

After my two-day excursion up north, I was thrown back into the thick of things to make up for lost time. Kathy Bennetts, a tiny Australian from Bill Forsythe's company in Frankfurt, is here to rehearse *in the middle*, and once again, I realise how wonderful it is to get information about a work from someone who is steeped in its style. Kathy travels all over the world teaching Bill's ballets, and she has a real skill at passing on corrections without implying that the initial attempt was dire. Having her here reminds me how difficult the transference of physical knowledge is without human contact. You can learn the steps from a combination of video and dance notation, but that's a bit like learning to speak a language phonetically, with no idea about what the words actually mean. And as a learning tool, both video and notation have their drawbacks; most performances and rehearsals contain errors – it's a rare show indeed when absolutely everything goes according to plan and you aren't forced, at some point, to make compromises. Take *Rite of Spring*, for instance. The video archives contain two versions, one from the sixties, of Monica Mason, who created the role. This one is undoubtedly correct (Monica is about the only person who could give a consistently accurate performance) but aside from the authentically grainy sixties quality, it fails to take into account any changes Kenneth MacMillan made in the choreography between then and his death, in 1992. The later version, from our last revival, is of a stage rehearsal where the dancer can only be described as 'losing it'. Stravinsky's music is complicated at the best of times, but on a bad day . . .

Dance notation, such as the Benesh system we use, is obviously less prone (though not immune) to error, as it isn't subject to the 'single chance' syndrome. The notator works in pencil until they're sure they've got it right, and the eraser is a wonderful thing. But although notation can record movement perfectly, neither video nor notation can convey the impetus and the intellectual stimulation behind the movement, and so often this is what makes it interesting. It's like the difference between a straightforward reading of a story, and an interpretative rendition of it. One is just words, the other draws you in and forces you to live, for a brief time, inside someone else's head. Certainly for the dancer, the difference between doing something 'because you're told to' and doing it for what could be a mass of other reasons – emotional, intellectual or physical – is huge. In three days, Bill's choreography has gone from being fun to being fascinating. And I am considered (not by Bill, I'm sure) to be something of a local expert where his choreography is concerned. I've worked with him on and off for about seven years, dancing in all three of the Forsythe works that The Royal Ballet has in its repertoire – *Herman Schmerman*, *middle*, and *Steptext*. Imagine how it must feel for a dancer who has never worked with Bill before. Of course, it might be that as it's new, it's interesting anyway, but I doubt it. Forsythe choreography without thought behind it can become a bit of a knees-up, and just kicking your legs around is fun for about five minutes.

Kathy's presence in the studio has helped to give our work intellectual muscle.

Despite these long rehearsal days, I fitted in two very different evenings at the theatre. On Thursday I went down to Croydon, to the Fairfield Hall, to hear one of my nephews and my niece in the Bromley Borough Schools' Prom. I'm becoming a regular there. Last year my niece was singing at the same event and this dutiful aunt went down to hear her. It's an extraordinary evening – five hundred children on the stage making live music, both in their own groups and as part of a very impressive whole. As they ranged from age six to sixteen, the standards were variable, but to me, and to all the other relatives who packed the hall, this was of course the least important thing. What really mattered was the experience, the discipline involved to get the music up to standard, the dependence on others to create something worth listening to, the sense of achievement when after months of rehearsals, there was an end product of which they could rightly be proud. Last year they sang *Captain Noah and his Floating Zoo*, a Joseph Horowitz composition which I sang at White Lodge over twenty years ago. (And I remembered most of the words. Wouldn't it be useful if we could wipe our own internal hard drive from time to time?) We were accompanied back then by our excellent, kilt-clad, Scottish music teacher, Alistair Cameron, but in Croydon, they boasted none other than the eighty-something-year-old Mr Horowitz himself at the piano.

The Bromley Borough Schools' Prom should be required viewing for Education Minister David Blunkett and his cabinet colleagues. No one in the Fairfield Hall on Thursday could possibly doubt the importance of musical (and artistic) education and the benefits it brings to children above and beyond the ability to simply 'strum a tune'.

There were some wonderfully touching moments as these young people struggled to harmonise together, particularly the little blonde girl who played with the Princes Plain Primary School Steel Band. She started off with a huge grin on her face, but as the piece progressed, the grin appeared to alter into a grimace. My sister and I couldn't decide whether she had a cold, or whether she was crying. We settled for the cold, but when the piece finished, her teacher (and conductor) gave her a big, sympathetic hug. After a few seconds of exchanged whispers, it transpired that her drums had been mounted the wrong way round; her left hand was having to play the right drum, and vice versa. I'm not sure if it crossed her mind that turning her back on the audience would automatically put the situation to rights – after all, she *was* only about six. She just bravely struggled on through her tears and made it to the end. Needless to say, when the news broke, she got the biggest round of applause of the evening, and the audience demanded that she was given a second chance. She smiled as if her cheeks would burst.

It's curious and heartwarming, this British ability to sympathise when people (even six-year-olds) refuse to be beaten by circumstance. I was reminded of Niccy Tranah, on the first night of *Giselle* in Hammersmith, when every time she put her foot on the floor it slid from beneath her. Despite the excellence of the rest of the cast, the audience saved their loudest cheers for Niccy.

Last night, at the opposite extreme of individual artistry, I saw the penultimate West End performance of Antony Sher in *Cyrano*. I saw an *Omnibus* programme about this back in October. David Bintley choreographed *Cyrano* for us a few years ago, but it somehow failed to establish itself into the repertoire. What I didn't realise then, and nor did I get this from the Gerard Depardieu film, was just how very funny it is. Certainly in this production, by Gregory Doran, it was an evening of extreme emotions, from ribald laughter to tearing regret. Sher gave a searing performance – something to be treasured.

But it took me a while to make the adjustments needed to watch live theatre rather than dead television. The first ten minutes had me fidgety and restless, unable to narrow my focus to the level where words rather than actions can be absorbed and understood. So much of television and film engages us because of what we see – who does what to whom. Even the wordiest of books – *Howards End*, for instance – are translated on to film as a story of events, things that happen on the outside, rather than a story of ideas, things that happen on the inside. If you're reared on a diet of smash hits and blockbusters, the subtler delights of a concept brilliantly embroidered with mental rather than physical fireworks will have a very hard time making any sort of impact at all.

A sudden quandary has been thrown in my way, and I'm forced to play mental games with myself as I try to decide whether or not to apply for the soon-to-be-vacant position of Director of the Royal Ballet School. Dame Merle Park, after being in charge for fifteen years, has reached retirement age, and I'm being lobbied from various corners to 'throw my hat in the ring'. I'm told that one person has already said publicly that I will be the person who takes over. I'm in so many minds about it, and the old habit of prevarication is crippling me. Why do I find it so hard to make a decision on this? Surely I should be able to choose one option over the other? The problem probably lies in the fact that where my career is concerned, I've never really had to make decisions. I've simply rolled down a pre-ordained route from White Lodge, through the Upper School and into the company, where I remain. In my outside life, I take decisions regularly and feel very comfortable about it. Public roles don't seem to pose problems. It's those little life choices that do. Give me the pick of two equally attractive outfits, for instance, and I'm pained with indecision. Sweaty palms, palpitations, does my bum look big in this, and so on. Other 'decisions' – writing books or speaking at the Oxford Union, for instance – were not choices between two options, unless you count not writing books and not speaking at Oxford as options. They were invitations that I either accepted or refused. I'm now at the point of thinking that I should at least *apply* for Dame Merle's job, so that the decision takes on reality. What to do? I call my friend David and use him as a sounding board.

Of course, it isn't just about taking on a new job. It's about giving up the old one. I have only ever danced, and even while I have momentarily been a 'bestselling author', I have still known that at the root of it all, I am a dancer. It's how I define myself, and the first time that dancing was temporarily withdrawn (through injury) I lost more than physical ability. I lost my identity and sense of worth. Back then, in the early nineties, I couldn't have begun to contemplate a life without dancing. What I did was entwined with who I was. Now, partly because I have so many other interesting things to do, I can *contemplate* a life away from the stage, but it's very hard to know just how much I'll miss it until it's gone.

I live my life by two strangely connected codes of conduct; an overarching sense of justice, and the tummy feeling. I don't think the former will help here. Applying or not applying would both be equally 'just' actions. But the second might give me some clues to which route I should go down. If I can seriously contemplate shifting careers, taking on the responsibility of educating the next generation of dancers and not feel that sickness in my stomach which signals unease, it might be the right thing for me to do.

16th February 1998, London
So today the *Guardian* runs an article entitled 'Top Pay At Crisis Opera House'. It complains that in the financial year leading up to closure,

salary levels at the 'crisis-torn' Royal Opera House were far higher than at similar arts institutions. *Similar* arts institutions? Like which? Does it make the comparison with truly similar arts institutions worldwide, Milan's La Scala, The Paris Opéra, or New York's Met, for instance? You bet it doesn't. Instead it tells us that thirty-three people at the Opera House last year received salaries in excess of £50,000.

Let me just say straight away that I am not amongst the lucky thirty-three, but can we take a reality check here? This is the week that Ruud Gullit, ex-Manager of Chelsea Football Club, tried (and admittedly failed) to get his salary increased to £38,461 a *week*. In the plethora of press coverage that ensued, *The Times* published a list of weekly salaries: Bernie Ecclestone (Formula One) receives £1.04 million a week, Jim Fifield (Chairman, EMI Music) gets £110,000, Alan Shearer's footballing skills earn him £70,000, and the *average* premier league player takes home £6,350. Per *week*.

Does no one else see a discrepancy here? The Royal Opera House is at the top of the premier league of arts institutions, countable on the fingers of one hand; The Royal Ballet is the Formula One of the dance world. Its employees and its managers should be well above average. How are we supposed to attract top-class administrators to look after the place if the salaries are not in line with the real, commercial world? Who is going to come and manage the Opera House for a tiny *fraction* of the money they could expect for running a similar enterprise in the private sector? Does it make sense for the *Guardian* to complain on its front page that they're not up to the job, and then, a week later, suggest that the Opera House's management team should, between them, take home less than a single, average, football player? I don't think so.

And how are we going to retain the cream of talent if artists aren't rewarded at the sort of levels they could expect to earn abroad? A dancer's life, like that of a champion footballer, is pitiably short. Could you blame any of our leading dancers if they finally decided to give in and accept the tempting offers they regularly receive from companies abroad?

Talking of tempting offers; in the end I avoided, once again, having to actually *make a decision*. I came home during the afternoon (hours away from the final deadline) still undecided about whether or not to send in an application to the recruitment agency dealing with the appointment of the new Director of the Royal Ballet School. For some reason I decided that before I did so (delaying tactics) I would return a call I'd received last week from a person whose name was unfamiliar. Call me psychic, but who else could it have been but the agency, contacting me about the position. So, a decision deferred yet again.

At work, we're about to embark on the Dance Bites tour, with a repertoire which is mostly very modern and very Deborah Bull. My work-load depends entirely on the programme we're doing at any given point. If we're performing a triple bill of contemporary work for instance, I'm likely to be dancing in one or two of the pieces. Ten years ago I would have been involved in all three. I no longer perform at all in some of the big, popular classics. These days, I'm only involved with the warhorses if I dance the leading role. As ballet regulars will be aware, although I dance Odette/Odile in *Swan Lake* and Aurora in *Beauty*, the other big ballets are not in my repertoire. I've grown used to having more free hours in the week to deal with all my other commitments; teaching, writing, Board memberships and a lot of speaking, but at the moment, with Dance Bites about to be served, I'm dancing for six or eight hours a day. It's playing havoc with my other life, but I am, nevertheless, enjoying it; dancing is still what I do before everything else.

Middle is still not quite polished to performance level, but with Kathy Bennetts' help it's come on leaps and bounds in the last few days. It's not stamina that I'm lacking, just familiarity. Dancing a new role is a bit like learning a new language. I've got to the point where I'm pretty accurate on the grammar and the pronunciation is passable, but I'm just not fluent yet, and my accent leaves a lot to be desired. I'm dancing *middle* like I speak Norwegian, and I'm not happy about it. *Nei. Det er ikke så godt.* Rehearsing it is the only thing that will help, and we have three more days, and three more full calls. My toes are firmly crossed (which probably isn't helping at all).

17th February 1998, London
I'm beginning to hear rumblings around Barons Court about an upcoming *World in Action* television exposé of the Royal Ballet School. Presumably this is Act Two of the press fiesta that surrounded last May's dismissal of Linda Goss, a teacher at White Lodge.

'They' have already been in touch with several girls from one particular graduating year – all of them classmates of an unhappy student whose parents were vociferously outspoken on the Linda Goss episode. Unfortunately it doesn't seem as if 'they' are terribly interested in portraying a balanced picture. No one has contacted successful graduates of the school, nor the several thousand unsuccessful graduates who would regard their time at White Lodge as a transforming experience and some of the best years of their lives. And although the producers have been offered the opportunity to give another side of the story – wheel in Deborah Bull on behalf of the pro-White Lodgers – my phone has not yet rung.

As with every other area of life, the question of 'correctness' has interesting ramifications in a training establishment like the Royal Ballet School. Let me say straight away that I am absolutely *not* in favour of bullying. But I think we have to look carefully at what bullying is. If a child is told off three times by the same teacher for misbehaving, is that bullying? Is that harassment? In my day, it most definitely was not. No child likes being told off – it's humiliating and embarrassing precisely because it brings home to the child the fact that his or her behaviour really is unacceptable. But when I was at school, there was no question of running off, crying 'harassment'. I'd misbehaved, and I'd been reminded of it. End of story. Nowadays, in our increasingly litigious society, children (and their parents) are all too conscious of telephone hotlines and bodies set up with the sole purpose of receiving complaints.

And of course there is the added complication that most of the children who go through the school will not achieve what they (or their parents) so desperately want. Professional contracts are few and far between; in the year I graduated, I was the only one of a dozen talented girls to be offered work with The Royal Ballet. Bitterness, in such cases, would not be out of place.

Well-intentioned outsiders, in an effort to support the school, like to offer a defence theory. They say that in order to achieve the heights of perfection that world-class ballet dancing demands, there is no option but to push students right to the limits of their endurance. There is sometimes an unspoken inference that a little bit of bullying might actually be acceptable. I completely disagree: I was never bullied, yet I worked like the original little Trojan to constantly, constantly improve. I did it because I wanted to, and what's more, I was surrounded by plenty of others with the same ambitions. The school is packed to the gills with girls and boys who are there because they *want* to be there, because they are driven to dance. Where that resolve is so great, there's no need to bully. It's more like turning a tap. No pressure, just a gentle touch, and out pour endless quantities of enthusiasm and dedication. And if the student does not have that resolve, the only people at fault are the parents who have sent a less than willing child to a school which never promises to be anything but demanding.

I fear that the *World in Action* programme will do White Lodge a damaging disservice and portray it in a completely unfair light. And when it hits the fan, we'll all need protective clothing. Oh, you can already see the links forming in the public mind: White Lodge – child abuse, Covent Garden – financial abuse. The abuse of power in these élite art forms.

19th February 1998, London

Thursday, and my friends at Rolls-Royce are on alert. I am still in constant communication with Richard Charlesworth, Head of Public Affairs, as I've been invited to help launch the Silver Seraph at a further series of big events; customer and 'society' launches around the world, and the biggest trade show of them all, the Geneva Motor Show in March. Today, Richard was hassled. An American auto magazine had leaked details of the Silver Seraph, still cloaked in mystery, not only giving away its name and its vital statistics, but blowing the cover on the new Bentley Arnage into the bargain. The New York bureau of London's *Times* picked up on the story and the motoring correspondent was forced to follow suit and leak as well. Inevitably, it made front page news. Apparently the American magazine got hold of the details from a dealer who had, on request, simply faxed them over to the reporter. Since we've all been sitting on the story for months and not telling a soul, it does seem a letdown. The embargo is due to be lifted in only ten days' time. In some ways it isn't surprising; everyone at the Opera House who knows about my special relationship with Rolls-Royce has been amazed that such a secret could have been kept under wraps when every sneeze at Covent Garden is echoed in the headlines. The world may now know the name of the car in advance of its public unveiling in Geneva, but what they have yet to find out is that my name is linked to it. Deborah Bull *is* the Silver Seraph.

At work today we had the final dress rehearsal of the Dance Bites programmes, and on Monday we take to the road; Sheffield, Blackpool, Bath and High Wycombe and a day trip to Geneva thrown in just for me.

It's all finally coming together. Despite Jonathan Cope's optimism about his rate of recovery from a very long illness, it was decided that it was unwise for him to rush back to partner me in Cathy Marston's piece, *Words Apart*. I'll be dancing, as I thought, with Chris Saunders. At this first showing to the rest of the company, Cathy's creation received lots of peer praise, the kind that's hardest to get, and highest in value to a performer. (It's not always the hardest to come by – there are invariably kind words for a débutante or an underdog, but when you get to my ripe old age, people tend to imagine you don't need the kudos any longer. You're one of a kennel of top dogs, and people usually only comment when they think something is exceptionally fine.) So soloist Peter Abegglen's 'your butt looks great in that costume' was much appreciated.

I'm gradually getting my legs around *middle*, and we have one more chance to run it before the first night. I shall use the rehearsal to try to tone down the effort a little. There is always a tendency to force your way through unfamiliar steps – not unlike that dreadful habit of speaking louder to foreigners in the belief that it will somehow help them to understand more clearly what you're trying to say. Unfortunately, I think I'm a much better dancer when I relax a bit. One of my best ballet teachers, Nancy Kilgour, said exactly the same thing to me when I was about fifteen. 'Deborah,' she said, 'you're a much better dancer when you don't try so hard.' Twenty years on, and I'm still trying hard to put Nancy's advice into practice.

In the afternoon I popped in to see Pat Kavanagh at Peters, Fraser and Dunlop, with a view to discussing what might come next in my life. It always makes me smile to say 'my agent'. The word conjures up visions of a grand Diaghilev figure negotiating an increased pointe shoe allowance, whereas in fact, unlike other dancers, I've never had a 'dance' agent in my life. Pat is my literary agent, and I suppose it's interesting that I should be discussing my future with her and not the ballet Board. She asked if I had any interest in choreography, and I started to make my excuses: 'Well, not really, I mean I *have* thought about it but really I'm not convinced . . .' She stopped me. 'It's all right, Deborah. You're allowed to have *one* thing you don't want to do.'

Talking of Boards, yesterday I had the chance to meet Lord Eatwell, the new Chairman of the ballet Board, and the Opera House's recently appointed Chairman, Sir Colin Southgate. Along with Vivien Duffield, Chair of the Opera House Trust, and Michael Berkeley, the composer, the sole survivors of the Select Committee's December report, these four make up the complete Royal Opera House Board at the moment. There are plans to enlarge it (whilst guarding against too unwieldy a group) and in a full company meeting, Lord Eatwell was interested to hear whether we dancers had any thoughts about possible appointments. He's particularly interested in having younger representation, and in an open defence of the people I admire who are over fifty, I felt compelled to suggest that being old doesn't necessarily prevent you from having young ideas. It's nice we were consulted, but I'm wary of the concept of governing by opinion polls. I always hope that there are people around whose ideas are *better* than mine. And in the absence of anything like the real subsidy necessary to run an opera house, I am also conscious of the need for the Board to be able fund-raisers. I know we don't like that idea, but we have to face reality. Where would our future lie without the millions of private pounds which former Board members have conjured up from various sources? Some people might find this type of talk distasteful, but the beauty of this patronage is that those millions of pounds (or the bricks and mortar they purchase) automatically become public funds, making the Opera House available to everyone, whether they pay fifty quid or a fiver for the pleasure. This is one of those economic tricks of light which people who decry élitism fail to see.

20th February 1998, London
At last a cessation in the media's hostilities against the House. Perhaps a truce is in sight? Unlikely. Richard Morrison's article in today's *Times* may not signal a total ceasefire, but it demonstrates an unforeseen streak of humanity in the ranks of the Opera House's massed persecutors.

He opens by asking that we at last consign to history an episode which, however good, bad or ugly it may have been, has come and gone. 'At some stage, the people who really care about musical life in Britain start to resent the endless sniping at this easy target by MPs who are themselves mostly abject under-achievers. What happened at Covent Garden last year is history. It stank, but it's over.' He goes on to suggest that we now switch our attention to the future, and proceeds to give some sensible and interesting thoughts on what that future might (or could) hold.

In his diagnosis, what the place lacks is a charismatic figurehead, an artistic leader of 'compelling vision' who will point the way forward. He may be right, but remember that such a person has to be found at the bargain basement price of under £50,000 a year. So if that person is out there and looking for a change of job, let's keep our fingers crossed that they've taken the arts world vow of poverty.

Never mind that Morrison completely and utterly in seven

(admittedly short) columns ignores the very existence of The Royal Ballet (most people do). Never mind that he completely ignores the existence of ballet altogether. He offers sympathy, reason and a kind word, and I shall include him in my prayers from here on in. (Unless, of course, he slides back into the media slough of despond.)

Come to think of it, I've met Richard Morrison before. Two years ago, in Norway, The Royal Ballet opened the Festspillene i Bergen with three performances of Twyla Tharp's *Mr Worldly Wise*. The *Festspillene* is a big date on the Bergen calendar, and the Bergensere don national costume, the *bunad*, in its honour. It was the first time the company had performed in Norway since the fifties, and we went down a storm. Morrison was there to report on our triumph. At a luncheon given the day after the opening by the British Ambassador to Norway, Torje (dressed splendidly in his *bunad*, vaguely military and very formal, offset by a jaunty red waistcoat) was seated next to Richard Morrison. When Morrison's column appeared the following week, it mentioned the ballet performance only in passing. The rest of it was devoted to a description of Torje's splendid outfit, and their exchange about his unusual work, attending to the health and fitness of Britain's most famous rock star, Mick Jagger. Morrison isn't quite sure if this is Norwegian humour, and wonders whether he should respond with '. . . and I am Keith Richards' personal chaplain'.

25th February 1998, London
Dance Bites has me in its jaws. Today I'm back in London after two days in Sheffield, catching my breath before I head off tomorrow morning to Blackpool, where the tour continues. I've survived the busiest two days of the schedule, and it should be easier from here on. (As long as you don't include the 'mad dogs and Englishmen' dash to the Geneva Motor Show next week between performances in Bath. I know that sounds crazy. Just wait for it to come.)

Torje (home for a brief weekend before heading off for Tokyo via, of all places, Guyana) came with me to Sheffield on Monday morning. I must confess I hadn't realised just how far it is to Sheffield. I thought it was about two hours – I think anywhere in the UK can be reached in about two hours – and I took a deep breath when I looked at the map and discovered it was more like four. So we left home earlier than I wanted to, at about 8 a.m., and even so, arrived with only minutes to spare before class began. I found the theatre at 12.57 p.m., checked into the 'Fonteyn' dressing-room (honestly, that's its name) and was in class by 1.00 p.m.

The Lyceum Theatre in Sheffield is beautiful – a gorgeously restored Victorian gem, with modern dressing-rooms added on in the past couple of decades. It works well, both front and back of house, giving the artists and the audience the best of their respective worlds. But in common with most theatres in the UK (I am ashamed to include London's Royal Festival Hall here) it doesn't have a good enough rehearsal studio. There is actually a room at the Lyceum to rehearse in, but the floor is best quality concrete covered in ultra-shiny lino. Not the best combination for dance – too hard for jumping and too slippery for pointe shoes – and I restricted myself to barre and a stretch.

As always, the first day of the tour is the hardest, involving a stage rehearsal in the afternoon as well as a performance in the evening. As soon as class was over, we all had to get into full costume and make-up for the press photographers. Well, I would have got into full make-up, if there hadn't been a mix-up with the shoe bags. When I pulled mine out of the wicker skip, it contained some mouldy old cards, a tutu signed by Jennifer Penney and 18-year-old dessicated make-up sticks. I knew this might happen when I packed up my Opera House dressing-room back in May at the closing of the House. Somewhere, there is a bag full of the stuff I need. Out of necessity, and raiding the make-up in my handbag, I went for the 'heavy day' look, more supermodel than ballerina.

This double dose of dancing, rehearsal followed closely by performance, makes for a long day indeed, and I don't really approve of using up the energy stores hours before a show. But the choreographers obviously wanted to see their new pieces on stage for the first time, so there was no choice but to dance Cathy Marston's piece, *Words Apart* full out. The rehearsal gave us a chance to get used to performing here. I had forgotten that the Lyceum has a raked stage. At the Opera House, it is flat, as are most of the theatres we dance in. Consequently, when we come to a theatre which is raked, you suffer something akin to a bad case of seasickness, hangover and jet lag rolled into one. You really do feel in the middle, somewhat elevated, and out of sorts. We're only talking about a slight gradient here – it's hardly a 1:1. But it's amazing how a little adjustment at ground level alters your sense of balance. The body can get used to anything though, and by Tuesday evening's show I was feeling almost at home. Which is not a bad thing. It will stand me in good stead for the second half of this week, up at the Blackpool Grand. Now *that* is a rake and a half. It's a bit like dancing on the slopes of Gstaad, and makes Sheffield seem as flat as Norfolk. I'm being extra careful on this unfamiliar territory, as rakes can reawaken dormant injuries.

The first night had its fair share of traumas and company casualties, one back spasm and one twisted ankle, and by Tuesday afternoon we had lost two dancers from the cast of *middle*. As it happens, they were dancing together, so we could do a straight swap with the second cast. That meant that Jenny Tattersall, a second year *corps de ballet* dancer, was thrown on in her first solo role with the minimum of rehearsal and, fortunately, the maximum of cool. It's not an easy piece to dance in the best of conditions and with full preparation. It requires technical strength and a mature confidence. But Jenny took the stage as if she'd been dancing the ballet for years. It was lovely to watch, and if I'd been wearing a hat, I would definitely have taken it off to her.

Tuesday as a whole wasn't any easier than Monday. We had two shows, matinée and evening, and because the assembled dance press were stopping off in Sheffield to review us on their way back from the première of Northern Ballet's *The Hunchback of Notre Dame* in Leeds, the first cast danced in both performances. A tough day, coming as it did after Monday's double effort. But there were no new casualties to add to the injury list, and at 10.30 p.m. Torje and I hit the road for another four-hour drive, back to London. A bit of a diversion, considering my next date is north of here, in Blackpool, on Thursday. But various people have been trying to arrange meetings with me and Wednesday was the only day this week I could guarantee would be clear. Several Little Chefs later, and relying on caffeine, we arrived home at 3 p.m., exhausted.

Four hours later I was up and driving Torje to Victoria Station. He is flying off to Guyana, and as I have a day off, I would have liked to take him all the way to the Gatwick to spend more time with him. But Michael Berkeley, who is interviewing me for Radio 3's *Private Passions*, has been called to an emergency Opera House Board meeting, forcing him to shift our appointment forward. I don't like the sound of unscheduled Board meetings. Something must be about to break.

27th February 1998, Blackpool
A night off in Blackpool. The mind boggles at the prospect of what I might do with it and settles eventually on the safe option of an evening in my room at the Imperial Hotel, a cold M & S supper and a chance to catch up with some writing. Oh, the glamour of touring.

I took the train up here yesterday morning, another four-hour journey, but it seemed a much better idea than driving. I love my little red car (*min røde bil*, as Torje and I call it) but I don't like to take it for long motorway trips on my own. I trust it completely not to break down, but I don't trust my own ability to stay focused for several hundred miles at the wheel. So fellow dancer Chris Saunders and I met at Euston and arrived in Blackpool at 2.15 p.m., fifteen minutes after the class started. Had we taken the earlier train, getting us here in time for class, the fare would have been about £130. By leaving an hour later, the fare dropped by an incredible £100, to £33. A breakthrough discovery; not only does it make more sense *physiologically* to warm up closer to the show, it also saves you money on British Rail. That doesn't excuse their bizarrely confusing tariffs.

After Wednesday's bright and brilliant sunshine, the hailstorm that met us at Blackpool was a bit of a shock. This week, it really is grim up north. The sea is a furious grey mass – bubbling stew and dumplings – and the wind is sharp as a knife. It makes me shiver to think what Radio 4's shipping forecast will sound like tonight. Like Sheffield, Blackpool boasts another gem of a theatre, but this time, the audience get a better deal than the artists. The dressing-rooms are reminiscent of old Covent Garden, cramped, suspect décor, dodgy plumbing, so naturally we all feel perfectly at home. And the raked stage is downhill all the way. For some reason I seem to have got used to dancing on the *piste*, as the show was the best yet. Hardly an ideal preparation, four hours on a BR train, but I must have done something right, as it all worked beautifully. And today's local paper called me a 'statuesque centrepiece' and a 'pin-up principal'. More, more, I love it.

The national papers (at least the ones I read) concentrated on yesterday's surprise announcement that Keith Cooper (Director of Sales and Broadcasting) and Richard Hall (Director of Finance) have been sacked from the Opera House. Richard Hall is a relatively new figure on the scene. In fact for the best part of a year, the House was without a Finance Director, a condition which received special censoring from Gerald Kaufman. Keith, on the other hand, has been around for quite some time in a variety of guises. He came to us from English National Opera and the Coliseum, where his innovative marketing campaigns had attracted all the right sort of attention. His major starring role at Covent Garden was in the television series *The House*, when he dismissed an employee on camera and split the viewing nation into Keith Cooper lovers, the minority, and haters, the majority. He then moved sideways, from 'Director of Corporate Affairs' to 'Sales and Broadcasting'. Title changes like this are often a sign of instability in one's foothold in a big organisation like the House. But his dismissal has come as a total surprise to us all. No one up in Blackpool knew anything about it, and I guess it explains the extraordinary Board meeting on Wednesday, and why my appointment was rescheduled with Michael Berkeley, one of the House's non-executive quartet.

I also read in today's paper that the average Manchester United fan spends £1,374 annually on his match tickets and merchandise habit. £1,374 a year? £115 a month? Does that take football supporting into the realms of élitism? You could see at least two ballet performances a week for that kind of money, and still have change for a 'Gotta Dance' T-shirt and a pint on the way home.

March 1998

Another stopover at home and a chance to do a quick batch of whites and coloureds before I head off again, this time to Bath. It is Sunday. A day of rest. I had only two appointments: the first was a rehearsal at two o'clock at the Royal College of Music for Tuesday's 'away day' to Geneva, where the new Rolls-Royce Silver Seraph will be launched. At Ackergill, back in January, I was accompanied by just four musicians. This time the performance has developed into a two-course offering, Aaron Copland's *Fanfare for the Common Man*, followed by Handel's 'Let the Bright Seraphim', and I have a singer, four brass players and three percussionists behind me. How very exciting. I guess we're going to have to make a fair amount of noise to quell the thronging motoring masses and the swimsuit lasses in Geneva, but I can advise against being in a rehearsal space 20 by 10 feet with that much decibel power going through you. My ears are ringing six hours after the rehearsal. I do feel extremely proud that I will be the person who reveals the Seraph to the world. (OK, I know it's been leaked, but I don't count that. Tuesday is her birthday and I am the muse who will summon her to life.)

At about 3 p.m. the door burst open and a breathless trumpeter came in. 'Bloody countryside march,' he swore, then took off his jacket to reveal a full Metropolitan Police uniform. He had been delayed by a spot of trouble amongst the quarter-million people and the 80,000 Range Rovers which had converged on London today to draw attention to the plight of the countryside. I haven't quite worked out how he manages to be both a serving officer as well as a student at the RCM, but he sure plays a mean trumpet.

Unfortunately I ran into trouble with the countryside march too. I left the college in South Kensington at 3.30 p.m., imagining (oh, foolishness) that I could cross the park and be home by 4 p.m. It's not, in the normal course of things, an unreasonable timetable, but it didn't take into account that there were a quarter-million extra Barbours (and their wearers) in town today. I was diverted via wherever it was they had all come from, and arrived home closer to 5 p.m. One photograph later, for the *Sunday Times* column, 'My Hols', and the evening was mine.

3rd March 1998, Bath – Geneva – Bath

The last thirty hours have been an exercise in how to live life dangerously. This exceptional year in the life of The Royal Ballet hasn't exactly been overloaded with performances, but unfortunately, Rolls-Royce chose to launch the Silver Seraph in Geneva on one of the few days that we have a matinée *and* an evening show – in Bath. Jeanetta Laurence and Anthony Dowell, against all their better instincts, generously agreed to look the other way and allow me to fly to Geneva on Tuesday morning, having danced in Bath the night before – as long as I was back in Bath, in the same theatre, for the performance at 7.30 p.m. – that evening.

This hard-to-believe (and even harder to achieve) itinerary required military precision and was at the absolute mercy of air traffic control in the air space between Geneva and London. Now I fly a lot, but this one even has *me* shaking my head in disbelief. It all started yesterday lunchtime, when I drove down to Bath with Niccy Tranah. On the way, my ever faithful Mazda developed a suspicious-sounding rattle. As I will be out of circulation during working hours tomorrow, I abandoned it at Niccy's hotel in Bath's Royal Crescent, in the hope that she might have some time to get it fixed. As usual, there was a stage call in the afternoon, and I spent the hour or so between rehearsal and performance reciting the mantra of the travelling guest artist: shoes, tights, costume, wings (this one is optional), hair-piece, head-dress, ribbons, pins, bobbins and bows, up and down the body until I was certain I couldn't have left anything out. One extra item which is rarely required – double-sided tape. My Seraph costume was made in a bit of a hurry, and it doesn't quite fit; the strapless bodice has a tendency to travel south. The endlessly helpful staff at Ackergill tried all manner of tinkering and tightening, but so that the car was the *only* thing to be revealed in performance, I resorted to using double-sided sticky tape, and securing the costume in place with a strip of tape just above my right breast. It worked like a dream. It left a raw bruise, but the skin grew back, eventually.

After Monday night's performance at about 10.30 p.m., I leave the stage door, tucked down an alleyway at the side of the theatre, expecting to find a waiting minicab which had been arranged to take me to

Heathrow. To save time tomorrow, I will stay at the airport overnight and take the first flight to Geneva in the morning. There, at the end of the passage, stands a Bentley in midnight blue. Feeling like Mathilde Kschessinska, Russia's grandest ballerina and mistress to Tsar Nicholas II, I settle into the back seat, fondle all the gadgets and chat on the phone all the way to the airport hotel. I check into my room at the Edwardian Radisson, blowing the fuse so all the lights refuse to operate and with it blowing my cover as the glamorous ballerina. It takes all the concentration I can muster to force myself to go to sleep. Even then I wake up three hours later, full of excitement at the trip ahead. When the alarm beeps rudely at 6 a.m., I look more like the back end of a bus than the ornamental front of a Rolls-Royce.

The outbound flight goes smoothly and according to plan. Above the clouds, the light turns out to be perfect for doing my make-up. The schedule is tight, tight, tight, and there's not a moment to lose. We land in Geneva on time. One down, one return flight to go. If I don't make it back in time for the show in Bath tonight, the company will never let me do anything quite so hairbrained again. Sometime during the journey, I finally start to accept that I really *am* going to Geneva. It has all been such a spider's web of ifs and buts that right up to the last minute I expected my mobile phone to ring with the news from Bath that somebody's ankle or back had gone and I had to return posthaste. But when I left the theatre last night I checked that everyone was in fine form; I can only hope they woke up in the same state this morning.

In Geneva, another Bentley, this one deepest burgundy and chauffeured by an elegant young man with strikingly aristocratic hands, delivered me across the road from the airport to the Expo Hall. It was all working out so far. The hall is a vast and amazing place and, unlike similar events at home which would sport spunky titles like 'Motor 98', this one is elegantly styled '*68ème salon international de l'auto*'. I have only once been to anything remotely similar, when I went to see a pre-production version of my little *røde bil* at the Earls Court Motor Show. I can't say I enjoyed it – an alien world of fast food and shell suits. But *le salon* was fairly civilised, although I suppose it does help to be whisked past security and on to the Rolls-Royce stand. The stand itself was wonderfully sparse, in marked contrast to the bustling and gaudy displays of the other manufacturers with their scantily clad girls on bonnets. At one end was a raised stage where the new arrival lurked shyly behind modesty screens. The empty floor space would soon be invaded by hundreds of photographers who were waiting nearby, cameras focused and lying in wait for the clock to strike one. I had the inevitable shock of seeing for myself just how little of the stage is left when you agree to share it with a Rolls-Royce weighing in at two and a quarter tonnes, but in true professional style I walked the course and worked out where adjustments would have to be made in the choreography so that I will walk and not limp into the theatre in Bath this evening. At Ackergill, the Seraph was hidden at the rear of the stage; here in Geneva it was draped in silk and placed centrally on a revolve which would eventually tilt to 35 degrees and continue to rotate the car at that precarious angle. My task was to make the dance work, no matter how or by what means, despite the fact that the revolve mechanism left a sizeable and dangerous gap between one half of the stage and the other. I saw there was a challenge ahead and set about solving it.

Richard Charlesworth took me to my changing-room and warm-up area: a stock cupboard about 2 by 4 feet, with a corridor cleared between the boxes where, if I really held my turn-out, I could manage a full *plié* in second. It's a good job they signed me and not Pavarotti, as he wouldn't have made it through the door. I warmed up like Nijinsky in *L'Après-midi d'un faune*, all hieroglyphic and in flat relief. Just before one o'clock, Joanne Lunn (the singer) and I took the stage. A gong called the crowd to attention. You could feel the anticipation swelling in the hall, and even before we moved, the flash guns were hard at work. The fanfare sounded its opening theme and I swung round into the first of several 'spirit of ecstasy' poses, to an accompanying chorus of photographer's motor drives. We were off. Yesterday, at the obligatory decibel monitoring session which took place while I was in Bath, the percussionists were nudging the levels of acceptability even though they were doing little more than lightly tapping their instruments. They wisely avoided playing them full out. Today, unfettered by authority, they let rip. The hall filled with the spine-tingling splendour that only live music can provide. All the chattering stopped. Dancing over the cracks in the stage felt a bit like crossing a glacier, but I was told afterwards I looked so self-assured that no one doubted the whole thing would be a triumph. They obviously didn't notice my downcast eyes, studiously measuring my every step. To quote the American ballerina, Merrill Ashley, 'so it works to paint eyeballs on your eyelids, then.' My final task was to change from muse to midwife, unfurling the silk shroud and unveiling the Seraph, bottom first, in an automotive breach birth.

The audience loved it; it's weird that this inconsequential trade-show appearance between my performances in Bath will put me on more front pages and television stations than anything else I am ever likely to do.

At the end of it all, the photographers wanted me back in what is fast becoming my trademark pose. I *bourréed* myself into the ground, each shimmering step heavier and more painful than the last, and had a brief taste of what a life hounded by paparazzi must be like. 'Over here, darling . . . look this way, love . . . to your right . . . one more . . . give us a bit of cleavage.' All right, I made the last one up.

By 2.30 p.m. my fifteen minutes of fame was over. I was back in the burgundy Bentley with the beautiful chauffeur and heading for the airport. Now I'm *en l'air* writing it all up, and still on schedule for this evening's performance in Bath. I have a moment of panic when the captain announces that due to strong winds in London our take-off will be held up for an hour. Help! My schedule is suddenly *en l'air*. But it seems that he manages to bully Geneva's air traffic control into halving the delay, and we are now *en route* with an estimated arrival time of 4.10 p.m. If I am very unlucky the plane could be forced to chase its tail over Heathrow for a while, but *el capitain* assures us we will be on the ground no later than five. Then it's up to the midnight-blue Bentley to spirit me to the theatre in Bath by the half. I know that my alternate casts will be cursing me if I'm not there by the end of the matinée, but at the moment I have no way of getting in touch to reassure them. The sign says the use of mobile phones is not allowed.

The joke on the Rolls-Royce stand today: apparently Mercedes have had to withdraw their new, smaller model from the show as it failed the 'elk test', i.e. can the car take the evasive action necessary to avoid a stray elk and still remain upright. Apparently it couldn't. In response to the Seraph, firm, solid, and pronounced by *Autocar* today as the 'best car in the world', it's rumoured the elks have been forced to introduce a Rolls-Royce test.

4th March 1998, London
I made it to the theatre last night exactly as Carole Parkhouse, stage manager, called the half, and danced the evening performance direct from the '*68ème salon international de l'auto*'. The only gifts I managed to bring back were golden boxes of triangular Toblerone which I distributed to my alternate casts. The performance went off according to plan and afterwards, dangerously exhausted, I drove myself one more

time along the M4. Two hours this time, my trusty Mazda still rattling like a bag of loose cutlery, and back into town. I arrived home in the early hours to scribble down this close to an eventful day. My own bed, and a day off ahead. Do I have any meetings?

5th March 1998, London
I found half an hour during breakfast this morning to watch the video of Monday evening's *World in Action* exposé of the Royal Ballet School, a guaranteed fast route to indigestion. Once again I was amazed by the power of the media to distort and its clever knack of creating instant villains. The programme opened with grainy black and white images of White Lodge in the rain (or they hadn't cleaned the camera lens – it wasn't easy to tell). The voice-over said something like, 'this school costs more than Eton, and you're paying for it.' 'Oh here we go,' I thought, 'lights, camera, hatchets.' The disembodied voice continued: 'What role do anorexia, bulimia and bullying play at the Royal Ballet School?' And every time we heard those three words spoken as a whole, the 'bal' of the ballet was spat out like a sour grape.

Using evocative monochrome 'reconstructions' of dancers closing cubicle doors and opening toilet lids, filmed as though by a hidden camera, it told the story of three ex-students who had unhappy experiences at the school. The girls stayed the entire course, and if there is a story to be told then theirs is perhaps more relevant, even though I have strong doubts about the *overall* accuracy. The boy profiled stayed for two months, and described the initial audition as 'very frightening – there was a panel of eleven watching you – there were lots of people there'. Forgive me for stating the obvious, but a child that doesn't like to be watched is perhaps not ideally suited to a life on the stage.

If the programme had wanted to present a balanced picture, it would surely have talked to a greater range of dancers, ones who had succeeded, ones who hadn't, and ones who had moved on to different careers but still value the years they spent at the school. Instead it raised an important issue and then sacrificed it to the easy option of tabloid sensationalism. And using actresses to speak the alleged words of pupils at the school and 'some of Britain's most successful dancers' is a cowardly way of arguing a case if ever there was one. It struck me as fictional small-screen drama rather than responsible journalism.

But all this is predictable – after all, the mixture of lost hope and tabloid TV is a potent device we see every night on the box in the corner of the sitting-room. What was inexcusable was the participation of other professionals in the dance world, in a sort of 'ganging up' (again) against the entire Royal Ballet organisation. And the nonsense they spouted – for instance, muscles being 'built up' in the wrong shape, and this from a medical professional who should know that our muscles develop pretty much according to a genetic game plan. And as for the claim that another leading school teaches a method that has been around 'a lot longer than the Royal Ballet School', well, for the record, the Royal Ballet School currently teaches a syllabus based on the Vaganova system, a Russian teaching system which dates back just about as far as ballet (in its current form) goes.

But the final blow to the programme's credibility came with the juxtaposition of two comments; one, that it was possible to create beautiful long muscles through ballet training because they do so at the 'elsewhere' school, and two, that if things didn't change we would soon be facing a situation where the dancers in British companies would have to be supplied entirely from abroad. The irony of this, that not only are none of the leading dancers at 'elsewhere's' affiliated company trained by their school, but at the time of writing, none of them are British, was ignored.

Of course there are issues to be addressed about technique and training. Great strides are being made in the understanding of the demands of classical ballet, and newly acquired knowledge needs to be filtered through into the schools. It is this aspect of the job that most interests me about the soon-to-be-vacant Directorship of the Royal Ballet School. But *World in Action* is not the place for debate on turn-out and *tendus*, and their benefit or lack of benefit to the health of impressionable young students. It's a matter for those people who really know about these things, whichever company they are linked to.

The programme left me feeling very angry, most of all about the divisions that exist within the classical ballet establishment. Surely we would be taken more seriously, in this time of crisis in the arts, if we spoke with a united voice? All the forces seem to be working against us at the moment, at a time when they should all be pulling together.

8th March 1998, London–New York
Another plane, and another chance to take stock. It seems that the only time I catch my breath these hectic days is when I am *forced* to sit still, held captive in a plane, train or automobile seat. I have even taken to

making phone calls on the five-minute walk between my flat and the underground station, but as yet I haven't succumbed to the temptation of calling people from the car. Much too God-fearing a citizen for that.

Right now I am on the way to the States for the *Totally Fit* tour. I'm not quite sure why *The Vitality Plan* is being released by DK in the US under a new name, but I suspect it has something to do with the way Americans mispronounce their 't's. *Todally Fit* wouldn't work back home, and *The Vidalidy Plan* just doesn't cut the mustard over here. I'm not sure I'm really looking forward to the next few days. An American book tour sounds terribly grand and frightfully big time, but I suspect it will mainly be a lot of travelling, a lot of talking and very little in the way of glamour. Worst of all, my dear friend Shelley Washington, ex-Twyla Tharp dancer and now Twyla's assistant, is leaving New York today and returning on the 18th, the day I depart. Oh well, at least my friends from Rolls-Royce will arrive next week, so I can play with them. Typically, Torje and the Rolling Stones have finished their shows here in North America and have moved on to Japan. When I go to Japan, for the R-R Silver Seraph launch next month, they will have flown to South America. Where in the world is Torje and my love life?

The second week of Dance Bites drew to a close yesterday with two performances at the Swan Theatre, in High Wycombe. I made a double trip down the A40, listening, red-faced, to a programme on Radio 4 about the overuse of the private car. Months ago, I agreed to speak about dancers' health to a group of employees from the pharmaceutical giant, Glaxo Wellcome, our sponsors, who were coming to see the show. The talk was scheduled to take place yesterday morning at 11 a.m. Inevitably, by the time yesterday came around I was up to my eyeballs and I would have loved a morning in town to get things done before my flight to the US. But a commitment is a commitment, so I drove there, gave the talk, and hurtled back again. Aarrghhh. For the second time in my burgeoning speaking career I abandoned written notes, although the improvisation was totally unplanned. I had left my hastily scribbled cue cards in the dressing-room. But it didn't matter. I have talked so much recently about dancers, fitness, and diet that I could probably do it on autopilot. And I did. Angela Coia (one of our two physiotherapists) gave the professional's viewpoint, and then, together, we fielded questions from the audience. Amongst them was an ex-dancer from English National Ballet. She said that she recognised the situation I have frequently described, the dancer's love/hate relationship with food, the fear of looking in the mirror, and the pressure dancers put on themselves to stay reed thin whatever the cost. Like me, she had spent much of her career fighting a battle between two selves, the 'thin' one, in control and able to renounce the urge to eat, and the 'fat' one, for whom food and eating were an unbearable and all-powerful force. She worries now that despite the good advice that is available, it won't be taken on board if an influential dance teacher takes a different line. She's right, of course, and although hearing the facts from a practising principal dancer gives the right message a greater chance of taking root, a student subjected daily to contradictory advice will need a huge amount of individual clear-headedness to stay on course.

After the talk I drove back home along the A40, the poor car still rattling like an old jalopy, and spent a couple of hours sorting out my suitcase. Difficult to know what to take, as I'm scheduled to appear in all three of my current hats: Ballet dancer's tiara, author's crown of thoughts, and Rolls-Royce muse wing. I stuck to my usual criteria. Continue adding outfits until the case won't close and never, ever take one black suit when you can fit in three. But which three?

Case closed, at about 5 p.m. I got back into the car, crossed my fingers and drove to High Wycombe for the performance. I was convinced that with my extraordinary record where anything mechanical, electrical or automated is concerned I was due for a breakdown round about Beaconsfield, but the little *røde bil* gallantly held out all the way there and back. As a reward I promise I will give my Mazda the attention it deserves the minute I am back in London for more than twelve hours at a stretch. At the Swan, I danced the final pair of eighteen ballets of the last two weeks. Dance Bites has played to packed houses in Bath and High Wycombe, and *Words Apart* collected an impressive and gratifying set of reviews. Boxes and shoe bags back in the skips, the company is now headed for Turin, Italy, where I'm not involved. I will join them in Frankfurt, Germany, on the 24th.

Before I left home I had a surprise phone call from Lord Eatwell, Chairman of the ballet Board. Might I have offended him in the recent company meeting by suggesting his attitude was ageist? It seems I can relax. He took my comments in the spirit in which they were intended. He asked me to go up to Cambridge to meet him when I return from the US, but didn't say why. We managed to arrange a time between an appearance on Carlton Food Network on the 20th, for the DK book, and a meeting with Sir Richard Eyre, in relation to his report on the Opera

House, on the 23rd. While we've been dancing away over the last three months, Richard Eyre has been continuing his investigation into the House, conducting a wide range of interviews with interested parties. One of his working group has insisted he talks to me.

10th March 1998, New York – Boston – Atlanta
Back in the USA, never mind Totally Fit. My life is totally mad. I began to suspect this sometime during the process of applying full TV make-up to a jet-lagged face at 5 a.m., and it was confirmed by the run of events that followed.

I arrived in New York on Sunday afternoon. Yesterday morning, Lucy Kenyon, of DK publicity, picked me up from the Carlyle Hotel (at last, luxury) and took me to a local television interview in Connecticut – in a white stretch-limo. I had read an article on the plane by one of the Two Fat Ladies, the cookery writers, about their own US publicity tour, and like me they had been amused to be collected (out of necessity?) in one of these vast cruising gin palaces. They are irredeemably seedy, with their dreadful decanters of cheap spirits, flashing disco lights and myriad tissue boxes. It smelt of dank carpets. I hovered above the seat and we set off for Connecticut. Two blocks later the panel separating us from the driver slid to a close. I guess he's seen it all, but I'm not sure what he expected Lucy and me to be getting up to on a Monday morning.

Twenty-four hours on and I'm in Boston. My press escort, Ginny, picked me up from the hotel at 6 a.m. this morning and we headed off for a live breakfast TV show, on location at the World Gym in Somerville, Mass. Being up before 8.30 a.m. is such an achievement for me that I was momentarily crestfallen to see from the number of cars in the parking lot that several other people were sharing my moment of virtuous triumph. Inside the gym, a vast universe filled with row upon row of exercise machines of every make and description, people were cycling, climbing and running themselves awake before heading (presumably) to the office. I say in *The VP*, now *TF*, that it doesn't matter what time of day you exercise, but personally I can think of nothing worse than working out as the sun is rising. But I guess it all comes down to personal preference – I would think nothing of exercising at eleven o'clock at night, when, I guess, all these early birds are sound asleep. After all, I do it for a living.

Vic, the cameraman, was waiting for us at the juice bar, but there was no sign of the show's host, Mariellen. I got my kit off (again) and donned the coral two-piece. She appeared eventually, blonde, big haired and smiley, and threw Ginny into a panic by announcing that our slot had been rescheduled. This threatened my appearance on *Matti in the Morning*, the number one drivetime radio show in the Boston area. A compromise was reached; I would do the 'taster' with Mariellen, dash over to be interviewed by Matti, then sprint back in time for Mariellen's main 'hit' at 7.35 a.m., just as the exercisers at home were stretching and yawning into gear. The 'hit' was all of three minutes – three minutes to distil the essence of *Totally Fit* and convince Greater Boston that it really couldn't do without the book. The things you do to hawk your wares.

After a brief pause for breakfast we headed off to *Doctors on Call* to prerecord for their Sunday show. Being greeted by a doctor wearing more make-up than me before ten in the morning might have been the final straw, but I had Smoki Bacon still to come. The doctor himself turned out to have layers of knowledge beneath all that make-up, and it was such a relief to have a conversation with someone who understands the issues in the book and asked interesting questions. On top of this, he loved *Totally Fit* and said how rare it was to see all the relevant information gathered together in one volume.

Next stop, with half an hour to spare, was Louis of Boston, the world's most beautiful and trendiest clothing store. A taut assistant dressed in black greeted me with 'Good afternoon, madam, I love your Dries shirt.' The bargain I snapped up in Wimbledon is turning out to be a calling card in America.

At one o'clock I was due at Café Rouge for lunch with Smoki Bacon and Dick Concannon. Smoki and Dick have a weekend show, one segment of which is lunch with a celebrity. Me, in case you were wondering. These guys are the archetypal American TV hosts, everything their names lead you to expect. The interview itself lasts about ten minutes – Dick asks the questions and Smoki (aged 70) operates the camera. It reminded me of those myriad 'public access' television channels in New York, where you make your own programme and buy a slice of air time to show it. You quickly understand why everyone can be a star in America. There used to be one channel which was so outrageously pornographic (for free) that I guess either Mayor Guiliani or the pay-as-you-yearn porn kings shut it down. It was still broadcasting when the company visited New York in the early nineties, and groups of dancers would turn up for work red-eyed from the joint effects of staying up late and crying with laughter at the antics on air.

Apparently Smoki and Dick are a bit of an institution here in Boston, and I liked them a lot. Once the camera was turned off, the conversation roamed freely over a fascinating range of topics, proof once again that age is not a barrier to youthful thinking. Sadly, the lunch was dreadful. I left a sizeable portion of an overstuffed sandwich on my plate, probably fuelling any suspicions they might have had that the healthy and happy eater I proclaim to be doesn't practise what she preaches.

My final stop in Boston was at *Talk America*, a nationally syndicated radio chat show hosted by Chuck Gustasson. He and I had a great 40 minutes, and it was such a relief not to have to try and sell the book while some producer is making fast and furious circles with his hand – the international sign to 'wind it up'.

I barely made the plane to Atlanta, but I am now safely on board and looking forward to an early night. Tomorrow the bandwagon starts again.

13th March 1998, New York
Back in New York, and enjoying a pace slower than the last few days. Atlanta was pretty much the Southern counterpart of the day in Boston. I got into trouble for not wearing a bra under the Dries shirt, on local television's *Peachtree Morning*. I didn't have a bra with me, and as I don't really have anything much to put in one, I very rarely wear them. I couldn't see what all the fuss was about. But looking around me, I could see that this is Bible belt country, and all the other women were demurely buttoned up and ruffled to the neck. I pancaked my nipples and kept my jacket tightly closed.

Just two interviews today in New York, and a chance to catch up on news from both the Opera House and the South Bank. North of the river, there have been more shake-ups, this time in the Marketing Department. When Keith Cooper's departure was announced a couple of weeks ago, one of the Board was quoted as saying that there would be 'more to follow'. Always an ominous statement. There will be nervous weeks ahead for us all as employees try to gauge just how many more. When will all this end?

On the South Bank, the latest news is that Chris Smith has put an end to the prevarication over the Richard Rogers redevelopment by announcing that the bid for Lottery funding has finally been turned down. I haven't managed to get hold of a British newspaper yet, but thanks to various friends and their e-mail servers I'm getting the story from two angles, inside and out. They aren't too dissimilar, except that the press appear to be linking the departure of Sir Brian Corby, Chairman of the South Bank Board, with the Arts Council's decision that it can't afford to fund the redevelopment. Everyone on the Board (and in higher places) has known for ages that Corby intended all along to step down this summer. He has done sterling work as Chair over the last eight years, all unpaid and all in addition to however else he earns his crust. Rumours are now centring on Nicholas Snowman, the Chief Executive. Although why a rejected Lottery bid should have to result in his resignation I don't know.

A press release from the Department for Culture, Media and Sport manages to put an optimistic spin on the South Bank affair, dropping in the rejection of the Lottery bid as background information for its own announcement of a 'new strategy for the future of the South Bank Centre'. Someone once told me that in Russian, the same word is used to mean both 'crisis' and 'opportunity'. Perhaps I could find out what it is. Cropportunity? In the current arts climate, it could soon turn out to be the most popular neologism in the English language.

Talking of new words, I have another one. Over the last couple of months I have discovered an unremarked sub-culture which, like an iceberg, reveals only its uppermost 10 per cent. It continues actively and subliminally around us whether we see it or not, yet we are only ever conscious of the end result. It is the underground life of the talk show. I have barely scratched the surface, yet I have already discovered a network of oversized TV studios, each one a composite of various bits of our life; the place where we cook, the place where we sit, the place where we eat and exercise, except that each location is honed to perfection, cushions permanently plumped, drapes and furnishings tastefully co-ordinated, and cookers that never need cleaning. The squeaky clean image on the screen throws our own domestic chaos into even darker relief. Or at least that's how it seems. Behind the scenes, it's every bit as disordered and madcap, if not more so. However liveable it all looks, it's an environment incapable of supporting human life. It is virtual life, full of virtual people. At the studio I visited in Atlanta, for instance, the oversized American fridge was heavily padlocked, presumably to guard against the entire crew's eating disorders. I feel certain that this sub-culture and its effect on people's aspirations would warrant further study, and I have even come up with a name for it. I'm booked to appear on the Sybil Tonkonogy show (via telephone hook-up) on the 24th of this month. Now, I don't know if Tonkonogy is really Sybil's name. But even supposing it does its duty as a surname, it isn't working nearly hard enough. I suggest hijacking it to name a course of study on the 'sofa chat show' culture. Ladies and gentlemen, I give you Tonkonogy, and the spin-off doll that goes with it.

19th March 1998, New York–London
The second week in New York flew by. I had a computer crisis, turning my laptop on back at the Carlyle to discover that the screen had gone dark on me. I searched frantically for a dimmer switch, couldn't find one, so resorted to calling Torje in Japan and soliciting his expert help. 'Darling, how do I turn up the brightness on the Toshiba?' 'You don't, it's preset. And why are you asking me this at 3 o'clock in the morning?' But as usual, he responded valiantly in times of a Deborah Bull crisis, talking me through all the options and concluding, sadly, that it was time to replace the machine. My blood ran cold. I don't do computer purchases. Torje does. I knew that a Fifth Avenue salesman would think all his Christmases had come at once if he saw me walk through the door. It might be the only part of my life where this applies, but where computers are concerned, I might as well have 'naïve' tattooed across my forehead. So Torje called a store he knows in New York and organised everything for me. All I had to do was jump in a cab and pick it up. After the most expensive computer set-up session ever, on the phone between New York and Japan, the Toshiba 'young pretender' was ready for action. 'Ol' blind' was packed up to travel home.

I managed to fit in some theatre, although all the shows I really wanted to see were booked up months in advance. Despite a narrowly averted strike by the Musicians Union, Broadway seems to be in great shape. The big hits are *Titanic*, the musical, and Disney's *The Lion King*. *The Sound of Music* has just been revived. Doesn't sound very healthy, put like that, but there's a whole host of interesting stuff going on which seems to be very well supported. I certainly couldn't get tickets, and even the concierge at the Carlyle couldn't help. So I settled for a David Mamet play, *The Old Neighborhood*, with Patti Lupone. My life seems to be going full circle. In spring of last year I went to see Patti in *Master Class* in London. I enjoyed the Mamet, but I wish someone had warned me I would need a phrase book. American is one thing; Jewish-American is another. The first section went completely over my head. Things looked up when Patti came on. I know opinion is divided over Patti

Lupone: Actress? Singer? Neither? Both? But I found her a riveting performer, and even now, a week later, I can clearly recall the intensity of her playing.

In a few days' time I have to be back on-stage with The Royal Ballet in Frankfurt, so despite a horror of the ballet world's 'open classes', I decided to take the plunge and try out Broadway's 'Steps' studio. American dancers do open class all the time. In England it would be fairly unusual to find Darcey Bussell or Sylvie Guillem popping round the corner to Pineapple Studios in Covent Garden. When I was a gal I was an avid consumer of these kinds of open classes, which might explain why I dislike them so much now. Back then I would even go to Brian Loftus' class at Urdang Academy in Covent Garden on a *Sunday*. But generally we all take the class the company provides, whereas it is quite normal for a dancer in New York City Ballet or American Ballet Theatre to go seek class elsewhere. 'Steps' is apparently the most popular venue at the moment, so I headed there for about 10.30 a.m. I figured that must be the time everyone in the world does dance class. I was right, although some dancers turned around and retraced their steps when they found out the regular teacher had been replaced. The stand-in was considered too slow. I reasoned that this was surely a relative judgement, and as I had no idea how fast a normal American ballet class might be, I decided to go ahead and give it a try. In truth it was a bit slow, but it was nevertheless very hard and very strengthening. I rather enjoyed it – perhaps I need to take things a little more slowly these days. The class was packed with every shape and size, evidently ranging from the professional to the absolute non-starter. There was a worrying sprinkling of emaciated youngsters, too.

The Rolls-Royce team, complete with my now regular partner, the silver enamelled Silver Seraph, arrived on Tuesday the 17th, for the New York launch. I had to go off to New Jersey for a live TV programme, but I joined the R-R group for a late dinner. There was no rush. We were scheduled to rehearse on a specially constructed stage in the Seagrams Building on Park Avenue at 1 a.m. During dinner, the phone rang. Change of plan – 2 a.m. Bleary-eyed, we dragged ourselves over there to find a half-built stage. It didn't look like anything was going to happen before 3 a.m., and sure enough, nothing did. 4 a.m., and still no action. We gave up and went home to bed.

So I was Miss Cheerful herself, next morning, when the *Columbus Dispatch* called at 9 a.m. I tried to remember what *Totally Fit* was all about, and afterwards went straight back to sleep. You can imagine how thrilled I was when my publicist, Lucy, called half an hour later to let me know how much the *Dispatch* had enjoyed talking to me. Yeah. Thanks, Lucy. ZZzzzzzzzz. The book part of this tour was over, and I could turn my attention to the R-R launches over the next forty-eight hours.

Rolls-Royce had devised a schedule which was a masterpiece of intricate timing, with opportunities unlimited for things to go wrong. On paper, it works fine: New York launch at 6 p.m. Wednesday evening, catch the 10 p.m. flight to London, arrive at 9 a.m. Thursday morning, London launch at 6.30 p.m. Thursday evening. What could be more simple? A single continent, for a start.

The first hiccup was completely unexpected; a plane crash-landed at Manchester Airport, closing it down and leaving the Chief Executive of Rolls-Royce, Graham Morris, stranded on the wrong side of the Atlantic. There was nothing to be done about it, and Ian McKay, Director of Product Strategy and Marketing, deputised, stepping gracefully into his shoes. The event finished at 8 p.m., and two hours later, we were due to take off for Heathrow. As there was no room for error, we were all geared up for a quick get-away (a runner, as they say in Rock 'n' Roll). Unfortunately, at 8.30 p.m. we were still huddled in the rain, waiting for the limo which, despite its extraordinary size, had managed to vanish off the face of the earth. With our luggage. Several phone calls later, we found it, and made the trip to JFK in record time.

At the airport, I noticed that the woman who checked us in had a picture of the Seraph peeping out from her wallet. I couldn't resist asking why, and she opened it up to reveal an entire illustrated wish list. 'This is where I'm gonna live; this is gonna be my car; this is my yacht; and this will be my pool.' Unfortunately, her affection for the car didn't help to sort out various ticketing dramas, and it was 9.59 p.m. before we crept, sheepish and apologetic, to our seats on a flight that was being held at the gate. 'Would the last remaining passengers' and so on. After last night's all-nighter, it wasn't long before all six of us were curled up, fast asleep.

We landed at Heathrow at 9.30 a.m. the following morning, and I popped home for a couple of hours' rest. We were scheduled to rehearse at the Dorchester at 4.30 p.m., and what do you know? At 6 p.m., as the first guests were clawing at the door, the car was threatening to crash through the revolving stage. The edge of the revolve was proving incapable of supporting the car's weight, and it had to be repositioned in the centre, shifting me and Ashley's choreography sideways. It didn't matter. I still had more room than Geneva, and probably more than Blackpool, now I come to think of it.

Through jet lag and exhaustion I danced away, and it all came off, eventually, without a hitch. At 10.30 p.m. the taxi dropped me home and I dragged myself round the corner to Cullens, unable to contemplate tomorrow's early start without milk in my tea, then crawled home to bed.

20th March 1998, Nottingham – London

Back to *The VP* publicity. Today I have been up to Nottingham, to record four snippets for Carlton Food Network. The interviews continue; another continent, another telly, exactly the same format. Tonkonogy. I think I'm on to something with my nascent thesis on the inner workings of the chat show culture. Today, the plan was that I would cook four recipes from *The VP*, but as I hastily pointed out to the producer on the telephone, (a) I don't cook and (b) *The VP* doesn't have recipes. It's all about eating to your taste within certain guidelines but *without* recipes. The producer convinced me there would be plenty of opportunities to make that point, and as for my kitchen phobia, well, a home economist does all the cooking anyway. So at 11 a.m. I boarded the train to Nottingham. The taxi which took me from the station to the studio displayed the awesome notice 'SOILING: any person or animal who soils the cab will be subject to a surcharge of £25'. I tried not to.

At Carlton, scheduled for a 2 p.m. start, I was kept waiting until at least 3.30 p.m. by a 'very famous chef' who was driving everyone mad. When I finally got into the studio I was so determined to make my 5.30 p.m. return train that I performed flawlessly, if you don't count referring to a lime as a lemon. Twice. But all things considered – New York, Boston, Atlanta, New York, London, Nottingham – I think I'm coping pretty well.

I spent the train journey home scouring the papers to try and find out what is going on at the Arts Council. Gerry Robinson is already in there, although not yet officially, and looking to shake it up. I heard rumours last night that the Council itself is to be 'slimmed down'. I guess that doesn't mean they're all getting free copies of *The VP*. In the end, unable to find anything more than a 'news in brief' snippet, three lines in *The Times*, I called the Council's Press Office from the train. Unfortunately, the snippet was about the extent of the press release, so I was none the wiser. I need to know what's going on here. This could affect me.

21st March 1998, London

I have just been up to Cambridge for my meeting with Lord Eatwell, planned on the telephone two weeks ago. It was never clear just what we were to meet about, but after a while he laid his cards on the table. He has asked me how I would feel about becoming a member of the ballet Board, a position never before held by a dancer in the company. This would put me in an unusual position. What will other people think? Does it mean I will finally be my own boss? I have asked him to give me a little time to mull it over, but I do feel a duty to do everything I can to ensure that The Royal Ballet survives this stormy period in its history. I believe Dame Ninette de Valois' vision for the company to be bigger than any single figure who may have been attached to the Royal Opera House, and if I have any chance of aiding the ballet company through these difficult times then I don't feel I can turn it down. Of course, it may be that after Richard Eyre reports we will all be turfed out anyway.

Last Sunday's *Times* had a front page story speculating that the long-awaited Eyre report would recommend privatisation of the Royal Opera House as the way forward. The article suggests that the theatre will be sold off to a commercial leisure company, but a certain amount of control retained over ticket prices and artistic output. Having watched this country's beautiful cinemas turned, one by one, into bingo halls during the seventies and eighties, are we now to see a similar fate befall the Opera House? I can see the flashing neon signs already: Mecca presents The Royal Ballet in some extravaganza or other. Or perhaps we will see Disney take it over in time to transfer *The Lion King* from Broadway to Covent Garden. Either way, I would like to know just what sort of strong-arm tactics could be employed to force a 'commercial' organisation to keep a ceiling on ticket prices and a bottom line on artistic standards. No truly commercial interest would sign the sort of contract that limited the return they could expect from an investment unsupported by public subsidy. And using public money to subsidise seat prices under current legislation would be outside the Arts Council's remit. The Council is prohibited from funding commercial ventures.

The *Independent* has a different suggestion, that the opera company would have its funding cut while the ballet retains its subsidy, and the Opera House would be funded directly by the government as a receiving house for both companies. It makes the point that the House itself could not easily be sold off as it has been the recipient of so much Lottery funding.

But both news reports raise the same question: Where does the money come from? If ticket prices are artificially depressed – great idea, nothing against it – then someone will have to make up the short fall. Who? Nowhere, but nowhere in the world of opera and ballet do the sums add up. Different countries find different ways of dealing with this, but a wing and a prayer is not usually one of the options.

And a note to David Lister, arts correspondent of the *Independent*: You know jolly well that the Opera House Board is not made up of 'many of the great and good of the arts world'. You've been following the saga closely enough to be well aware that at present, the Board is made up of a grand total of four. Great and good they may be. Many, they are not.

23rd March 1998, London
Another year older. I have just filled in a survey on the tube and noticed that I have moved one box further in the great pigeon holing of life. I can no longer tick the 25–34 age group. I've moved into the 35–44 bracket. Blimey. How did that happen? Last time I looked I was 21.

I have also realised with a jolt that table dancing is out of the question as an alternative career. Today I bought *The Stage*, whose arts news has been bang on this year, in an effort to find word about the implications for us of Gordon Brown's budget. No luck, so I flicked through the employment pages instead. All the adverts seeking dancers (mostly for cruise liners and clubs) stipulate that applicants must be under the age of 35. I've missed my chance. I guess I'm more of a laptop dancer than a lap dancer, so it's no great hardship. I suppose there's always a career for me as a touch typist.

I'm on my way home from a meeting with Sir Richard Eyre; the name becomes flesh at last. He's a strikingly good-looking man with such an air of weariness that I wanted to gather him up and take him home for a hot dinner. I was surprised to have been asked to contribute to the ongoing debate over the Opera House's future which will form the basis of his report. But apparently various people had assured him that he really must hear what I had to say on the matter. Bowing to the suggestions, he invited me to the Department in Cockspur Street to meet him. In truth, I'm not sure I added anything useful to the hours of lobbying he must have endured from the dance world, and frankly, he seemed worn out by it all. I can't imagine he hasn't already heard every argument there is to make, every possible way of combining companies, theatres and orchestras. His notebook must look like the menu at Pizza

Hut; deep pan with black olives and extra pepperoni, or would Sir prefer the olives on a thin crust, without the cheese? Although I have thought about it as much as anyone over the last six months, with the possible exception of Sir Richard, I haven't come up with anything wildly radical myself. For what it might be worth, I added my piece, but whenever I defend our position in the House, I can hear the immortal words of Mandy Rice Davis: 'She would say that, wouldn't she?' But perhaps it's worth a reminder that whilst we don't particularly want to be thrown out of the House after working for a quarter of a century to get it right, English National Opera don't want to move in, either. I've racked my brains to come up with the thunderbolt of genius that will solve the problem at a stroke, but I haven't found it. Judging from the careworn look of Sir Richard, neither has anyone else.

This modern day Solomon didn't give much away, but I got the impression that he has concluded that without the possibility of extra funding, there are few options preferable but to maintain the status quo. As interesting as it must have been to carry out what could prove to be no more than a theoretical exercise – Chris Smith is not even guaranteeing that he will act on the findings – it must sometimes feel to Eyre like a thankless and hopeless task. I'm not convinced my contribution made it any easier.

I came home and packed another suitcase. After little more than a weekend back in England, I'm off to Germany in the morning to catch up with the company.

25th March 1998, Frankfurt, Germany
The opening night of *Sleeping Beauty* in Frankfurt and I am writing this between appearances as the Fairy of Passion in the Prologue and the Bluebird in Act Three. It feels like groundhog day; the familiar strains of Tchaikovsky and the stacks of pastel tutus could indicate any city, any tour of the last five years – Washington, New York, Madrid, Costa Mesa – except that today had a distinguishing feature that sets it apart. We lost yet another Chief Executive. Mary Allen, after a short seven months in office, has resigned. Amazing. All in all, she was with us almost twice as long as Genista McIntosh, who took over from Jeremy Isaacs last January and resigned in May.

I am at a loss to understand just what is going on here in my own organisation, yet I'm sure that tomorrow's papers back home will have plenty to say about it. Throughout this entire year, what has struck me more than anything else is the contrast between the amount of information the outsiders seem to have about the inner workings of the House and the little we insiders know. I'm glad I'm not at home, because someone would be bound to ring me up asking for an astute observation or a pithy quote, and frankly, I'm totally lost for words. I have absolutely nothing of intelligence to add. I just keep hearing echoed paraphrases of Oscar Wilde: 'To lose one Chief Executive may be regarded as a misfortune; to lose both looks like carelessness.'

The press release was faxed to us along with a note from Mary Allen. The first told us that the Chief Executive had resigned as a result of differences of opinion about the direction in which the House should go. It also announces that Pelham Allen (well, that'll save on the cost of new stationery – a bit of Tippex should do it) will act as Chief Executive until a replacement can be found. Pelham came to us from Coopers and Lybrand, specifically to sort out the Royal Opera House's precarious position. Doctoring sick businesses is his speciality. In her personal note, Mary urges us to keep the faith, as it were, and to give Pelham the whole-hearted support we gave her. I guess hidden somewhere between the lines is the truth of just what has gone on, but it seems incomprehensible to most people that she should have survived the onslaught of Operation Kaufman only to succumb to some other, less public, internal pressure later on. In fact, that seems to be the most common reaction tonight – surprise at the timing rather than at the news itself. Sooner would have made sense. Later would have made sense. Right now leaves us puzzled. Once again we have lost our rudder in a fierce and ongoing storm, and I guess a small but select bunch of MPs have pulled on their dancing shoes to dance, yet again, on the grave of the Opera House.

26th March 1998, Munich, Germany
In Munich, on an overnight trip from Frankfurt and a day release from The Royal Ballet, I am introducing the Seraph to the locals. Like the Opera House, Rolls-Royce are undergoing changes at the top as well. The company has been on the market for three months now, and yesterday's paper reported that Volkswagen have finally opened the bidding. Everyone expects BMW to follow suit, sparking off a battle of the Teutons for a British crown jewel. One of these upcoming German events would be the perfect setting for an announcement of new ownership, and I wonder if we will see additions to the guest list either here, or in Berlin next week.

We had a wonderful launch tonight in the Nymphenburg Porcelain Factory, providing me with the once in a lifetime opportunity to dance as a bull in a china shop. The unveiling of the car took place in the kiln – it's bigger than it sounds – and allowed us to make stunning use of an overhead gallery in yet another variant on the original choreography. The stage was about the tiniest yet, but by shifting most of the steps on to the diagonal (sorry, Ashley, needs must) it turned into one of the best shows we've given. Part of the thrill of these launches is making it work in changing conditions, refusing to be defeated by whatever challenge the different venues throw up. And the other part of the thrill is being transported around in chauffeured Bentleys. This is not an act of extravagance on the part of my employers. Bentleys and Rolls-Royces are what they have to hand, and using them for transport is obviously going to be cheaper than renting a Fiat Uno or a Volkswagen Polo for the day.

27th March 1998, Frankfurt, Germany
The Rolls-Royce sale is hotting up. As anticipated, BMW today joined VW in a race to secure the company. Over drinks last night there was much speculation and coded conversation. Graham Morris, the Chief Executive, has flown back to London with every expectation of an early announcement next week, so Tuesday's Berlin launch may be either overshadowed or overcrowded.

The word from my friends in London (the source of all my information about the House) is that there is nothing unexpected in Mary Allen's departure. She and the Board have been disagreeing for some time, and those in the know have been aware for a while that her exit was on the cards. How come we in the company are always the last to find out?

Mary is the subject of some unwarranted sniping in the press. As far as I am aware, Kaufman's report was not binding in law, yet Mary's decision not to abide by his findings is being added to a list of complaints against her. The words 'goalpost' and 'moved' are dancing an uneasy *pas de deux* in my head. She accepted the position of Chief Executive in good faith and gave it her very best, quickly gaining the trust and support of the House and sticking with us through some very tough times. Now the Board has changed the job description and wants someone new to fill it. Is it right that she should be pilloried by the press because her feet don't fit the new order?

I had a brief glimpse of a newpaper article by Gerald Kaufman, explaining 'Why It Was Right That Mary Allen Should Go'. I'm not sure I like this new trend of politician as media pundit. I wouldn't like my bank manager to hijack a column in the *Evening Standard* explaining 'Why We Shouldn't Extend Deborah Bull's Overdraft'. This government's constant self-justification suggests a lack of self-belief to me. We (and they) have to accept that the government we voted in will take and make decisions on our behalf, God help us, and we don't need to know about the click of every cog and the turn of every wheel that goes into it. Imagine a judge leaving the High Court, whipping off his wig, and saying to the waiting reporters; 'Bloody hell, he was a right one, that Fingers McGee, if I'd had my way, I'd have had his head off.' There's a Russian *répétiteur*, Aleksander Agadzhanov, who often takes my rehearsals. If I reveal any of the faff and fuddle that goes into a finished step, he complains to me 'too much kitchen'. Too much kitchen, New Labour, too much kitchen.

30th March 1998, Frankfurt, Germany
Woke up to see a poor replica of me on the TV – you know, the silver one, six inches tall, which graces the bonnet of the Rolls-Royce. She was illustrating the morning's top story, the agreed sale (subject to shareholder agreement) of R-R to BMW. As we predicted, today is D-Day. A car owner's consortium back home, a well-meaning group of Rolls-Royce and Bentley enthusiasts, hasn't quite given up yet in their attempt to acquire the marque, but most people doubt they can match the economic might of the German suitors.

In the continuing saga of our own changes at the top, Pelham Allen, our latest Chief Executive, came to address the company on Saturday. It was a generous and much appreciated gesture, flying over to Frankfurt simply to introduce himself and offer a degree of reassurance in the light of this week's surprise event. He laid his cards on the table, and the company admired his honesty. He hails very much from the world of commerce, not art, and freely admits that he has never seen a ballet in his life. But he has seen several companies teetering on the brink of disaster, and his speciality is pulling them back from the precipice. As fixers go, he's rumoured to be one of the best. He has plans to go ruthlessly through the organisation from top to bottom, weeding out inefficiency and updating archaic practices. Just eight days a week, then. Afterwards, he took a seat out front to watch his very first ballet performance. I hope he enjoyed it. He will leave tomorrow morning before I have a chance to find out.

Several people have since told me that for the first time this year, they feel a burgeoning sense of security. My fingers and toes and arms and knees are now crossed. I'm tied up in knots in the hope that all will be well. Could we have finally touched bottom, or are there fathoms further to go? After all, there is still the Richard Eyre report to come in May. Might this be the beast from twenty thousand leagues below?

At the theatre, I did class at 5.30 p.m., just before the show. Halfway through, one of the boys sidled up to me. 'Psst, you got any bananas?' I felt like a drug pusher on the streets of King's Cross. 'I can let you have one. Come to my room after class.'

April 1998

The last four weeks have felt like a sequence from *Around the World in Eighty Days*. My schedule is starting to resemble an airline timetable. I packed my case and left Frankfurt last Tuesday, flying to Berlin for *another* Rolls-Royce launch. A Jaguar, for some strange reason, collected me from the airport and took me to the Adlon Hotel. I haven't been to Berlin for several years; the company performed in both the East and the West during the eighties, but I haven't been there since that memorable afternoon when the wall came tumbling down. I wonder if other people of my generation remember where they were when they heard that the Berlin Wall was finally being torn down. It certainly sticks in my mind as a JFK moment. I was driving along the Marylebone Road on the way to the Opera House, and heard the news on Radio 4. I parked in the car park (those were the days – in the new Covent Garden, we'll fight for parking meters along with the rest of you) and rushed around trying to find someone to tell, someone who would find the event as exhilarating as I did.

The Adlon is right by the site of those reunification celebrations, at the Brandenburg Gate. It was built at the beginning of the century and it's recently been restored to its prewar glories after decades of neglect. The R-R event was taking place in the ballroom and I went straight in, as I always do, to check out the stage. Nice size, but a polished wood surface which threatened to up-end me before I took my first step. So in yet another variant on 'let's adapt Ashley's choreography' I danced in bare feet. I love dancing shoeless; pointe shoes trigger a Pavlovian (the dog handler, not the dancer) response of 'pulling up', away from the floor, in true classical ballerina style. It's perfectly appropriate most of the time, but modern choreography often calls for a more grounded, earthy approach, and taking your shoes off is an easy way to get there. To substitute for the silver tights and shoes I normally wear, I issued a challenge to the hotel's concierge (at 6 p.m.): find me some silver make-up, *bitte*. They rose to it magnificently, and half an hour later, room service arrived with a tub of Kryolan and a make-up sponge. Now that's the mark of a great hotel.

For this performance, the musicians who played in Geneva and London were airlifted into Berlin. I don't mind dancing to tape – it's one way of ensuring a consistent tempo – but it was wonderful to go back to live music and feel a collective shiver as the percussionists set the show in motion. Afterwards, when the guests had all gone, Joanne Lunn, the soprano, and the musicians gathered round the piano and improvised into the night. From jazz and pop to classical. *Lieder* and lighter. The R-R contingent huddled around a table at the other side of the room, talking serious business. With BMW entering a period of exclusive negotiations with Vickers, Rolls-Royce's parent company, I think we all know what they were talking about.

The next morning I was up at very silly o'clock to fly back to London for the briefest of stopovers before catching a plane to Hong Kong in the afternoon. We arrived, twelve hours later, at ten in the morning, feeling less than terrific. I'm in a time zone unknown.

I was last in Hong Kong with The Royal Ballet in 1983. The trip is nothing more than a hazy memory, but I'm sure I didn't find the place quite so Chinese. This may have been because we arrived there at the end of a nine-week tour which included three difficult weeks in Beijing, Shanghai and Canton (all very Chinese) and the British aspects of Hong Kong would have shone like beacons in the night.

But my first impression today was that Hong Kong seems to have become overwhelmingly Chinese in the few short months since Britain handed back the colony to mainland China. I suddenly remembered Torje's story about the abandoned sugar cane factories in Hawaii. In the years since they were closed down they have been reclaimed by the jungle to such an extent that you could walk right over them and not know they were there. Perhaps it isn't fair to judge the place on the appearance of its airport. It's very much on its last legs, and no money is likely to be spent on improvements when a brand spanking new one, designed by Norman Foster, is due to open this summer. It's one of those 'busing' airports – the planes park up wherever they can find a space and double-ended 'push-me-pull-you' buses transport passengers to the terminal. The place looks like a Sainsbury's car park on a Saturday morning, with rows of dormant jets plus several operative ones nosing around looking for empty bays. 'Go on, you'll get it in there, right hand down a bit . . . Oops. Sorry.'

I didn't see much of our last outpost of colonialism on this twenty-hour trip. The only bit I saw in daylight was the road between the airport and the hotel. But I saw enough to know that Hong Kong is crushingly overcrowded, with roughly the same population as Scotland living in a tiny fraction of the space. Massive housing developments line the roads, batches of five or six identical lego blocks designed by the presenters of *Play School*, stark oblong boxes with rows of black dots for windows.

We transferred straight to the Hyatt Hotel, a chic but soulless place which was providing both the performance venue for the R-R launch and a bed for the night. This was to be our only double show; a matinée for the press; and at 7.45 p.m., a performance for the invited guests. We went straight into a rehearsal, to co-ordinate music and lighting and check out the floor. The event was taking place in the lobby, so the challenge of the day was to cope with a highly polished marble surface. Funnily enough, it was much less slippery than it sounds. With a liberal sprinkling of powdered resin to give me grip, I was able to keep my pointe shoes on. (As much as I like feeling the air between my toes, it's more befitting to the grand scheme if I'm on *pointe*.) Rehearsal over, Joanne and I went up to our rooms, thinking we might catch up on a little sleep before the first performance. I normally try to adapt immediately to local hours, but as these few days are completely twilight zone, I decided it wouldn't hurt to try and take the edge off my tiredness. I looked at my watch and realised it was already 1 p.m.; as I need a couple of hours to warm up and get ready, there was no option but to keep going. I ordered a pot of coffee and started on my make-up. By now the floor was moving, through grogginess, not technical design, and I had serious doubts about whether or not I would remain upright. But I managed, and the photographers got their shots. Between performances I had an hour in bed and felt much better for it. We even stayed awake long enough to get out of the hotel for dinner in town.

Another early start next morning saw us *en route* to Tokyo. Northwest Airlines obviously have the same policy as I do, adapting straight from the outset to whatever time it is at the point of disembarkation. So at 8.45 a.m. we were expected to tuck into pasta with a chicken and barbecue sauce. Yuck. I know this will come as a shock to anyone familiar with my eating habits (and by now, that includes most of the nation) but I *turned the pasta down*. I longed for a simple bowl of Tesco Healthy Eating Muesli.

The Tokyo event, the grand finale of the R-R tour, turned out to be the grandest by far. We were whisked straight from the airport to Happo-en, a banqueting suite in Meguro, an exclusive district of Tokyo.

As I've come to expect in Japan, we were looked after superbly, although there was still a lingering element of the all too familiar 'performers come last' syndrome. I would never demand special treatment, but if I've been asked along to dance, I tend to have a few simple expectations, like a space to dance in, for instance. As it was, the Silver Seraph was centre front on a (relatively) vast stage, leaving me plenty of room behind and to the sides, if I didn't mind being obscured by a lead player in heavy metal. I minded, but as a request to reposition the car was greeted as if I'd asked them to shift Mount Fuji, I dusted down my flexibility, again, and made it work. I was forced to compromise the steps once more to counter backstage intractability. It didn't help that by now we were all drained of our last few drops of energy. The course of true art never did run smooth for this girl and her Rolls-Royce.

It was definitely an 'all stops out' event. We even had a thirty-piece orchestra, so Handel's 'Seraphim', as well as Copland's *Fanfare*, were played to their full grandeur. The orchestra had rehearsed the complete version of the Handel, ABA, whereas we have been doing the A section only. Not a problem, we lied, and I set about adapting Ashley's choreography for the final time so that it wasn't too obvious that I would be dancing the same steps twice. I solved the conundrum pretty neatly by wearing my flowing draperies throughout the first A section. I usually remove them right at the beginning, but dancing with wings gave the piece a totally different look and saved the Japanese audience from two and a half minutes of original Deborah Bull choreography. The B section, slow and stately, was easily dealt with by a rather nice improvisation on 'statues I have known' up on the raised podium at the back. As this elongated version was now running at about ten minutes, some creative posturing served both to save my breath and transfer the attention for a while to the soprano, Joanne Lunn.

We both had a shock when right at the end of the rehearsal, car revealed, the orchestra struck up again with Enya's 'Orinoco's Flow'. As they played, I was supposed to draw Joanne through the crowds and lead the audience out into the garden, where there were two more Seraphs parked up on the gravel. It's the cherry blossom season here in Tokyo, and once everyone was outside, the trees and the cars were to be illuminated at our command. It all sounded dreadfully tacky, but we had little option but to agree to it. I had got nowhere fast on my earlier suggestion of moving the car to give me a little space, and besides, someone had worked very hard on this scenario and was presumably rather proud of it. The show went on as they wanted it to.

Now I'm flying home to London for a single meeting before I head off for a much needed holiday in Rio de Janeiro. Sadly, my brief relationship with Rolls-Royce is over, at least for the moment. Despite the various challenges thrown up by eight different venues and a breathtaking schedule stretching out over the last few months, I shall only remember an enormous, unexpected and unprecedented amount of fun. My secret fantasy, that I'd be presented at the end of it all with my own car to keep, didn't come to pass, but I did get a Spirit of Ecstacy in porcelain to put on my mantelpiece.

5th April 1998, London
I don't know what I'd have done without the South Bank press office during my months out on the road. They continue to send me a collection of cuttings every week which have been my only way of keeping abreast of arts news here in London. This week's were the most bizarre to date (and believe me, they face strong competition). Sometime, while I was aboard yet another long-haul flight, speculation was gaining pace amongst those in the know that the new Chief Executive/General Director of Covent Garden would be none other than the man who currently holds our fate in his hands – Sir Richard Eyre. It is only speculation, and we all know that at least 50 per cent of what we read in the papers has about as much relation to the truth as I have to the Queen Mother. But I must say, it has a pleasing ring to it. A White Knight to the rescue. The whole Covent Garden affair, from Genista McIntosh's resignation back in May, through near-bankruptcy in November, Kaufman in December and now Mary Allen's departure has so much of the soap opera about it that it somehow seems to cry out for an ending with its seeds sown early on in the plot. Who better to take control than the one person deemed worthy enough to undertake an unbiased and objective assessment of the House? The triumph of good over evil. The only other ending with enough suds to fit is the opposite one, where Keith Cooper, recently departed marketing man who starred in television's *The House*, rises again, stages a coup at Covent Garden and seizes control.

But as we all know, despite the way it has looked this year, life doesn't have the same structure as a soap opera. There's neither order, nor circularity, and logical endings occur by coincidence, not design. Art is there precisely to tease meaning from that chaos. Nice as it might be to work under Sir Richard Eyre, it's unlikely that anything quite so predictable will take place. If it's a question of life, not art, expect nothing but the unexpected.

Thursday's papers carried an open letter to Richard Eyre from Mary Allen. I was glad to see that she is still very much alive and kicking, despite the kicking *she* has received in the media over the last few days. She puts forward publicly the points that she would have raised with him privately at a meeting last week, had events not taken the turn they did. Once again the words 'Coliseum' and 'dance house' met in the same sentence. I'm not sure that it's anything more than received wisdom, this idea of the Coli as the perfect theatre for dance. As a member of the audience, I don't think any such thing, and once I took the plunge and owned up to this particular bit of heresy, various other people started coming out of the woodwork to agree with me. It's not so much a question of the stage. I'm sure it's a perfectly nice stage, but as 25 years (at least) of expertise have gone into designing the new stage at the Garden, I think we might assume *that* will be pretty nice too. It's more to do with the theatre as a place to watch dance. The cliff edge perspective from the upper (and cheaper) levels at the Coli gives me not only a very weird view, but a headache, too.

11th April 1998, Rio de Janeiro, Brazil
At last a real break and, moreover, the longed-for opportunity to meet up with Torje again. It is Easter Saturday and for six days now I've been in Rio de Janeiro, where the Stones are performing tonight. The company has a few days off which, added to the long Easter weekend, translates into a whole week's holiday. It's come as a blessing. I've been sleeping for the entire Brazilian nation and I still feel exhausted. The last month's schedule is finally catching up on me. I flew here on Monday, after squeezing in a meeting with Bob Lockyer of the BBC about the dance on television project. I must confess I thought my inchoate television career was dead rather than dormant, as it's been so long since it was last discussed. But there seems to be a good possibility that a one-off 'pilot' will be shown at Christmas, and the idea of the dance series itself is still very much alive.

Rio is hot and busy, and Copacabana beach is better in Barry Manilow's version than it is in real life. (I know, that's saying something.) I don't like holidaying in cities, especially when it's 30°C in the shade. So I was very relieved when we were whisked out of town to visit a friend's *fazenda* about three hours' drive from here, up in the Brazilian highlands. The country is dotted with these ranches, built for the coffee plantation owners towards the end of the last century. This one is less ostentatious than some, a simple, low-level building settled in the natural basin of three overlooking peaks. But in matters of taste, it's utterly exquisite, and the silence is deafening. And we are away from it all.

Here in South America, the band is plagued by the ever present, prying lenses of the paparazzi, and the hotel back in Rio is under surveillance day and night. Life in the fast lane might sound exciting, but the reality isn't quite so good. Dancers very rarely attract the same attention as rock and film stars. Perhaps only Rudolf Nureyev, with his combination of charismatic beauty, jet-setting lifestyle and exotic past has ever become tabloid fodder in the way the Stones are. The rest of us drift in and out of the spotlight, glamorous between the hours of 7.30 and 10.30 p.m., but totally anonymous the rest of the time.

14th April 1998, in flight, Rio–London
I'm flying home from Rio. It sounds like a song of regret, and it is. It's been great to see Torje and catch another *Bridges to Babylon* concert. Several thousand Brazilians jumping up and down and punching the air in time to the 'get no' of 'Satisfaction' is definitely an experience to remember. It's very strange, though; wherever I go, I'm always told, 'oh, you should have been in Buenos Aires/Las Vegas/Hawaii, and felt the atmosphere there.' Apparently I miss the really good shows. Well, they must be good, as this one was amazing. Bob Dylan opened the show, and returned later on for a joint rendition with the band of 'Like a Rolling Stone'. (As Mick used to say on the last tour, 'Here's one Bob wrote for us years ago.') It was an historic moment, two great rock legends up there on the stage together. Before I left home, Culture Secretary Chris Smith was in trouble again, this time for refusing to make qualitative judgements between John Keats and Bob Dylan. I don't want to enter the debate here, but I can say that Dylan, singing in Rio together with Mick and the boys, seemed a pretty poetic couplet to me.

Now I am thinking about catching up on the sleep I failed to get last night. We arrived back at the hotel from a concert in Sao Paulo at half-past three in the morning, and by the time I had packed it was gone four. My obligatory midnight pee took place at nine in the morning, and I was horrified to realise that was it for the night. Time to get up. The plane

I'm on at the moment will land in Frankfurt in about eight hours' time, at 5 a.m., from where I'll catch the early bird special to London. I reach Heathrow Airport at 8 a.m., and class starts at 10.30 a.m. I don't know what the rehearsal schedule holds for me, but I sure hope no one crosses my path round teatime. I should be seriously tetchy by then.

After a lovely week away from it all, I have various London issues running through my head. I haven't even been able to log on all week, so absolutely anything could have happened while I've been gone. It's been a blissful news blackout, but I'm sure I must have missed something important. There's a small handful of things for me to deal with when I get back; an interview with the governors about the Directorship of the Royal Ballet School, and a BBC television proposal which has to be put down on paper and submitted by the beginning of the week. The treadmill starts to crank up.

15th April 1998, London
I did miss something important while I was in Rio. Nicholas Snowman, Chief Executive, will be leaving the South Bank after all. Unfortunately I'm a bit late on this particular piece of news, as it was announced while I was incommunicado in Rio. Being on the Board, it isn't a complete surprise, but the confirming faxes and phone messages came to my home while I was out of the loop. The papers have been touting it for a while, and if he was going anywhere, it was always going to be back to the Glyndebourne Festival Opera, where his career began. In some ways, his will be a hard act to follow. His decade at the South Bank has been one of artistic innovation and financial stability and the search will start almost immediately for his successor.

The game of musical chairs continues. Now there is another top seat vacant at a British arts institution and a speculative list of candidates has already been drawn up from the floating pool of currently available artistic front men (and women). The papers do make me laugh. I have watched them harass Nicholas, suggesting with and without subtlety that the Lottery bid would lead to his demise. Now, less than a month after the Arts Council gave its final, negative, verdict on Richard Rogers' glass wave, Nicholas is moving to a job which has been advertised for the best part of the last six months. Yet the commentators try to imply that his appointment is all part of a 'deal' to clear the decks at the South Bank and make room for someone else. Everyone knows (or should be able to imagine) the selection process that precedes an appointment at this level.

Suggesting that this sort of bartering might have gone on is insulting both to Nicholas, whose track record in the arts world is not undistinguished, and to George Christie, who would never hand over Glyndebourne quite so lightly.

16th April 1998, London
Back to technological reality with yet another machine breaking down on me. The computer I'm writing on now decided to do something terminal the day before I flew to Rio, but I checked it into computer hospital while I was away and by the time I returned it was fully recovered. I thought I must be through my quota of breakdowns, but this morning I left the house only to find the car wouldn't start. Cured of its rattle in my absence, the garage had kindly driven my little red car back home and parked it outside my flat. This morning I turned the ignition key and instead of turning over as normal its starter motor ticked like a clock. I called the garage from the car and let them listen to it over the phone. Flat battery. If I wasn't a girl I would have known that. So now I have to (a) locate Torje's charger, remove the battery and put it on charge for twenty-four hours; (b) call the recovery service and get them to tow it to the garage where they can boost-charge it for me; (c) find a friendly neighbour to give me a jump (offers on a postcard, please); or (d) cry. I haven't made up my mind yet, but (d) sounds good.

I felt like crying at work, too. I have spent the last ten days recovering from my whirlwind schedule, and unusually for me, I have done absolutely nothing physical. (I don't count white water rafting in Brazil.) Today I felt seriously unfit, but at least everyone was in the same boat after a week away. We had a two-and-half-hour rehearsal for *Birthday Offering*, a Frederick Ashton ballet that was made in May 1956 for the twenty-fifth anniversary of the Sadlers Wells Ballet. In October of that year, the company was awarded the Royal Charter and became The Royal Ballet. This year we are reviving *Birthday Offering* for Dame Ninette de Valois' centenary on June 6th. It is famous in the history of The Royal Ballet for fielding seven ballerinas in the same piece, originally Margot Fonteyn, Svetlana Beriosova, Elaine Fifield, Nadia Nerina, Rowena Jackson, Beryl Grey, and Violetta Elvin. Each ballerina has a solo variation, and they are all complete gems of Ashton choreography. Unfortunately, I don't think any of the solos are up my particular street, and I have been cast in the Nerina role, the one in which I feel least comfortable. Nadia Nerina was renowned for her amazing elevation. She was the original Lise in *La Fille Mal Gardée*, and her jump was as strong and as light as any man's. Once, in *Swan Lake*, she substituted thirty-two *entrechat six* for the more usual *fouettés* in the black act. Most women couldn't do thirty-two *entrechat six* in a lifetime, let alone at one of the most exhausting moments in all of classical ballet. Her variation in *Birthday Offering* is one long jump, from start to finish, and because of my prolonged ankle injury, I haven't jumped seriously for about three years. I felt like a fraud even attempting it and I'm sure Monica Mason, who was taking the call, picked up on my negative vibes. But I think what really held me back was a vivid memory of the last revival of *Birthday Offering*, round about 1984. I was a *coryphée*, one rank above *corps de ballet*, and although I hadn't exactly made my mark in the company, I must have showed *some* kind of promise. Yet when the cast sheet was posted, my name wasn't on it. I certainly wouldn't have expected a performance of any of the solos, but as almost everyone else with two arms and two legs was down to learn a role, I took the exclusion rather badly. I even went as far as registering a complaint, but it didn't get me anywhere. I was told that I just wasn't right for *Birthday Offering*. The judgement clearly took root; fourteen years later it popped up again, nicely developed into a fully fledged hang-up. I'm not sure I'll be able to shake it off.

After rehearsals, discussion in the canteen at Barons Court was about a recent television programme on Rudolf Nureyev. There was much surprise that in an interview he gave before his death, he described his technique as 'unremarkable'. Dancers usually think of Nureyev as the man who invented technique. Before he defected from the Soviet Union to the West, male dancers were generally stylish, but – how to put this? – less than athletic. Margot Fonteyn's previous partners, Robert Helpmann and Michael Somes, are remembered for their partnering skills and their compelling theatricality; Helpmann even went on to enjoy a second career as an actor. But watching them on film, you really feel as if you are peering into a bygone era. It's hard to see any link between them and the dancers of today, the Jonathan Copes and Inaki Urlezagas. They dance as if in black and white, classy, yes, but predating the glorious technicolor of Nureyev's repertoire of fireworks. Nureyev literally exploded into the middle of all this, with a vocabulary of steps that had never been seen on this side of the East/West divide, and the great thrust forward of male dance technique in the sixties owes a massive debt to him. He swept up Fonteyn, aged forty and on the verge of retirement, and carried her into a second career even more glittering than her first. The photographic evidence speaks for itself; in the early pictures, she inhabits the black-and-white, fifties world of Somes and Helpmann, perfectly at home in the archives. A few years later, her technique has blossomed into full colour and the bridge between Fonteyn and the likes of Viviana Durante and Darcey Bussell becomes clear.

Not many people know this, but when Nureyev gave his final performance at the Royal Opera House, I was his partner. Admittedly, there were no pointe shoes and tutus involved, but nevertheless, I think this entitles me to my own tiny footnote in dance history. Towards the end of Fonteyn's life, when illness was robbing her of both her health and her finances, the company gave a gala performance of *Romeo and Juliet* to establish an endowment fund for her. By then, Rudolf was well beyond dancing Romeo, so he danced the secondary role of Mercutio. I was his harlot.

17th April 1998, London

Hope springs eternal at work with the birth of the first of this year's vintage crop of babies. Sean William Cassidy was born yesterday to his proud parents, Nicola Searchfield and Michael (Stuart) Cassidy. I gather the actual event was long, drawn-out and painful. I hope to be spared the details.

Until yesterday we had five dancers and one physiotherapist all expecting babies this year. Now there are four. It isn't an easy decision to make, taking a year out of a short career to have children, and destroying, at least temporarily, all the hard work that goes into the creation of a dancer's body. And then there is the rebuilding process following delivery. All that work, when the maternal hormones must be screaming 'stay at home, stay at home'. But dancers are probably the most determined and focused people you are ever likely to meet. Nicola Roberts, for instance, was back on stage dancing Giselle only four months after her son Jordan was born. In order to keep the lay-off as brief as possible, most of the mothers-to-be are doing class as long as they can, sometimes days before delivery, and the sight of five dome-like stomachs lined up at the barre is both charming and comical, like five of Peter Mandelson's 'baby domes', or a line-up of teletubbies. They seemed to announce their pregnancies within weeks of one another, so I guess the babies will come thick and fast now, giving a whole new meaning to the term 'baby shower'.

21st April 1998, London
Yesterday's gossip, today's news, and even then it didn't get to me until about six o'clock this afternoon. I'm afraid that once again your woman on the inside has singularly failed to be one step ahead of the rest in reporting Opera House developments. But I've got used to being the last to know anything about the Opera House, and as usual, I heard the latest news while I was over at the South Bank, for another Board meeting.

Anyway, the long and the short of it is that the Opera House has acquired an Artistic Director, at least for an interim period of two years. Note that this is not a General Director, the post which is being advertised, nor a Chief Executive, the post where the vacancy exists, which so many have attempted to fill and so few have remained in. But nevertheless, we have someone at the helm to steer us through the rest of closure and see us back into the new House. The really good thing about the appointment of Richard Jarman is that he appears to have an equal history in both opera and ballet. As much as I like the idea of an artistic guru at the top, I harbour a niggling worry about whether such a figure exists outside the world of opera. There has been a dearth of such people within ballet since Diaghilev shuffled off his famous overcoat. I can only think of someone like John Drummond, for instance. But the media's list of prospective candidates for the Opera House hot seat rejected him as being 'too old'. The rest of the list was exclusively operatic. This isn't necessarily a problem – a good brain is a good brain – but there's a feeling historically within the House of ballet 'taking second place' to opera, and having an established 'opera man' at the top might have revived this particular complaint. Jarman has worked within the last decade at Scottish Opera, English National Ballet and the Edinburgh Festival, so he seems to bring wide experience to the post. Those in the know say he is 'very good news'.

Further on the subject of new appointments: yesterday morning I had my interview for the position of Director of the Royal Ballet School. I had been hoping that by now I would have a clearer idea of whether or not I want the job. Or perhaps it would be truer to say I had been hoping that by now I would have discovered I really *do* want the job and could make a decision about it. Unfortunately that doesn't seem to have happened. As much as I see what a wonderful opportunity it is, I can't help but feel that it has come at the wrong time for me. At the moment my nets are cast wide; I'm trying my hand at everything and loving it. The idea of narrowing my focus to one project leaves me with a sense of sadness as to what I might be missing. It's not that the job scares me; there is lots of work to do, and I would love to dirty my hands doing it. But not now. A few years on, maybe, but not now. Of course, it's unlikely that the job will be available in a few years' time, so the whole thing is a bit like a game of pontoon. Should I stick or twist? It has been an enormous compliment to be considered for such an important role, but in the end, the tummy feeling made the decision for me. At the moment, it just doesn't feel right. I shall stick.

And of course there is the dancing. When I got home, Jeanetta Laurence called to say that Anthony Dowell wanted a word. I spent a nervous five minutes wondering what I had done wrong before he called back. In fact it was good news; in next season's revival of *Mr Worldly Wise*, Twyla Tharp would like me to take over the part Darcey Bussell originally created. I accepted without a thought for the fact that a few hours earlier I had been discussing a job which would have meant me hanging up my toe shoes for ever. Looks like I'll be dancing away for a while yet.

24th April 1998, London
Today's papers report on Grey Gowrie's unusual farewell to the Arts Council. He has been its Chairman for four years now, through last May's change of government. The emotion of the occasion has inspired him to verse, not, so I read, his first foray into the form. Amongst his other accomplishments, he's a published poet. The extract in *Arts Council News* is accompanied by an open letter to the Council in which he celebrates the highs and chronicles the lows, chief amongst which are what he calls the 'Royal Opera Company Titanic' and his personal grief at the loss of an 'outstanding' former Secretary-General, Mary Allen. I rushed back to my files to check on the acrimonious exchange between the two of them which was played out in public last month through the pages of *The Times*. But the letter is not a chance to gripe; its tone is resolutely positive, and this makes a rather nice change. Like many commentators, I'm guilty of seeing the current plight of the arts in the gloomiest of lights. He's not exactly a man of the people hailing, as he does, from the Upper House. In a famous riposte to a journalist who questioned whether the arts were really in touch with the rest of the world, he apparently said, 'My dear, we don't live in a *tour d'ivoire*.' That sums him up nicely. But Gowrie has an ability to see art today as part of the great scheme of things, the successor to yesterday and the precursor of what is to come, an in-depth understanding of its place in history, and

this I'll miss. We still don't know what the future Arts Council will look like under its altogether different new Chairman, Gerry Robinson.

28th April 1998, London

Two very short rehearsals this week, with Monica Mason, to try and get my legs better acquainted with the steps they are going to dance in *Birthday Offering*. I was every bit as uncertain about the solo as the last time I rehearsed it, and in a classic delaying tactic, I wandered over to the piano, to have a look at the pianist's music. As many of the scores date back to the very first rehearsals, in this case, fifty-two years ago, they can be fascinating, littered with the choreographer's notes on tempi, or the names of the dancers on whom the ballet was created. The score revealed that the music for Nerina's variation is called 'La Grêle'. I asked Ghislaine Thesmar of the Paris Opéra, currently teaching the girls classes for the company, what *la grêle* means. In her almost perfect English, she said, 'you know, the little hard rain . . . rice balls.' Hailstones. I'm a dancing hailstone, and suddenly the solo makes thundering sense. My delaying tactic has given it a whole new emphasis, a means of linking the physical difficulties with an intellectual idea. At last I've found a weapon to ward off the ghosts of the previous casts, and a way to dance it for myself.

Bumped, unexpectedly, into Mary Allen, in the corridors of Barons Court. She was in the building to visit the company physiotherapists, as she's still suffering from the knee injury that she brought with her to my DK book launch back in January. We had a brief chat, and I teased her gently, asking her to promise that she wouldn't publish *her* book before I publish mine. The papers have been full of speculation that she will go public with the diary she admits she kept during her tenure at the House, but I can reveal here that at the moment, she has made no such decision, although she hasn't ruled it out either.

She's not the only person to be thinking about 'air-kissing and telling'. Keith Cooper is in discussion about an updated version of *The House*, the infamous television series that went behind the scenes at Covent Garden and stunned the nation by revealing Jeremy Isaacs – *without his shirt*. As a shocking silver-screen moment, it comes second only to that scene in *Fatal Attraction*, where Michael Douglas cavorts in a disco in a V-neck Pringle. At present, Keith is waiting tables at his boyfriend's restaurant in West London, courting publicity as he takes his orders; my spies tell me that he has been spotted lunching with Genista McIntosh, and on this particular occasion, we don't think he was doing the serving. As the spy said (I'd love to claim it as mine, but I'm too honest), 'I'd like to have been a fly in that particular soup.'

29th April 1998, London
Rushing out to the private view of the Anish Kapoor exhibition at the Hayward Gallery on the South Bank last night, I listened to a telephone message from John Eatwell, Chairman of the ballet Board. The message said he needed to talk to me, without saying why. When I came back from dinner I picked up my e-mail. It included a note from a journalist friend: 'What do you think of the new ballet Board?' As it didn't say, 'How nice that you are on the ballet Board,' I began to put two and two together and worked out what John might want to tell me.

This morning I spoke to him. There has been a change of plan, and after further discussion it has been decided that there won't, after all, be a dancer on the ballet Board. Naturally, I'm disappointed.

But he has an alternative idea to put to me. The new Opera House (if it still belongs to us by the time it is rebuilt and reopened) will have not only the main auditorium and a studio theatre, but a third performing space converted from the largest of our rehearsal studios as and when it is needed. It will have flexible bleacher seating, a full lighting rig, public access, and it can be used for almost anything: educational events, choreographic workshops, lecture demonstrations as well as small-scale performance. It should be the access point of the building for a large sector of the public, with tickets cheap enough that they aren't beyond *anyone*'s means. John and I, in our previous conversation, were both very excited about the possibilities it will open up for the artists. Now he has asked me to think about what might go on there. I was rather taken aback at first – after all, this came entirely out of the blue – but after a few minutes the ideas started to flow. There are so many issues in the House and in the ballet company which attract criticism, warranted or other-wise, which a space like this could positively counter. Choreographic development for a start. There has long been a dichotomy between the need to sell tickets and the need to develop new choreographers. The main auditorium isn't always the most suitable place for testing out new ideas which could be either triumphant or disastrous. A space over which the dancers feel some sense of ownership, one where there is limited fear of failure, would perhaps encourage choreographers to take greater and more thrilling risks. And knowing as I do how appalling facilities are throughout the rest of the arts world, it would be terrific if the studio could be open to others when The Royal Ballet is away on tour. With a bit of drive and determination, the possibilities for this space could be endless, and it could give huge credibility to Covent Garden as a major mover within the arts community.

30th April 1998, London
My photocopied clippings from the press office at the South Bank this week nicely juxtaposed a piece from the *Telegraph* on Gerry Robinson's takeover at the Arts Council with an article from *Classical Music* about the Department of Culture, Media and Sport's first Annual Report. While Robinson in Great Peter Street is telling us he has no time for 'waffle' and promising 'there will be no more wordy policy statements', over in Cockspur Street Chris Smith is issuing reams and reams of the stuff. Stressing as keywords 'access, excellence, education and creativity', he says: 'These stand as the aims of our policy and they are aims which resonate across every other department of government. I want to see the DCMS as a dynamic force at the centre of government. Making a significant addition to the quality of life in every community in Britain, providing jobs, generating wealth, contributing to the perception of our country, at home and abroad, as a nation which recognises and celebrates creativity and talent in all its people.'

Laudable aims, in a great and wordy policy. But this is the problem with laudable aims. When you write them down they start to sound wordy. You can't talk about the value and the purpose of the arts without straying away from facts and figures and on to words, and, worse still, words which attempt to verbalise the realms of the 'spiritual'. Immediately, we're on dangerous ground. The 'spiritual', as proscribed by E.M. Forster's Dolly Wilcox, for whom 'spooks and going to church summarized the unseen', is perfectly acceptable as after-dinner conversation. We are quite prepared to listen to (and believe) any amount of nonsense about 'spooks' and the 'church' of the nineties; blue triangles, colonic irrigation, astrology. There are thousands of people out there who link their self-development to total, unmitigated nonsense gleaned from star signs, fortune-telling and numerology, but suggest that art can make any sort of a difference, and we're laughed out of court.

In this midst of all this I continue to search for a balance; to keep my head above the threatening swell of populism and its tendency towards the lowest common denominator, without ever losing sight of the need for art to connect – with everyone – which is our entire reason for existing.

May 1998

1st May 1998, London

To celebrate the end of my first year dancing away from Covent Garden, I went to visit the building site which, in eighteen months' time, will be the reincarnated Royal Opera House. Given the turmoil of the last year, who can say what will go on there, or who will run it?

I've hardly been to Covent Garden in the ten months since we last performed there, and, as an area, I can't say I miss it. It's changed so much that it's barely recognisable as the theatre district on which my teenage dreams were founded. Yet the Opera House stands defiantly in the middle of it all. Kitted out with steel-capped wellies, fluorescent jacket and hard hat, I'm led through a barrage of security checks and on to the site itself. What I see is something quite vast, but not a place vast enough to be home to Chris Smith's three-in-a-bed scenario (an equation, I suspect, which has long been abandoned). The site stretches from the piazza at the south to Floral Street at the north. It's a hive of activity, and in the unseasonable sunshine the builders climb fearlessly along steel girders and smile for my camera, probably delighted that at last one of the promised dancers has shown up to check out their work.

Before my eyes, this artistic Legoland is coming together, and the building is shooting up in little pockets around the periphery. There is an immense hole in the middle where the art will be, almost like the void that fills the Opera House's future at the moment, as we await the Eyre report, due out this month. At the rear of the site, butting on to the market, is the 'James St corner', the part which will be home to The Royal Ballet. For the last sixteen years, we have had two studios at the Opera House. In a year's time, we will have five. It's the furthest advanced of all the various constructions, and up on the fourth floor one of the ballet studios is nearing completion. You can see it taking shape, with wonderful glass windows overlooking the piazza and enormous silver tubes – part of the 'comfort-cooling' system – extending in every direction across the ceiling. Gone, we hope, are the days when post-global warming summer temperatures would leave us – literally – gasping for breath. There is even a terrace, exclusive to the ballet, where we can snatch some fresh air on the days when the schedule holds us captive from 9.15 in the morning to 10.30 at night. In the old House we would emerge from these thirteen-hour stints blinking like moles. Four floors below, at stage level, the dressing-rooms are also close to completion, with twentieth-century plumbing, windows that open and, best of all, space and light. One of them is even fitted out, mirrors, lights and shower room in place, like a theatrical 'show home'. I can't say I'll miss the communal showers, six scaled-up shower heads in an eight-foot square space and a floor that was permanently ankle deep in other people's used bath water.

Inside the white stuccoed House which has graced so many front pages over the last, turbulent twelve months, I wandered through unrecognisable corridors and barren stairwells, thick with the dust of a century, into the auditorium. I've lived amidst domestic building work before. I like to think I know a thing or two about 'stripping out'. But I was totally unprepared for what I saw. Despite the fact that the auditorium will eventually re-emerge 'untouched', all that remains to identify it as the theatre I have known for eighteen years are the crescent-shaped tiers of the pit lobby, stalls circle, grand tier and balcony, or what Torje, with his background in football, refers to as the 'terraces'. Amongst the grime and the rubble they retain the faintest trace of their former grandeur, with the 'gilded girlies' still gripping precariously the balustrade, as if overseeing, with some kind of grief, the chaos below. But even *they* have dressed down to match the builders; their wings have been clipped and taken into storage. Their arms, after a century of supporting a pair of heavy chandeliers apiece, have been relieved of their burden and given a couple of years off. I look directly upwards and see that the newly gilded dome, the only finished element, is concealed behind an enormous dustsheet. It will remain under wraps like a treasure, until the builders move out. Apart from these few hints of its former and future splendour, I could be looking at any refurbishment of any building, anywhere.

Only once did I feel my own ghost hovering, as I stood at the spot in the stalls circle where, until last year, I and other dancers who weren't involved in the day's schedule would congregate to watch the rehearsal on-stage. But there was no stage and, anyway, no pass door to access it, just a solid, unbroken wall where the red curtain used to hang. I longed suddenly to get back to what we called normality, to life in the House, a regular routine of dancing here, not dancing away. A familiar landscape of five minute calls, dressing-rooms, waiting in the wings and taking the stage.

I wander outside, quite disorientated by the mixture of the new Garden to come and the old House under refurbishment and I notice this stretch of wall, visible along the northern boundary, which gives one of the few remaining clues as to the site's history. It's the wall which runs along Floral Street, and in marked contrast to the building materials of the nineties strewn around the place, it's five storeys of flimsy Victorian brick. It looks every bit as fragile as the current situation which surrounds the Opera House. Yet the wall has been there since 1858, the year when Edward Barry's Royal Opera House was built. Like a defiant motion that this House will stand, it's not going anywhere.

Epilogue

It's just over a year since I started this diary, and what a year it has been. I have used up another passport, stamped with an itinerary which will have travel agents salivating at the thought of the commissions it earned. Touring in all its forms seems to have taken over my life; Royal Ballet tours, book tours, speaking tours, Rolls-Royce tours and always, in the background, Torje's absence, on tour with the Rolling Stones. I can't remember staying in one place for more than a few days.

Certainly, I could never have predicted that the first twelve months in the wilderness would have proved so dramatic for the Opera House. Last May, Genista McIntosh was (as far as we knew) happily at work in the Chief Executive's office, the development scheme was full steam ahead, and the money that would fund it was either in the bank or firmly pledged. Little did we know that Genista would be replaced not once, but twice within the next ten months. We didn't know that bankruptcy was on the cards, that Gerald Kaufman had a Select Committee inquiry up his sleeve which would dispatch an entire Board, gummed to death by the report with 'no teeth', or that a year on, our new home would hang in the balance as we nervously await the announcement of our fate from the pen of Richard Eyre.

The Opera House may have brought much of this on itself: Gerald Kaufman would certainly have us believe that. But out in the big world, things haven't been going so well for the arts, either. New Labour, twelve months into its first term of office, may have announced its quiet satisfaction with the way things have gone, but Tony Blair has singularly failed to justify the faith certain prominent artists very publicly placed in him. Once his election victory was secured, the Downing Street invitations, previously flowing like water to the culturally cool and hip, mysteriously dried up. *I* never received one. Revenue funding to the arts has continued to decline, as it did under the previous administration. But whereas John Major cushioned the cuts with the introduction of cash from the National Lottery, Labour has treated the 'goose that laid the golden eggs' to a virtual hysterectomy. In the past few months, the voices of dissent have started to make themselves heard. At first there were low grumblings, then a public dousing of John Prescott, by a pop personality, at Alexandra Palace. When comedian Ben Elton, Mr Left himself, started to knock Labour on television in the way he used to reserve for the Tories, we knew the honeymoon was finally over. The arts have had enough of promises unfulfilled. Perhaps sensing this watershed, Blair unexpectedly invited a prestigious handful of serious arts figures to a Downing Street meeting on the eve of publication of Sir Richard Eyre's report.

When *The Eyre Review: The Future of Lyric Theatre in London* finally arrives, six weeks behind schedule, it is read as a vigorous and convincing defence of public subsidy for the arts. It voices eloquently many of the things I've been thinking and saying throughout this year. It temperately points out the excesses of the past whilst offering little in the way of a practical template for the future. Yet Eyre's review can be welcomed, precisely because he confirms what we've been saying all along. A decision has to be made; we either believe that artistic creativity is a life-enhancing affirmation of humanity, as essential to the soul as oxygen is to the body, or we don't. If the vote is *for* art, then we have to be willing to pay for it, because in the absence of sufficient subsidy commercial pressures are allowed to impinge too heavily on creativity, turning art into mere entertainment. Fun, yes, box-office, certainly, but not the same thing as an artistic experience. At some point, the government will have to stop writing off claims of underfunding throughout the arts world as mismanagement and accept that if you want accessible world-class art at the Opera House, or anywhere else, you have to pay for it. The tug of war and the inevitable bad publicity continue.

The Opera House's future may still be on shaky ground, Torje may still be on foreign soil, but other elements of the year have tied themselves up more neatly. My car is rattle free, my computer is fixed and, aside from an overnight trip to New York to appear on *Good Morning America*, I'm blissfully enjoying an extended period at home, hours at the keyboard as well as a daily routine of classes and rehearsals which will soon culminate in a month of performances at the Coliseum. The Royal Ballet School has found itself a Director from Australia, Gailene Stock. Rolls-Royce has been sold, not, as we expected to BMW, but to the makers of the people's car, VW. My BBC project has become a reality and I'm furiously working away on a script for filming in August. The South Bank Board is actively seeking a replacement for its

Chief Executive, Nicholas Snowman, and reworking the redevelopment once again to come up with a scheme which is achievable under the New Labour, New Lottery regulations. Dame Ninette de Valois, the founder of The Royal Ballet, celebrated her 100th birthday on June 6th by attending an afternoon performance in the studio theatre at White Lodge. I *did* dance in *Birthday Offering*, despite all my misgivings about the role, and Madam, talking loudly throughout, made her customary comments on each dancer as they took the stage. She didn't disappoint me. 'Who's this? Who? Deborah Bull? Oh, yes. I always meant to write to her father about that name.'

One development this month was totally unexpected. On June 4th, I was standing in the garden of Danesfield House, one of several 'country house' hotels within an hour's drive of London. I was there to do, of all things, a fashion shoot for *Hello!* magazine, having refused repeatedly, point blank, to allow their camera to invade my home. Dressing up in glamorous frocks was the compromise we reached. I am looking splendid in a vast red and black dress by Tomasz Starzewski, with matching, wide-brimmed hat. My mobile phone rings.

'Deborah? Deborah Bull? This is Chris Smith's office. Is this a good moment to talk? The Minister would like a word.'

'Er, yeah, I guess so.'

I try to replace the two-foot wide creation on my head with my 'serious person in the arts' hat, all the time wondering just what Chris Smith could possibly want to speak to me about. He comes on the line before I have worked it out, and before I have remembered how you are supposed to address a member of Her Majesty's government. He goes straight to the point. As we don't really know each other, there is no scope for the normal niceties which are used in opening conversations. And as I have been writing about him and his decisions over the last year in the abstract, it strikes me as very strange to be talking to him in person. He is calling because he would like me to consider serving on the new Arts Council. I don't remember too much of what came after that. I was so taken aback that it was filtered through a thick haze of disbelief.

I struggled over a long weekend to work out what my answer would be. I had three separate questions, ideological, practical and personal. Do I believe in Gerry Robinson's vision of the future? Can I stretch the hours in the day to encompass my life as a ballet dancer as well as a role on the Arts Council? And by running my life in this reverse order – most people move on to councils and boards once they have earned their fortunes and their lives ahead are secure – am I compromising my life beyond the tutu?

Finally I have to make the big decision, and I realise my life over the last year has been leading up to this. I tell him yes. Yes, because I'm committed. Yes, because I'm sick and tired of feeling impotent in the face of decisions about the arts. Yes, because I'm deeply concerned to secure the future of art in this country, believing passionately in its power to change people's lives. And yes, because at this time of change it seems to make much more sense to be on the inside rather than the outside.

I've learnt the first law of public life; never answer the phone to the Minister in the middle of an *Hello!* shoot. Brickbats and abuse are bound to follow. A year ago, I was waiting in the wings to be on-stage and dancing away, as the Opera House curtain came down for the last time. In twelve months I've moved centre stage in a far more serious drama and I don't know how it will end. The script for the new Arts Council has yet to be written. Despite the mixed reviews I've collected for my latest role, a role I have yet to perform, I stand by my decision.

My life, like the Royal Opera House itself, is nothing like it was a year ago. It's undergone a process of refurbishment, some of it, from the ground up. I've become more politicised, pulled into a process which I've blithely danced through for much of my career. Will it take me further away from dancing? Maybe, eventually. What began as a year about dancing away has become a year about moving my life away from what it was to what it might become. These days I dance in a world elsewhere.